To Pam, Sept. 9, 2011
From Alice Torth

Pam,
Best Wishes
from
Michael Riedler

THE BEST OF
Cottey Cooking

THE BEST OF
Cottey Cooking

*Favorite Recipes from
the Celebrated Cuisine
of Cottey College*

by Michael Richardson

Published by
Rust Publishing MOKS, LLC
P.O. Box 247
Nevada, MO 64772

Manufactured by
Favorite Recipes® Press
P.O. Box 305142
Nashville, TN 37230
800.358.0560

ISBN   978-0-9845283-0-1

Written by Michael Richardson
Foreword by Helen Washburn, Ph.D.
Photography by Kenny Felt
Designed by Ryan Wallace

Printed and assembled in the USA
First printing 2010

Dedicated to Lorraine,
Rachel and Parker.

66 One cannot think well,
love well, sleep well, if
one has not *dined* well. **99**

VIRGINIA WOOLF

CONTENTS

ACKNOWLEDGMENTS

It takes the help, support and talent of so many people to complete a project such as this. It is humbling to realize how many things one can't do well, yet it is quite gratifying to work with a group of individuals who are willing to share their skills, their time and their passion towards a common goal. I have so many to thank for the evolution and completion of this book. My sincere thanks to the P.E.O. Sisterhood, the alumnae and the students who have expressed interest in and support of our dining staff and food offerings at Cottey. You are truly the inspiration for this book. To Michelle Hart, and then Linda Russell, for your early work in helping me find a publisher and typing the recipes. Even though the project ultimately went in a different direction, I am very thankful for your time and your commitment. Many thanks to Mary Haggans, my boss, who has given me the time and the freedom to attend to the demands of this project; to Dr. Judy Rogers for your support and belief in this book; to Jean Foster and Steve Reed for your time spent searching for publishers; to Jean Foster for also proofreading many areas of the book; to Becky Kiel and Debbie Garten for allowing me to have my own private table in the library archives for months to research records and pour through old photos; to Seth Barrett for your professional, yet easy going manner in helping me put this project on a sound financial footing; to Kendall Vickers for your advice and sound legal counsel throughout; to Barbara and Steve Wiseman for your talent in decor and food styling, as well as the use of your fabulous kitchen; to Karen Hertzberg for the generous loan of your beautiful china for the food shoot; to Lynn Wade and Sharyon Duke for your creative writing expertise. To Allison Fast, Cottey Alumna, and true supporter of the cause for your exacting and complete proofreading efforts. You were absolutely the right person to come along for this difficult task and I am grateful to you. To Dr. Helen Washburn for your willingness to write the foreward and illuminate the background and story behind this book. To Mark Richardson for your oversight of the design process and general support and advice to me, your brother. To Kenny Felt for your photographic talent — you can make, it seems, anyone look photogenic. You have played such an integral part in the design process. To Ryan Wallace for your expertise as the main contributor to the design and the professional layout of this book. I appreciate your talent, and for being on task from the beginning. It has been an honor to have you as a key member of the team for this project. To Julie Righter, the one who has helped me the most in a profound number of ways, to move this project forward on time and with a commitment to excellence. You faithfully met with me, encouraged me, opened doors for me and prodded this process along for months and months. You have been generous with your time and resources in seeing this project through. Through it all, I have gained a genuine friend. And, last but not least, I want to thank the staff at Cottey Dining for your daily commitment to the work you do, for the pride you take in doing your jobs, and for your efforts in keeping the food and service quality at such a high level. Without your consistent striving towards excellence, there would be little demand for a book such as this. Thank you!

FOREWORD

By Helen Washburn, Ph.D.

It is an honor to have been asked to write the foreward for Michael Richardson's cookbook of favorite Cottey recipes. So many of my memories, and those of Cottey's alumnae, revolve around the unique student traditions and activities in the dining room and the fine food served there by Cottey's loyal and conscientious food service personnel. From my first day at Cottey, I was impressed by the fact that the facility was called a dining room instead of a cafeteria. That name communicated a pride in the place as well as the quality of the food served there. Whether it is for a daily breakfast, lunch, dinner or special event, thoughtful attention to planning and food preparation always is given to assure that dining at Cottey is an enjoyable experience.

Michael Richardson's arrival at Cottey in 1993 was serendipitous and fortuitous. I believe he found his niche serving Cottey's students, faculty and staff, preparing elegant, creative cuisine for guests at the President's House, and impressing PEO officers and members who are frequent guests at the College. Cottey has a long history of providing superior food. Memories of this tradition often were shared with me by alumnae whom I met over the years I was at Cottey. Michael's efforts have continued the tradition of excellence.

Michael's training and experience as a chef are a source of pride to the Cottey community. His genuine interest in meeting the needs of students and matching their interests with the menus he prepares is extraordinary. Stories of his special attention to students are legend.

> **Michael's training and experience as a chef have been a source of pride to the Cottey community. His genuine interest in meeting the needs of students and matching their interests with the menus he prepares is extraordinary.**

Besides preparing tasty and healthy food that students enjoy on a daily basis, he goes above and beyond to provide dishes familiar to our international students and attends to the special requirements of students with food allergies and special diets. New and popular trends in food often are reflected in his menus. As every parent knows, accommodating to young people's food likes and dislikes is no easy task. Yet Michael's ability to relate to our young women, and his patient and sincere desire to consult with them on menu planning, has assured a satisfied and appreciative student body. He knows what he needs to do to please his customers and he succeeds.

Michael is an artist who expresses his talents through the preparation and presentation of food. He has applied his aesthetic sensibilities to everything from the appearance of the dining room to the way food is plated for special dinners. He believes that college food service should focus on quality. He has adapted to young people's growing interest in healthy eating. This has been reflected in his use of organically grown food and emphasis on the training of the staff in healthy food preparation. He even planted an herb garden outside Robertson Hall so he would have fresh herbs to use in his recipes.

Michael has been careful to preserve and even improve upon many of Cottey's dining room traditions. Although it is no longer practical to have sit-down dinners every night, Cottey continues to have special dinners to celebrate holidays, Founder's

Day when alumnae are on campus, Yellow and White dinner during graduation weekend, and most special of all, Hanging of the Greens prior to the Christmas break. In addition, a marvelous brunch is offered to students and their guests on Sundays. All students have the opportunity to experience a formal dinner with members of their residence hall suites in the Centennial Room, formerly the Red Room. Singing of Cottey songs traditionally has occurred during meal times. A unique Cottey tradition is for students to "scinermer-ink" unsuspecting male guests the first time they come to the dining room.

Over the years of his tenure at Cottey, there have been many requests for recipes by visitors to the College and by students, faculty and staff, so Michael has prepared a cookbook. I have my favorites and look forward to owning this book so I can prepare them in my kitchen. For those who, like me, have enjoyed meals in the Cottey dining room, you will want to add this cookbook to your library. Thank you, Michael, for your devoted service to Cottey and her students, and for devoting the endless hours and hard work required for the compilation of *The Best of Cottey Cooking*.

INTRODUCTION

By Michael Richardson

For almost two decades I have been on an enlightened and fascinating journey. I truly have enjoyed the challenge of consistently striving to provide tasty, healthy food and satisfying the ever-changing tastes of young women in a welcoming atmosphere. Of all the customers I have served over the years, the students at Cottey have proven to be the most rewarding to me as a chef. They are bright, fun, demanding yet appreciative, and they display a zest for life that is infectious to those of us who work in their midst.

My purpose in writing *The Best of Cottey Cooking* is to share the recipes that are a result of many years of creative effort to serve the best possible meals while maintaining Cottey's reputation for dining excellence. Furthermore, a significant portion of your purchase will be used to establish a Cottey scholarship fund for young women who seek a higher education but haven't the financial means.

My culinary journey to Cottey began in 1993, when I lived in the Chicago suburb of Glenview. I spotted a classified ad for Cottey College seeking a "Director of Food Service — culinary experience preferred." It caught my attention because, at the time, few institutions sought culinary professionals to run their food programs.

After learning there were 350 students enrolled at Cottey, I was able to determine the number of meals per day and staff needed for their program. Although I had never prepared college food, I felt that this would be both demanding and rewarding for me, if given the opportunity. After all, I had ample management experience, and if I could devise a program that could offer the tasty restaurant food I knew how to prepare, then it would be successful. I applied for the position and ultimately was pleased to accept an offer. Little did I know the extent of the challenges that lay ahead.

I arrived on campus in July of 1993 and heard with great interest the tales of life at Cottey food service, particularly during the era of Leonard Delano, who retired 20 years earlier. Under his direction, Cottey had developed an international reputation of dining excellence. I wanted to emulate that reputation, but knew little about the food preferences of young women.

I spent the first few years asking students a lot of questions, installed a suggestion box in the dining room and participated in a student-led food committee. I wrote recipes, and then more recipes, to meet the demands of an international student body on a 20-meal per week plan. I visited half a dozen other colleges to soak up their offerings, searched through books, magazines and cookbooks, pursued

> **Of all the customers I have served over the years, the students at Cottey have proven to be the most rewarding to me as a chef. They are bright, fun, demanding yet appreciative, and they display a zest for life that is infectious to those of us who work in their midst.**

recipes from church suppers, bed and breakfasts and state fair winners — anywhere I thought I could find recipes that students would like. And then I had to re-write the recipes, typically written to serve four, to ones that could serve 100.

As soon as my first fall semester at Cottey began, the vegetarian students asserted their needs. At the time, very little was available in cookbooks that would appeal to their young palates. I would light-heartedly joke that we had vegetarians who didn't like vegetables. Though a bit of an exaggeration, this wasn't far from the truth. During the first few years, I learned a lot and wrote hundreds of vegetarian recipes so that I could offer both a lacto/ovo entree (includes eggs and milk products) as well as a vegan (no animal products) entree at each meal.

We now serve vegetarian soups, sandwiches, pastas and an assortment of entrees drawing from American, Asian, Mexican, Indian, Italian and Mediterranean influences. It is an ongoing pursuit to provide enough variety on a daily basis to satisfy these students. My next recipe frontier is in the gluten-free offerings that many students now request.

The Best of Cottey Cooking contains the accumulation of my many years of recipe writing and includes many from my past as a restaurant chef. I also have included recipes from students and college staff who have inspired me and whose contributions are just as important to the success of Cottey's culinary reputation. This book includes the most popular dishes at Cottey from each category that we serve, and it is my sincere hope that the recipes within will be added to your repertoire of dishes for both daily cooking needs and for those special occasions when you want to spoil friends and family.

Where in the beginning of my life at Cottey I had re-written recipes that served four to those that would serve 100, I now have re-written these recipes into family-sized quantities for the home cook, with some improvements along the way. I shopped for all the ingredients at local supermarkets in our small town of Nevada and personally tested all of the recipes on an older stove and oven at home. I have written them to work for the average cook, and they will work well if the directions are followed in order. Though some ingredient lists may appear long, you will see them come together quickly in the skillet or bowl and are paramount to the flavorful success that follows.

I've always liked the way Julia Child would advise her readers in the process of cooking her recipes. For example, she says to read the recipe first, even if you're an experienced cook. Then visualize each step so you will know exactly what techniques, ingredients, time and equipment are required to avoid surprises. I agree with Julia. I also would add that it is helpful to measure out all ingredients before cooking — even setting out in order of use. This helps when the phone rings, or another interruption occurs, and perhaps you forget where you are in the process.

As Julia used to say, "try new recipes, learn from your mistakes, be fearless, and above all have fun." Now, if you'll excuse me, I've got something ready to come out of the oven.

THE BEST OF
Cottey Cooking

BREAKFAST/BRUNCH

MAIN DISHES

Egg Puff Casserole **V**

Bananas Foster Crepes **V**

Brunch Enchiladas

Brunch Strata

Hawaiian Bread French Toast
   w/ Fruit Salsa **V**

Swedish Pancakes **V**

Almond French Toast **V**

Blueberry Maple French Toast **V**

Breakfast Quesadillas **V**

Healthy Pancakes **V**

Honey Cinnamon Granola **VI**

COFFEE CAKES/ MUFFINS

Cream Cheese Swirl Coffee Cake **V**

Pistachio Coffee Cake **V**

Banana Bread **V**

Pumpkin Swirl Bread **V**

Cinnamon Swirl Bread **V**

Molasses Glazed Pecan Scones **V**

Orange Rolls **V**

Sausage and Cheese Scones

Orange Muffins **V**

Apple Streusel Muffins **V**

Blueberry Lemon Muffins **V**

Butterscotch Muffins **V**

Lemon Crunch Muffins **V**

Healthy Bran Apple Muffins **V**

Piña Colada Muffins **V**

Raspberry Cheesecake Muffins **V**

V Vegetarian
VI Vegan

EGG PUFF CASSEROLE

16–20 Servings

12 eggs
½ cup + 2 tablespoons all-purpose flour
2½ cups (24 ounces) cottage cheese, small curd, drained
2 (8-ounce) packages shredded cheddar-jack cheese blend
5 tablespoons butter or margarine, melted
½ teaspoon salt
3 tablespoons diced green chiles (optional)

Add chopped ham or cooked sausage crumbles to the batter if a meatier version is desired. Great for brunch or for a crowd. Recipe easily can be cut in half as well.

Preheat oven to 350°F. Beat the eggs until light and lemon colored. Stir in remaining ingredients; mix until batter is smooth. Pour mixture into a greased 9-by-13-inch pan. Bake for 40–45 minutes, or until golden brown and a tester inserted in center comes out clean.

BANANAS FOSTER CREPES

8 Servings

8 crepes

Filling Sauce

- 2 tablespoons + 2 teaspoons butter or margarine
- 1 teaspoon Triple Sec (or other orange liqueur)
- 4 tablespoons + 1 teaspoon brown sugar
  pinch ground cinnamon
  pinch ground nutmeg
- 2 tablespoons + 2 teaspoons half-and-half
- ¼ teaspoon cornstarch
- 2 firm bananas, halved lengthwise, then halved crosswise

Topping Sauce

- ½ cup + 1 teaspoon half-and-half
- ¼ teaspoon vanilla
- ½ teaspoon Triple Sec (or other orange liqueur)
- 4 tablespoons + 1 teaspoon packed brown sugar
  pinch ground cinnamon
- ½ teaspoon cornstarch

  whipped topping (optional)

Use the Swedish Pancakes recipe on page 25 to make the crepes. They can be made ahead and frozen. Ready-made, frozen crepes are another option, if available to you.

Lightly oil-spray an 8-by-8-inch pan or glass dish. Place the bananas, flat-side down, in the pan; set aside.

For Filling Melt the butter in a medium saucepan. Stir in the Triple Sec and brown sugar; cook on medium heat until sugar is melted. Add the spices and half-and-half; stir well to blend. Add just enough water to the cornstarch to make a pourable mixture and stir into the sauce. Cook until slightly thickened, about 30 seconds.

Pour sauce evenly over the bananas. Cover with foil, poke holes in the foil, and bake in a preheated 350°F oven for 16–18 minutes, or until bananas are softened but not mushy. Remove foil and let cool slightly.

For Topping In a saucepan, heat the half-and-half, vanilla, Triple Sec, brown sugar and cinnamon; bring to a boil. Mix cornstarch with just enough water to make a pourable mixture then add to the sauce, while stirring; boil until thickened, about 30 seconds. Remove from heat, cover and set aside.

For Assembly On a work surface lay out the crepes and place a banana piece on the lower third of each. Ladle 1 tablespoon of **filling sauce** over the banana, then roll up crepe tightly, folding in both sides to enclose the filling. Oil-spray a 9-by-13-inch pan and lay the rolled crepes, seam-side down, in the pan in a row. Top each crepe with 1 tablespoon of the **topping sauce**. Place the pan in the oven and bake, uncovered, for 10–12 minutes, or until crepes are hot (be careful not to overbake).

Serve crepes alone or with whipped topping.

BRUNCH ENCHILADAS

4 Large Servings

Filling

- 1 ½ teaspoons vegetable oil
- 2 slices bacon, diced
- 1 ½ teaspoons minced garlic
- ¾ cup diced onion
- ¼ cup finely chopped green bell pepper
- ¾ cup (3 ounces) shredded ham
- 1 ¼ cups shredded cheddar cheese, divided use
- 4 (8-inch) flour tortillas

Egg Mixture

- 3 large eggs
- 1 tablespoon all-purpose flour
- ¼ teaspoon garlic powder
  pinch cayenne pepper
- 1 ½ cups half-and-half

Spicy Cheese Sauce

- ¾ cup half-and-half
- 2 tablespoons salsa
- ¾ cup shredded cheddar cheese
- 1 ½ teaspoons all-purpose flour
  pinch salt

This casserole needs to chill overnight, so plan accordingly.

For Filling Heat the oil in a large skillet. Add the bacon and cook until just crisp. Add the garlic, onion and green pepper and cook, stirring often, for 3 minutes to soften the vegetables. Remove from heat and stir in the ham. Cool slightly.

Lightly oil an 8-by-8-inch pan. Lay out the tortillas on a work surface. Divide filling evenly among them. Top each with 3 tablespoons of the cheese (remaining cheese will be used later). Roll up tightly and place in the pan, seam-side down.

For Egg Mixture Beat the eggs until smooth. Add 2 tablespoons of half-and-half to the flour, whisking until smooth. Add this mixture, the spices and remaining half-and-half to the eggs, whisking until blended. Pour the mixture over tortillas in the pan. Cover and refrigerate overnight.

Remove pan from the refrigerator about 30 minutes before baking, then bake, covered, at 350°F for 40–45 minutes, or until a tester inserted in center comes out clean. Sprinkle the remaining cheese (from the filling) over the top and bake, uncovered, for 6–7 minutes to melt the cheese. Let rest for 10 minutes before serving.

For Spicy Cheese Sauce In a saucepan, heat the half-and-half and salsa over medium heat. In a small bowl, toss the flour and shredded cheese together. Add to the saucepan and whisk until cheese is melted and sauce is smooth. Season with salt to taste. Ladle the sauce over each serving of enchilada; sprinkle with cilantro if desired.

BRUNCH STRATA

4–6 Servings

Vegetable Mixture

  4 teaspoons vegetable oil
½ teaspoon minced garlic
¼ cup finely chopped green bell pepper
½ cup diced onion
  1 cup diced zucchini
  1 cup mushrooms, halved, sliced thin
¾ cup (3 ounces) shredded ham

Egg Mixture

  1 (8-ounce) package cream cheese,
    softened
½ cup milk
  4 large eggs
½ teaspoon salt
¼ teaspoon black pepper
1 ½ cups shredded cheddar cheese

A favorite of President Judy Rogers, the creamy texture combined with the sauteed vegetables makes this a special brunch offering.

Heat the oil in a large skillet. Add the garlic and green pepper. Cook for 10 seconds, then add the onion, zucchini and mushrooms. Cook for 3–4 minutes, or until vegetables are tender. Remove from heat and stir in the ham.

In a mixing bowl, beat the cream cheese and milk until smooth. Add the eggs, salt and pepper, and continue beating until blended and smooth. Stir in the cheeese, then the vegetable mixture.

Lightly oil-spray an 8-by-8-inch pan. Pour the egg mixture into the pan. Bake in a pre-heated 350°F oven for 30-35 minutes, or until a tester inserted in center comes out clean. Let stand for 10 minutes before serving.

HAWAIIAN BREAD FRENCH TOAST WITH FRUIT SALSA

4 Servings

8 slices Hawaiian bread, halved,
 sliced ¾ inch, left out to dry,
 uncovered, for 1 day
3 eggs, beaten
¾ cup milk
½ teaspoon vanilla
 butter or margarine, as needed
¼ cup powdered sugar

Fruit Salsa (optional)
1 ½ cups diced fresh pineapple
 (or use canned chunks)
½ cup fresh strawberries, rinsed, diced
⅓ cup fresh blueberries, rinsed
¼ cup sugar
½ cup pineapple juice
1 teaspoon lemon juice
¼ teaspoon vanilla

 butter or margarine, as needed
 pancake syrup, as needed

Most supermarkets carry the sweet Hawaiian bread in their bakery section. It makes a great French toast by itself or served with the fruit salsa.

For Fruit Salsa In a small saucepan, add the sugar, pineapple juice and lemon juice; bring to a boil. Boil for 8 minutes, or until reduced by about half. Remove from heat; let cool completely. Stir in vanilla; set aside. Combine fruit in a medium bowl. Toss with the cooled syrup; chill for 30 minutes. Strain before serving.

For French Toast Combine the eggs, milk and vanilla in a shallow pan. Heat a large skillet and add butter to coat the pan. Dip the bread slices in egg mixture on both sides and place in the hot buttered skillet. Cook for 2–3 minutes per side, or until golden brown, adding butter as needed. Top with butter and pancake syrup as desired; sprinkle with powdered sugar. Spoon strained fruit salsa beside the French toast on each plate.

SWEDISH PANCAKES

6–7 Pancakes (recipe can be doubled)

2 large eggs
1 cup milk
½ cup all-purpose flour
2 teaspoons sugar
1 tablespoon butter, melted
pinch salt

These pancakes are very similar to crepes. The cooking technique is the same and may take a few tries to get them just right. They are well worth the effort and are, for me, a favorite for weekend breakfasts. We had a student from Sweden who claimed they were as good as her grandmother's! Serve them with butter and pancake syrup, or jam.

Beat the eggs in a large bowl. Mix in the milk, flour, sugar, butter and salt (or place all ingredients in a blender and blend until smooth). Batter should be thin (if batter seems too thin, just whisk in a touch more flour).

Oil-spray a medium nonstick skillet. Turn heat to medium-high and wait for 2 minutes or so for the pan to heat up. Stir batter; pour ¼ cup batter into the heated pan. Immediately pick up the pan and swirl batter around to the edges until it firms up and is no longer runny. Cook for 1 minute, then remove from heat; carefully flip over the pancake and cook for 30–35 seconds more on the second side. Pancakes should have golden brown spots. Roll each pancake up loosely; place, seam-side down, in a heat-proof dish and keep warm in a 200°F oven while you prepare more.

ALMOND FRENCH TOAST

6 Servings

French Toast

- 6 slices Texas toast, crusts removed, left out to dry 4 hours (or overnight)
- 2 eggs
- ½ cup milk
- ½ teaspoon almond extract
- 2 tablespoons butter or margarine

Almond Butter

- 6 tablespoons butter, softened
- 1 tablespoon + 1½ teaspoons powdered sugar
- ½ teaspoon almond extract

  powdered sugar, as needed
  pancake syrup, as needed

This is definitely one of our most requested brunch dishes.

Slice bread diagonally for triangle shapes; set aside. Stir together the eggs, milk and almond extract and place in a shallow pan; set aside.

For Almond Butter Combine the butter, sugar and almond extract. Beat until smooth. Chill until slightly firm, about 10 minutes.

Meanwhile, heat 1 tablespoon of butter in a skillet. Dip 6 bread triangles into the egg mixture, turning to coat both sides. Cook in butter until golden brown on both sides. Transfer to a serving plate and keep warm. Repeat procedure with remaining bread slices, egg mixture and butter.

Dollop the center of each triangle with a teaspoon or so of the almond butter (or spoon almond butter into a pastry bag fitted with a decorative tip and pipe butter onto the center of each triangle). Sprinkle powdered sugar over all. Serve warm with pancake syrup on the side.

BLUEBERRY MAPLE FRENCH TOAST

16 Servings

French Toast

- 12 slices day-old white bread, crusts removed, cut into 1-inch cubes
- 1 (8-ounce) package cream cheese, cold, cut into ½-inch cubes
- 1 cup fresh or frozen blueberries
- 12 eggs
- 2 cups milk
- ⅓ cup pancake syrup
- ¼ cup sugar
- ½ teaspoon salt
- 2½ teaspoons vanilla

Sauce (optional)

- 1 cup sugar
- 2 tablespoons cornstarch
- 1 cup water
- 1 cup fresh or frozen blueberries
- ¼ teaspoon vanilla
- 1 teaspoon lemon juice
- 2 tablespoons butter, cold

Great to serve for Sunday brunch. You could leave the bread out to air-dry on Friday night, assemble the casserole on Saturday, then bake and serve on Sunday morning. The sauce in this recipe is wonderful ladled over each serving, however, you can use a purchased blueberry or pancake syrup with good results.

Place half the bread cubes in a buttered 9-by-13-inch pan. Cover evenly with the cream cheese cubes. Top with the blueberries and remaining bread cubes.

In a large bowl, beat the eggs, then add the milk, syrup, sugar, salt and vanilla; mix well. Pour over the bread mixture. Cover and **refrigerate overnight**.

Remove casserole from the refrigerator 30–40 minutes before baking, and then bake, uncovered, at 350°F for 20 minutes. Rotate the pan* and bake for 20–25 minutes more, or until a tester inserted in center comes out clean. It should be light brown; cover with foil if getting too browned. Let casserole rest for 20 minutes before cutting into servings.

For Sauce In a saucepan, combine the sugar and cornstarch; stir in the water. Bring to a boil over medium heat; boil for 3 minutes, stirring frequently. Reduce heat and stir in the blueberries; simmer for 10 minutes. Stir in the vanilla, lemon juice and butter, stirring until butter is melted. Serve sauce warm.

* Rotate the pan refers to turning the pan 180° (half a turn) to insure even browning.

BREAKFAST QUESADILLAS

4 Servings

6 eggs, lightly beaten
  dash salt
2 tablespoons salsa

2 tablespoons low-fat or regular
  cream cheese, softened
1 ½ teaspoons salsa

1 ½ cups shredded cheddar-jack
  cheese blend
4 (8-inch) flour tortillas
4 tablespoons vegetable oil

  salsa, as needed
  sour cream, as needed

Scramble the eggs in a nonstick skillet; season with salt to taste. Stir in the salsa and remove from heat when the eggs are just set.

In a small bowl, combine the cream cheese and salsa. Lay out 2 tortillas on a work surface. Spread half the cream cheese mixture on each tortilla. Top each with half the scrambled eggs, then cover with half the cheese blend. Place the remaining tortillas on top. Keep covered until ready to cook.

Heat a skillet with a thin layer of oil. Cook each quesadilla until golden brown on each side and cheese is melted; add oil as needed to the skillet.

Cut each quesadilla into 6 wedges. Serve hot with salsa and sour cream.

HEALTHY PANCAKES

10 Pancakes

3/4 cup all-purpose flour
1/2 cup whole wheat flour
1/2 cup toasted wheat germ*
 1 egg
1 1/4 cups vanilla soymilk (or regular milk)
 3 tablespoons honey
1 1/2 teaspoons baking powder
1 1/2 teaspoons baking soda
 1/4 cup canola oil
1 1/2 teaspoons vanilla
 3/4 cup fresh blueberries (optional)

These are flavorful and surprisingly fluffy in spite of the whole grain profile. If you use plain milk instead of vanilla soymilk, add an additional 1/2 teaspoon of vanilla.

In a large bowl, mix all ingredients until smooth. Pour batter by 1/4 cupfuls onto a lightly-oiled hot skillet. Cook until golden brown on each side. For blueberry pancakes, stir the blueberries into the batter just before cooking.

* Sold in glass jars and is available in most supermarkets. It has a nutty flavor in contrast to raw wheat germ.

HONEY CINNAMON GRANOLA

16–20 Servings (about 13 cups)

5 1/2 cups (18 ounces) quick oats
    5 tablespoons toasted wheat germ*
    1 cup sliced almonds
    2 tablespoons sesame seeds
    1 cup flaked coconut
    2 tablespoons ground cinnamon
  1/2 cup vegetable oil
    6 tablespoons honey
    3 tablespoons pancake syrup
    4 teaspoons vanilla
1 1/2 cups raisins
    3 cups raisin bran cereal

This granola is extremely popular among our students. This recipe can be cut in half. It also freezes well.

Preheat oven to 350°F.

In a large bowl, mix the oats, wheat germ, almonds, sesame seeds, coconut and cinnamon.

In a small bowl, mix the oil, honey, syrup, and vanilla until well combined. Drizzle into oat mixture and stir, using a rubber spatula or wooden spoon, until oats are evenly coated with honey mixture.

Transfer mixture to jelly-roll pans or cookie sheets, spreading into an even layer. Bake for 20–25 minutes, stirring the mixture twice during baking. Remove from oven when granola is lightly toasted and dry. Let cool. Stir in raisins and cereal. Store in an airtight container.

* Sold in glass jars and is available in most supermarkets. It has a nutty flavor in contrast to raw wheat germ.

CREAM CHEESE SWIRL COFFEE CAKE

1 10-Inch Cake

Filling

1 (8-ounce) package cream cheese, softened
3 tablespoons powdered sugar
2 tablespoons milk
½ teaspoon vanilla

Cake

2 cups all-purpose flour
1 teaspoon baking powder
1 teaspoon baking soda
¼ teaspoon salt
1 cup sugar
½ cup (1 stick) butter, softened
3 eggs
1 teaspoon vanilla
1 (8-ounce) carton sour cream

Nut Mix

¼ cup finely chopped pecans or walnuts
2 tablespoons sugar
½ teaspoon ground cinnamon

Icing

½ cup powdered sugar
½ teaspoon vanilla
1 tablespoon milk

For Filling In a medium bowl, beat the cream cheese, powdered sugar, milk and vanilla until smooth; set aside.

For Cake Generously grease and flour a 10-inch bundt or tube pan. Tap out excess flour. Stir together the flour, baking powder, baking soda and salt; set aside. In a mixing bowl, beat the sugar and butter until light and fluffy. Add the eggs and vanilla; mix well. Add dry ingredients alternately with sour cream; mix well. Pour half the batter into the prepared pan. Spoon the cheese mixture (filling) on top of batter in the center. Spoon remaining batter over filling to cover.

For Nut Mix Combine the chopped nuts, sugar and cinnamon, and sprinkle evenly over the top of the batter.

Preheat oven to 350°F. Bake for 40–45 minutes, or until a tester inserted in center comes out clean. Cool for 10 minutes, then remove cake by flipping over and tapping to release from pan.

For Icing Combine icing ingredients in a small bowl, mixing until smooth. Drizzle over cake. Serve cake warm or at room temperature.

PISTACHIO COFFEE CAKE

16–20 Servings

Cake

1 (18.25-ounce) box white
or yellow cake mix
1 (3.4-ounce) box pistachio
instant pudding mix
1 cup vegetable oil
6 eggs
1 (8-ounce) carton sour cream

Filling

½ cup (2 ounces) pecan pieces
1½ cups sugar
2 tablespoons ground cinnamon
2 tablespoons butter or margarine, cold

**Every cookbook should include
at least one recipe from the
author's mother-in-law, and this
is it. This coffee cake has been a
family favorite for years and has
been well received on campus as
well. It is very moist and has a
unique pistachio flavor.**

In a large bowl, combine all cake ingredients together; beat for 3 minutes (for stand mixer use paddle attachment).

Combine all filling ingredients in a food processor. Process using on/off turns just until mixture is the size of coarse crumbs (be careful not to over process).

Grease a 9-by-13-inch pan. Spread 2½ cups of the cake batter on the bottom of the pan. Sprinkle 1¾ cups of filling evenly over the batter, patting down to form a firm layer. Spread remaining batter over the filling to cover as well as possible (it doesn't have to be perfect), then sprinkle the remaining filling over the top.

Preheat oven to 350°F. Bake for 20 minutes. Rotate the pan* and bake for 16–20 minutes more, or until a tester inserted in center comes out clean. Let cake cool for 30 minutes or so before serving.

* Rotate the pan refers to turning the pan 180° (half a turn) to insure even browning.

BANANA BREAD

1 Large Loaf (or 24 muffins)

- 3 bananas, very ripe, mashed
- 2 eggs
- 1 ¾ cups all-purpose flour
- 1 ¼ cups sugar
- ½ cup vegetable oil
- 5 tablespoons buttermilk
- 1 teaspoon baking soda
- 1 teaspoon vanilla
- ½ teaspoon salt

I developed this recipe at home for our children when they were young. Now grown, they still love to have it when home. We sometimes bake it in the small loaf pans so that each person gets his or her own loaf for breakfast.

Preheat oven to 325°F. Grease and flour a 9-by-5-inch loaf pan.

Add all ingredients to a large bowl; mix just until combined. Transfer batter to the prepared pan. Bake until top is golden brown and a tester inserted in center comes out clean, about 1 hour and 20 minutes (for muffins, bake for 20–22 minutes).

PUMPKIN SWIRL BREAD

1 Loaf

1 (8-ounce) package cream cheese, softened
¼ cup sugar
1 egg, beaten

Dry Ingredients

1¾ cups all-purpose flour
1½ cups sugar
1 teaspoon baking soda
1 teaspoon ground cinnamon
½ teaspoon salt
¼ teaspoon ground nutmeg

1 cup canned pumpkin
½ cup (1 stick) butter or margarine, melted
1 egg
⅓ cup water

After tasting this bread at a local school fundraising event, I was hooked. With some digging and some convincing, I was able to obtain this recipe from the cook who prepared it. We serve it often at our Sunday brunch. It is the perfect quick bread to serve around the holidays.

Combine the cream cheese, sugar and egg; set aside.

Combine dry ingredients in a medium bowl. In another bowl, combine the pumpkin, margarine, egg, and water. Mix the dry ingredients into the pumpkin mixture until moist. Reserve 2 cups of batter.

Preheat oven to 350°F. Pour remaining batter into a greased and floured 9-by-5-inch loaf pan. Pour the cream cheese mixture over batter. Top with the reserved batter. Cut through batter with a knife several times to make a swirl effect.

Bake for 1 hour and 10 minutes, or until a tester inserted in center comes out clean. Cool for 10–15 minutes before removing from pan.

CINNAMON SWIRL BREAD

1 Loaf

Batter

½ cup (1 stick) butter or margarine, softened

2 eggs, beaten

2 cups all-purpose flour

1 teaspoon baking powder

1 teaspoon baking soda

1 ¼ teaspoons vanilla

¾ cup sugar

¼ teaspoon salt

1 cup buttermilk

Filling

1 ½ teaspoons ground cinnamon

6 tablespoons brown sugar

½ cup finely chopped walnuts

1 tablespoon butter or margarine, softened

Topping

3 tablespoons butter or margarine, melted

4 teaspoons sugar

½ teaspoon ground cinnamon

Preheat oven to 350°F. Mix all batter ingredients together. Pour half the batter into a greased 9-by-5-inch loaf pan. Combine all filling ingredients in a small bowl; sprinkle evenly over the batter. Top with the remaining batter. Cut through batter with a knife several times to make a swirl effect.

Bake at 350°F for 50–60 minutes, or until a tester inserted in center comes out clean. While warm, brush or spread melted butter over the top. Combine the sugar and cinnamon, and sprinkle evenly over the top. Remove from the pan and let cool on a rack. Serve warm or at room temperature.

We tried to buy a prepared cinnamon swirl bread to use for making French toast for special occasion brunches. We were unable to find a good one, so we created this recipe. We use it for a breakfast quick bread, or will slice it and dry it out to make the cinnamon swirl French toast as originally intended.

MOLASSES GLAZED PECAN SCONES

16 Wedges

Scones

  2 cups all-purpose flour
  1/2 cup packed brown sugar
  1 teaspoon baking powder
  1/2 teaspoon baking soda
  1/2 teaspoon salt
  6 tablespoons butter, cold, cut into 1/2-inch cubes
  3/4 cup pecans

  2/3 cup buttermilk
  1/2 teaspoon vanilla
  1 1/2 teaspoons maple extract
  2 egg yolks

Glaze

  4 1/2 teaspoons milk
  1 cup powdered sugar
  1 1/2 teaspoons molasses

Try these scones for a change from the typical muffins or coffee cakes. They are nutty and moist with a pleasant sweetness from the molasses glaze.

Preheat oven to 350°F. Bake the pecans for 6–7 minutes until lightly toasted. Let cool, then finely chop; set aside.

In a large bowl, combine the flour, brown sugar, baking powder, baking soda and salt; whisk to blend. Drop in butter. Using fingertips, rub in until butter is reduced to pea-size pieces. Or, use a stand mixer with the paddle attachment; beat on medium speed for 2 minutes or so until the butter is reduced to pea-size pieces. Mix in pecans.

In a medium bowl, whisk the buttermilk, vanilla, maple extract and egg yolks. Add to flour mixture. Toss with a fork until dough comes together in moist clumps. Gather dough into a ball. Press onto a lightly oil-sprayed baking sheet into an 8-inch round.

Bake for 20–22 minutes, or until a tester inserted in center comes out clean. Let cool for 15 minutes, then cut into 16 wedges. Separate the wedges from one another by about 1 inch.

For Glaze Combine the milk, powdered sugar and molasses with a whisk. Spread glaze generously over each wedge while scones are still warm (let glaze drip slightly over the edges). Cool completely; serve at room temperature. Keep covered so scones stay moist.

ORANGE ROLLS

9 Rolls

Rolls

1 (.25-ounce) package active dry yeast
½ cup warm water (110–115°F)
¼ teaspoon sugar
2 cups all-purpose flour
2 tablespoons butter or margarine, softened
1 tablespoon sugar
1 teaspoon salt
1 egg, lightly beaten

Filling

1 ½ cups powdered sugar
1 ½ teaspoons grated orange zest
3 tablespoons butter or margarine, melted
2 tablespoons orange juice

These rolls are prepared the same way as cinnamon rolls, but with an orange filling and icing.

For Rolls In a mixing bowl, add yeast and sugar to the warm water; let stand for 5 minutes. Add 1 cup of flour and the butter, sugar, salt and egg. Beat with a stand mixer, using paddle attachment, on medium speed until smooth. Stir in remaining flour, then add more flour as needed to make a soft dough. Turn onto a lightly floured surface; knead until smooth, about 2 minutes. Cover and let rest for 15 minutes.

For Filling Combine all filling ingredients in a bowl; mix until smooth, and set aside.

Roll dough into a rectangle about 14-by-7 inches. Spread with ½ of the orange filling, leaving a 1-inch border on long sides. Roll up, jelly-roll fashion, starting at long side. Pinch seam to seal. Cut into 9 equal slices and place, cut-side down, into a greased 8-by-8-inch pan. Cover and let rise in a warm place, free from drafts, for 30 minutes. Preheat oven to 350°F. Bake for 20–22 minutes until golden brown. Spread remaining filling over the top, as an icing, while rolls are still warm.

SAUSAGE AND CHEESE SCONES

12 Scones

1 ¾ cups all-purpose flour
¼ cup sugar
½ teaspoon salt
½ teaspoon onion powder
¼ teaspoon garlic powder
2 ¼ teaspoons baking powder
½ cup (1 stick) butter or margarine,
cold, cut into pieces
8 ounces (½ pound) breakfast
sausage, cooked, crumbled, cooled
1 ¼ cups finely shredded cheddar cheese
½ cup buttermilk

**These are best when served warm.
At Cottey, we split and fill them with
scrambled eggs and cheese slices to
make hot breakfast sandwiches.**

Combine dry ingredients in a mixing bowl. Cut in butter until it resembles coarse meal. Stir in the cheese, then the cooked sausage. Mix the buttermilk into the dough. Add more flour, in small amounts, if dough is sticky.

Dust work surface with flour. Knead dough briefly and press into a ¾-inch thick rectangle. Using the rim of a cup, or a 2½-inch biscuit cutter, cut out rounds. Gather up scraps and pat out dough to cut more rounds.

Preheat oven to 400°F. Place rounds on a lightly-greased baking sheet about 2 inches apart. Bake for 9 minutes. Rotate the pan* and bake for 9–10 minutes more. Transfer to a wire rack to cool.

* Rotate the pan refers to turning the pan 180° (half a turn)
to insure even browning.

ORANGE MUFFINS

12 Muffins

Batter

- 6 tablespoons vegetable oil
- 1 cup sugar
- 2 eggs
- 1 ½ cups all-purpose flour
- 1 teaspoon salt
- 1 teaspoon baking soda
- 1 teaspoon vanilla
- ¼ cup orange juice
- 2 tablespoons grated orange zest

Icing

- ½ cup powdered sugar
- 2–3 teaspoons orange juice

Use fresh squeezed orange juice for the best flavor.

Preheat oven to 350°F. Oil-spray 12 muffin tins, or line with paper baking cups; set aside.

For Batter Combine the oil, sugar and eggs; mix well. Stir in remaining batter ingredients. Spoon batter into the prepared muffin tins, filling them ⅔ full. Bake for 12–15 minutes, or until a tester inserted in center comes out clean.

For Icing Combine the powdered sugar and 2 teaspoons orange juice. Add more orange juice, as needed, to make a thick but spreadable icing. Cool muffins completely, then spread a layer of icing over each top.

APPLE STREUSEL MUFFINS

18 Muffins

Batter

    2 cups all-purpose flour
    1 cup sugar
 1 1/2 teaspoons ground cinnamon
   1/4 teaspoon ground nutmeg
    1 teaspoon baking powder
   1/2 teaspoon baking soda
   1/2 teaspoon salt
    2 eggs
    1 (8-ounce) carton sour cream
    1 teaspoon vanilla
   1/4 cup butter or margarine, melted
 1 1/2 cups, unpeeled, finely chopped apples

Topping

   1/4 cup sugar
    3 tablespoons all-purpose flour
   1/4 teaspoon ground cinnamon
    2 tablespoons butter or margarine,
        cold, cut into pieces
    1 tablespoon chopped flaked coconut
        (optional)

Preheat oven to 350°F. Generously grease 18 muffin tins, or line with paper baking cups; set aside.

For Batter In a mixing bowl, stir together the flour, sugar, cinnamon, nutmeg, baking powder, baking soda and salt. In a medium bowl, beat the eggs, then stir in the sour cream, vanilla and melted butter until smooth. Add the egg mixture and apples to the flour mixture. Stir just until batter is smooth. Spoon batter into the prepared muffin tins, filling them 2/3 full.

For Streusel Topping In a small bowl, stir together the sugar, flour and cinnamon. Using a pastry blender or fork, cut in the butter until the mixture resembles coarse crumbs. Stir in the coconut. Sprinkle a portion of the topping on each muffin.

Bake for 20–22 minutes, or until a tester inserted in center comes out clean.

BLUEBERRY LEMON MUFFINS

12 Muffins

Batter

1 3/4 cups all-purpose flour

1/2 cup sugar

2 1/2 teaspoons baking powder

3/4 teaspoon salt

1 teaspoon grated lemon zest

1 egg

3/4 cup milk

1 tablespoon fresh lemon juice

1/3 cup vegetable oil

1 cup blueberries (fresh or frozen)

Topping

2 tablespoons butter, melted

1/4 cup sugar

These are light and flavorful, offering a balance of tart lemon and the sweetness of blueberry, with sugar on top. If lemon is not to your liking, just leave out the juice and zest and you will have a good blueberry muffin on its own, with or without the sugar topping.

Preheat oven to 350°F. Lightly grease 12 muffin tins, or line with paper baking cups; set aside.

In a large bowl, stir together the flour, sugar, baking powder, salt and zest. In a medium bowl, beat the egg, milk, lemon juice and oil until smooth. Add the egg mixture to the flour mixture. Stir just until combined, being careful not to beat the batter too much.

Fold the blueberries into the batter. Spoon batter into the prepared muffin tins, filling them 2/3 full.

Bake for 20–22 minutes, or until a tester inserted in center comes out clean. Let cool for 15–20 minutes. Dip the top of each muffin in the melted butter, and then in the sugar.

BUTTERSCOTCH MUFFINS

18 Muffins

Batter

  2 cups all-purpose flour
  1 cup sugar
  1 (3.4-ounce) package instant
    butterscotch pudding mix
  1 (3.4-ounce) package instant vanilla
    pudding mix
  2 teaspoons baking powder
  1 teaspoon salt
  1 cup water
  4 eggs
  ¾ cup vegetable oil
  1 teaspoon vanilla

Topping

  ½ cup packed brown sugar
  ½ cup finely chopped pecans
  1½ teaspoons ground cinnamon

These muffins have their fans
among our students and staff.
They are moist and have a wonderful, crisp topping.

Preheat oven to 350°F. Lightly grease 18 muffin tins, or line with paper baking cups; set aside.

For Batter In a mixing bowl, combine the flour, sugar, pudding mixes, baking powder and salt. In a separate bowl, combine the water, eggs, oil and vanilla; stir into the dry ingredients just until smooth. Spoon batter into the prepared muffin tins, filling them ⅔ full.

For Topping Combine the topping ingredients in a small bowl; sprinkle generously over batter. Bake for 20–22 minutes, or until a tester inserted in center comes out clean. Cool for 5 minutes before removing from muffin tins.

LEMON CRUNCH MUFFINS

18 Muffins

Batter

2 cups all-purpose flour

1 cup sugar

1 (3.4-ounce) package instant lemon pudding mix

1 (3.4-ounce) package instant vanilla pudding mix

2 teaspoons baking powder

1 teaspoon salt

1 cup water

4 eggs

¾ cup vegetable oil

1 teaspoon vanilla

Topping

½ cup packed brown sugar

½ cup finely chopped flaked coconut

1½ teaspoons ground cinnamon

These muffins are very moist with a light lemon flavor and crisp topping.

Preheat oven to 350°F. Lightly grease 18 muffin tins, or line with paper baking cups; set aside.

For Batter In a mixing bowl, combine the flour, pudding mixes, baking powder and salt. In a separate bowl, combine the water, eggs, oil and vanilla; stir into the dry ingredients just until smooth. Spoon batter into the prepared muffin tins, filling them ⅔ full.

For Topping Combine the topping ingredients in a small bowl; sprinkle generously over batter. Bake for 20–22 minutes, or until a tester inserted in center comes out clean. Cool for 5 minutes before removing from muffin tins.

HEALTHY BRAN APPLE MUFFINS

12 Muffins

  1 cup buttermilk
1 ¼ cups bran cereal (shreds or flakes)
1 ¼ teaspoons baking soda
  1 cup packed brown sugar
  3 tablespoons applesauce
  2 eggs
2 ¼ teaspoons molasses
  1 cup all-purpose flour
  ¼ teaspoon salt
  1 cup finely chopped apple

This muffin is a personal favorite. It is moist and flavorful and "better for you" at the same time. The applesauce replaces the oil typically in muffin batter, and you can use only egg whites instead of whole eggs to lower calories more.

Preheat oven to 350°F. Grease 12 muffin tins, or line with paper baking cups; set aside.

In a medium bowl, combine the buttermilk, bran and baking soda; set aside. In a mixing bowl, beat the sugar and applesauce until smooth. Add eggs; beat until smooth. Stir in the molasses, then the buttermilk-bran mixture. Gradually add the flour, while mixing, then stir in the salt and apple.

Spoon batter into the prepared muffin tins, filling them nearly to the top. Bake for 20–22 minutes, or until a tester inserted in center comes out clean. Cool in pans for 10 minutes, then transfer to a wire rack or other cool surface.

PIÑA COLADA MUFFINS

12 Muffins

- 1 (18.25-ounce) package yellow cake mix
- ¾ cup water
- ½ cup flaked coconut
- 1 (8-ounce) can crushed pineapple, drained

We like to serve these as part of an assorted muffin platter because they are a nice change from the usual muffin varieties. These are moist and easy to make.

Preheat oven to 350°F. Lightly grease 12 muffin tins, or line with paper baking cups; set aside.

Combine the cake mix, water, coconut and pineapple to make a smooth batter. Spoon batter into the prepared muffin tins, filling them ⅞ full. Bake for 12–14 minutes, or until a tester inserted in center comes out clean.

RASPBERRY CHEESECAKE MUFFINS

15 Muffins

Batter

2 ¼ cups all-purpose flour

¾ cup sugar

¾ cup (1 ½ sticks) butter, cold,
   cut into pieces

½ teaspoon baking soda

½ teaspoon baking powder

¼ teaspoon salt

¾ cup (6 ounces) sour cream

1 egg

1 teaspoon almond extract

Filling

4 ounces cream cheese, softened

1 large egg yolk

2 tablespoons sugar

1 tablespoon + 2 teaspoons raspberry
   preserves (or strawberry)

These are as good as they sound
and not difficult to make. You basi-
cally dollup the cream cheese filling
over batter, dollop the raspberry
over that, then sprinkle with batter
crumbs and bake. We think they are
worth the extra "dolloping."

Preheat oven to 350°F. Grease 15 muffin tins, or line with paper baking cups; set aside.

For Batter In a mixing bowl, combine the flour and sugar; cut in the butter until crumbly. Reserve 1 cup for topping. To the remaining crumb mixture, add the baking soda, baking powder, salt, sour cream, egg and almond extract. Spoon batter into the muffin tins, filling them about ⅔ full. With damp fingers, or a greased spoon, press lightly in the centers to make a small indentation.

For Filling Stir together the cream cheese, egg yolk and sugar until smooth. Spoon about 2 teaspoons into the center of each muffin. Spoon a heaping ¼ teaspoon of preserves over the cream cheese. Sprinkle with the reserved crumb mixture to cover.

Bake for 20–22 minutes, or until a tester inserted in center comes out clean.

SOUPS/SALADS

SOUPS

Tortilla Soup
Vegetarian Chili
Minestrone Soup V V
Beer Cheese Soup
Baked Potato Soup V
Beef Stew
Beth's Ham and Bean Soup
Black Bean and Veggie Chili V
Chicken Enchilada Soup
French Onion Soup au Gratin
Gazpacho V
Macaroni and Cheese Soup V
Spanish Chicken and Rice Soup
Taco Soup

SALADS

Homemade Croutons V
Caesar Salad V
Greek Salad V
Mandarin Orange Salad V
Mary's Spinach Mushroom Salad
Black-Eyed Pea Salad V
Asian Coleslaw V
Sunny Broccoli Salad
Tabbouleh V
Artichoke Spinach Salad V
Angel Hair Salad V

V Vegetarian
V Vegan

TORTILLA SOUP

4 Servings

Tortilla Strips

6 corn tortillas, divided
4 teaspoons vegetable oil

Soup

4 cups chicken broth
2 tablespoons tomato paste
(or tomato sauce)
¾ teaspoon chili powder
¼ teaspoon ground cumin
¼ teaspoon garlic powder
½ teaspoon onion powder
½ teaspoon salt
⅛ teaspoon black pepper
¼ cup finely chopped onion
¼ cup finely chopped celery
2 teaspoons minced cilantro

Toppings

2 cups cooked chicken,
shredded or diced
2 cups shredded cheddar-jack
cheese blend
½ cup diced fresh avocado
¾ cup crisp tortilla strips

This is a wonderful "south of the border" flavored soup that can be individualized by adding an assortment of toppings at the table. A few are suggested. For a vegetarian soup, use vegetable broth in place of the chicken broth.

For Corn Tortilla Strips Preheat oven to 350°F. Cut tortillas in half, then cut into very thin strips. Place in a large bowl and toss with the oil to coat. Place strips on a baking sheet and bake for 12–15 minutes, or until golden and crisp; set aside.

Heat the broth in a soup pot. Stir in the tomato paste and all seasonings. Add the onion and celery; bring to a boil, then lower the heat and simmer, covered, for 15 minutes. Skim off any accumulated foam, then stir in half the tortilla strips and the cilantro. Cook, covered, for 10 minutes more. Serve in soup bowls with the toppings on the side.

VEGETARIAN CHILI

8 Servings

4 teaspoons vegetable oil

2 cups diced onion

1 ½ teaspoons diced fresh jalapeño

1 teaspoon minced garlic

1 (10.75-ounce) can tomato soup, water added

1 (1-ounce) package dried onion soup mix

1 (1-pound) can vegetarian refried beans

2 (15-ounce) cans chili flavored beans

2 tablespoons salsa

¼ teaspoon salt

1 ½ teaspoons chili powder

½ teaspoon ground cumin

¼ teaspoon garlic powder

½ teaspoon onion powder

This recipe was written for our vegetarian students and is inspired by a recipe given to me from Cottey's longtime chili afficionado, Bill Watkins, who cooked the chili for the campus chili feeds before retiring. As Bill would want it, you can add cooked, ground beef or venison to this recipe, if desired. If you do, omit 1 can of chili beans and add more chili powder to taste.

Heat the oil in a soup pot. Add the onion and cook for 5 minutes over medium heat, stirring occasionally. Add the garlic and jalapeño, and cook for 3 minutes more. Add remaining ingredients, stirring well to combine. Turn heat to low and cook, covered, for 20 minutes, stirring every few minutes to keep solids from sticking to the bottom of the pot.

Place in soup bowls and serve with assorted toppings such as shredded cheddar cheese, sour cream, chopped onion and chopped jalapeños.

MINESTRONE SOUP

8 Servings

1 tablespoon olive oil

1 ½ teaspoons minced garlic

½ cup diced onion

½ cup diced celery

⅓ cup carrot, peeled, quartered lengthwise, sliced thin

½ cup diced cabbage

⅓ cup diced zucchini

¼ cup dry red wine (optional)

3 cups vegetable or chicken broth

2 cups spaghetti sauce

½ cup peeled, diced potato

⅓ cup kidney beans, rinsed, drained

½ cup white beans, rinsed, drained

⅓ cup small seashell pasta

¼ teaspoon salt

⅛ teaspoon black pepper

1 large or 2 small bay leaves

2 teaspoons minced fresh basil (or ½ teaspoon dried)

1 teaspoon minced fresh oregano (or ¼ teaspoon dried)

½ cup grated parmesan cheese (optional)

Although not difficult to prepare, this recipe uses small quantities of several ingredients. You could double or triple the recipe and freeze the rest. You also can substitute equal amounts of other beans or vegetables as available. This soup is terrific on a cold winter day. Serve with rustic Italian bread.

Heat the oil in a soup pot over medium heat. Add the garlic, onion, celery, carrot and cabbage; cook for 3 minutes, stirring often. Add the zucchini and cook for 1 minute more. Turn heat to high and add the wine; cook for 1 minute, stirring often. Add remaining ingredients, except fresh basil and oregano (dried basil and oregano, if using, can be added here); cover and cook for 15 minutes over low heat. Add fresh basil and oregano and cook, covered, for 10 minutes more over low heat. Remove bay leaves before serving.

BEER CHEESE SOUP

8 Servings

1 ⅛ cups beer
6 tablespoons butter
6 tablespoons finely chopped onion
3 tablespoons finely chopped celery
3 tablespoons finely chopped carrot
3 tablespoons finely chopped
  green onion
  pinch dried thyme
6 tablespoons all-purpose flour
4 ½ cups chicken broth
1 ¾ cups heavy whipping cream
  pinch cayenne pepper
3 ½ cups shredded cheddar cheese

This is one of the soups most requested by students for the annual suite dinners in the Centennial Room (formerly the Red Room). Although some are disappointed that the alcohol cooks out, the beer flavor takes a back seat to the creamy, cheese soup and creates a winning taste combination.

Simmer beer, covered, for 10 minutes; set aside.

Melt the butter in a soup pot. Add the vegetables and cook for 6–7 minutes, or until almost tender, stirring often.

Add the flour to the vegetables. Stir frequently over medium heat for 4 minutes or so, then stir in the broth. Simmer for 10 minutes, uncovered, stirring occasionally. Add the beer, cream, cayenne and cheese. Simmer gently for 15 minutes, covered. Serve hot.

BAKED POTATO SOUP

8 Servings

Soup

  6 tablespoons butter or margarine
  ½ cup all-purpose flour
2¾ cups vegetable or chicken broth
  2 cups milk
  2 cups half-and-half
4½ cups peeled, diced baking potatoes
1¾ teaspoons seasoning salt
  ⅛ teaspoon white pepper

Toppings

  ½ cup green onions, sliced thin
  8 slices bacon, cooked crisp, crumbled
  ½ cup sour cream
  1 cup shredded cheddar cheese

Without a doubt, this is our most popular soup. Although fairly mild in flavor, it is sought after by many on campus for its comforting, creamy texture made complete with shredded cheese, chopped bacon, green onion and sour cream, or any combination thereof. Cottey uses vegetable broth for the benefit of vegetarians on campus, but chicken broth also works well.

Boil potatoes until just tender, about 10 minutes; drain and set aside (do not rinse).

Melt the butter in a heavy-bottomed soup pot. Stir in the flour and whisk until smooth. Cook this mixture (called a roux) for 2 minutes over low heat, stirring constantly. Gradually add the broth, while stirring. Add the milk and half-and-half; continue stirring until smooth.

Stir in the potatoes and seasonings (start with 1¾ teaspoons of seasoning salt, then add more to taste). Simmer on very low heat for 8–10 minutes, stirring often. Serve hot with toppings of choice on the side.

BEEF STEW

6 Servings

   4 teaspoons vegetable oil, divided
   1 pound beef stew meat, cut
      into 1-inch pieces
   4 teaspoons all-purpose flour
   1 cup diced onion
 1/2 cup diced celery
 1/3 cup peeled, diced carrot
   1 teaspoon minced garlic
 1/2 teaspoon seasoning salt
 1/8 teaspoon black pepper
 1/2 teaspoon dried thyme
 1/2 teaspoon onion powder
 1/4 teaspoon garlic powder
   2 cups peeled, diced baking potatoes
   4 cups beef broth
 1/2 cup water
   1 cup tomato sauce
 1/2 cup cut green beans (frozen or canned)
 1/4 cup frozen peas

You can prepare this stew all in 1 pot, but I prefer to brown the meat in a nonstick skillet, then add it to the stew. This is very satisfying, especially when the weather gets cold. Serve with some good bread and a small salad for a complete meal. This recipe can be doubled and it freezes well.

Heat 2 teaspoons of oil in a nonstick skillet. Pat the beef cubes dry with paper towels, then place in a bowl. Sprinkle the flour over the meat and stir to lightly coat. Brown the meat in the skillet on all sides; set aside.

Meanwhile, heat the remaining oil in a large soup pot. Add the onion, celery, carrot and garlic; cook for 2 minutes, then stir in all the seasonings. Cook for 1 minute, then add the potatoes, broth, water, tomato sauce and beef. Bring to a boil, then turn heat to very low; cover and simmer for 2 hours. Add the green beans and peas and cook for 30 minutes more, or until the meat is tender. Skim off any grease that has accumulated on top.

BETH'S HAM AND BEAN SOUP

6–8 Servings

4 cups chicken broth

2 (15.5-ounce) cans great northern beans, undrained

¼ cup finely chopped celery

2 tablespoons finely chopped carrot

¼ cup finely chopped onion

¾ teaspoon minced garlic

1 ham hock

dash black pepper

½ cup chopped smoked ham

Beth Kemper worked in our dining department for many years. Before she retired, she was the head cook. This is inspired by her recipe, which uses dried beans, soaked overnight. I have shortened the process by using canned beans with their liquid. We usually serve this with cornbread on the side.

In a soup pot, add the broth, beans, vegetables, ham hock and pepper. Bring to a boil, then lower heat; cover, and simmer for 1½ hours. Remove hock from soup; let cool. Cut any usable meat from the hock, discarding the skin, fat and gristle; add to the soup. Stir in the smoked ham and simmer the soup for 7–8 minutes more. Skim off any accumulated fat. Serve hot.

BLACK BEAN AND VEGGIE CHILI

8 Servings

1 tablespoon vegetable oil
1 cup diced onion
½ cup diced green bell pepper
½ cup diced red bell pepper
1 teaspoon minced garlic
1 cup diced zucchini
½ teaspoon salt
¾ teaspoon ground cumin
½ teaspoon dried basil
½ teaspoon onion powder
2½ teaspoons minced cilantro
2 cups vegetable broth*
1 (14.5-ounce) can diced tomatoes, undrained
½ cup tomato sauce
½ cup salsa
½ cup corn kernels (frozen or canned)
1 (15-ounce) can black beans, rinsed, drained
¾ cup water

This chili recipe was given to me by a student many years ago, and we continue to receive compliments on it whenever it is offered. Serve with some great bread for a filling meal. You can control the spiciness by the type of salsa used. Also you can cut back on the salsa and increase the tomato sauce if you prefer a milder flavor profile.

Heat the oil in a soup pot. Add the onion and peppers and cook, stirring frequently, for 4 minutes over medium heat. Add the garlic, zucchini, salt, cumin, basil, onion powder and cilantro, and cook for 3 minutes more. Add remaining ingredients and bring to a boil. Reduce heat to low and simmer, covered, for 20 minutes, or until the vegetables are tender.

* For vegetable broth, use vegetable bouillon, or a vegetable paste for broth, or canned vegetable broth, whichever is available locally. Also you can make homemade broth by cooking ½ cup each of chopped celery, carrot and onion in 4 cups simmering water until liquid is reduced by half; strain. You can double or triple this recipe and freeze for another use.

CHICKEN ENCHILADA SOUP

5–6 Servings

Soup

   4 teaspoons vegetable oil
½ cup diced onion
¾ teaspoon minced garlic
   3 cups chicken broth
½ cup all-purpose flour
   1 chicken bouillon cube
   1 cup milk
¼ cup salsa
¼ teaspoon salt
½ teaspoon onion powder
¾ teaspoon chili powder
½ teaspoon ground cumin
   2 cups shredded cheddar cheese
1½ cups cooked, chopped chicken

Toppings

   1 cup shredded cheddar cheese
   1 cup lightly crushed corn chips
½ cup salsa
½ cup sour cream

This is a popular soup among students and staff, and is a very festive dish when served with a variety of toppings on the side. You easily can convert this to a vegetarian dish by using vegetable broth and leaving out the chicken.

Heat the oil in a soup pot over medium heat. Add the onion and cook for 3 minutes, stirring frequently. Add the garlic and cook for 30 seconds, stirring. Mix the flour with 1 cup of broth, whisking until very smooth. Add the flour mixture and remaining broth to the onion mixture; bring to a boil. Boil until thickened, then lower heat and add the bouillon; simmer mixture for 5 minutes, stirring frequently. Stir in the milk, salsa and all seasonings. Gradually stir in the cheese; continue to stir until cheese is melted. Add the chicken; cover and simmer for 6–7 minutes. Serve with toppings of choice on the side.

FRENCH ONION SOUP AU GRATIN

2 Servings

2	slices French bread (½-inch slices)
1	tablespoon butter
1 ¾	cups onion, sliced very thin
1	(14-ounce) can beef broth
1 ¾	teaspoons au jus gravy mix
¼	cup water
¼	teaspoon dried thyme
⅛	teaspoon salt
	dash black pepper
1	cup shredded Swiss cheese
½	cup shredded mozzarella cheese

This recipe can be doubled or tripled. It is inspired by a recipe I prepared when working as the sous chef for a French restaurant in Charleston, South Carolina. It is almost identical, except that we used half grated Gruyere and half Emmanthaler cheese on top, in the Lyonnais style. The combination above is milder, more economical, and I found it to be better accepted by our students.

Place the bread slices in a preheated 350°F oven and bake for 6–7 minutes per side, until slices are dry and lightly toasted; set aside.

Melt the butter in a deep skillet. Add the onions and cook on medium-low heat until onions are golden brown and tender, about 20 minutes (the onions should brown gently and slowly — turn heat down if they are browning quickly). Add the broth, au jus mix, water, thyme, salt and pepper. Bring to a boil, then lower heat and simmer, covered, for 15 minutes.

Ladle soup into oven-proof bowls to within ¾-inch of the rim. Top each with a bread slice, trimmed to fit if necessary. Combine the cheeses and mound the bread with a generous amount of the mixture. Preheat broiler to 500°F. Place the soup bowls on a heavy baking pan and place under the broiler until cheese is bubbly and golden brown.

GAZPACHO

4 Servings

- ¼ cup diced onion
- ¼ cup diced celery
- ¾ cup peeled, seeded, diced cucumber
- ¾ cup diced green bell pepper
- 1 ½ cups diced ripe tomatoes
- ½ teaspoon minced fresh garlic
- ¾ teaspoon minced fresh parsley
- ¾ teaspoon minced cilantro (optional)
- ½ cup vegetable or chicken broth
- 1 ½ cups V-8 juice
- 1 ½ teaspoons Worcestershire sauce
- ¼ teaspoon hot red pepper sauce
- 1 ½ teaspoons red wine vinegar
- ½ teaspoon sugar
- ⅛ teaspoon black pepper
- ¼ teaspoon + pinch salt
- 1 ½ teaspoons fresh lemon juice

In a large container or bowl, combine the vegetables, garlic, parsley and cilantro. Stir in the remaining ingredients. Place mixture in a food processor in batches. Process with on/off turns just long enough to make small chunks of the vegetables, but not pureed. Stir well, then chill for 4 hours or overnight. Serve cold.

This is one of the few cold soups prepared in the Cottey kitchen. We offer this to the guests who attend the Vacation College program in May when the weather warms up. This recipe is inspired by one that my mother, Joan Richardson, made for gatherings in mid-summer. I remember that she served it in a clear glass bowl which accentuated all the soup's colors.

MACARONI AND CHEESE SOUP

6–8 Servings

- 1 (7.25-ounce) box macaroni and cheese dinner (elbow noodles)
- 1 (10.75-ounce) can cheddar cheese soup, undiluted
- 4 1/4 cups milk
- 1 teaspoon salt
- 1 teaspoon sugar
- dash white pepper
- 3/4 cup shredded cheddar cheese

This is true comfort food and is right up there in popularity with our baked potato soup.

Prepare macaroni and cheese as directed on the box, except omit the margarine called for in the directions. Add the soup, milk and seasonings. Bring to a boil, then lower heat. Cover and simmer for 8–10 minutes, stirring frequently. Stir in the cheese and heat just until cheese is melted (this soup will start out looking thin, but will thicken after several minutes as the cooked pasta expands). If soup thickens more than desired as it sits, just add more milk to reach desired consistency.

SPANISH CHICKEN AND RICE SOUP

8–10 Servings

- 4 teaspoons vegetable oil
- 2 teaspoons minced garlic
- 1 cup diced onion
- 2/3 cup diced celery
- 1/2 teaspoon garlic powder
- 1/2 teaspoon onion powder
- 1/4 teaspoon ground cumin
- 3/4 teaspoon chili powder
- 1/4 teaspoon celery salt
- 1/4 teaspoon black pepper
- 1/2 teaspoon sugar
- 1 tablespoon minced cilantro
- 2 tablespoons all-purpose flour
- 8 cups chicken broth
- 3/4 cup water
- 1 cup crushed tomatoes
- 1 (6.2-ounce) box 10-minute Spanish rice (with seasoning packet)
- 3 cups cooked, diced chicken

This soup freezes well. It tends to thicken as it sits overnight; just add more water or broth as needed to reach desired consistency.

Heat the oil in a large soup pot. Add the garlic, onion and celery; cook for 5 minutes over medium heat, stirring often. Add seasonings, sugar, cilantro and flour; cook for 2 minutes, stirring often. Stir in the broth, water, tomatoes, uncooked rice and seasoning packet. Bring to a boil, then lower heat. Cover and simmer for 10 minutes, or until rice is puffed and cooked. Stir in chicken and simmer, covered, for 5 minutes more. Skim off any accumulated oil that may rise to the top. Serve hot.

TACO SOUP

10–12 Servings

Soup

2 tablespoons vegetable oil
2 cups diced onion
1 ½ teaspoons minced garlic
1 ¼ pounds lean ground beef
1 ½ cups chicken broth
1 (15-ounce) can tomato sauce
1 (14.5-ounce) can diced tomatoes, undrained
3 (1-pound) cans medium chili beans, undrained
¼ cup medium salsa
4 tablespoons chopped green chiles
1 ¼ cups corn kernels (frozen or canned)
1 (1.25-ounce) package taco seasoning mix
1 (1-ounce) package ranch dressing mix
½ teaspoon onion powder

Topping

4 cups corn chips
1 ½ cups sour cream
3 cups shredded cheddar cheese

This is more like a chili than a soup. Though confusing, it doesn't seem to have affected its popularity as it has a strong following on our campus. You can increase the spicy heat according to your preference by using a hotter salsa and adding more green chiles. As is, it is medium-spiced. This would be great to serve at a super bowl party, a family reunion, or whenever a group is gathering. It also freezes well.

Heat the oil in a large soup pot. Add the onion and garlic; cook for 4 minutes, stirring often, over medium-high heat. Add the beef and cook until meat is browned, stirring to crumble meat. Stir in remaining ingredients. Bring to a boil, then lower heat immediately and simmer, uncovered, for 20 minutes, stirring frequently. Serve hot with toppings on the side.

HOMEMADE CROUTONS

2 Cups

  2 cups French bread, sliced ¾-inch,
    crust removed, cubed
  3 tablespoons butter
  2 tablespoons olive oil
  ¼ teaspoon dried basil
  ¼ teaspoon dried oregano
  ¼ teaspoon garlic powder
  ¼ teaspoon onion powder
  ⅛ teaspoon salt
  ⅛ teaspoon black pepper
  2 tablespoons finely grated parmesan
    cheese

French bread, Italian bread, or Texas
toast can be used to make these
croutons. They are superior to most
store-bought croutons. We make
them in 5 gallon quantities to use
for special buffets and suite dinners.
You can double or triple this recipe
and freeze them, although fresh is
best. If you do freeze them, bake
for 5–6 minutes in a 350°F oven
to re-crisp them.

Preheat oven to 350°F. Bake bread cubes on a baking sheet for
5 minutes, or until just firm.

Meanwhile, combine the butter, oil and all seasonings in a small
saucepan. Heat until butter is melted; keep warm.

Place bread cubes in a large bowl and toss with seasoned oil
mixture to coat evenly. Sprinkle with the parmesan and toss to
coat evenly. Place coated bread cubes back on the baking sheet
in one layer and bake for 5 minutes. Turn the bread cubes over
with a spatula and bake for 3 minutes more, or until golden
brown and crisp. Drain on paper towels; cool. Store at room
temperature in an airtight container.

CAESAR SALAD

12–16 Servings

Dressing

- 1 cup real mayonnaise
- 5 medium garlic cloves, peeled
- 1 tablespoon + ½ teaspoon Worcestershire sauce
- 2 tablespoons lemon juice
- 3 tablespoons grated parmesan cheese
- ¾ teaspoon onion powder
- 1 teaspoon seasoning salt
- ½ teaspoon salt
- ⅛ teaspoon white pepper
- ½ cup olive oil
- ¼ cup milk

Salad, per serving

- 2 cups chopped romaine lettuce
- 1 tablespoon grated parmesan cheese
- ½ cup croutons, preferably homemade

Many people have told me over the years that this is it — that there is no need to look further for another Caesar dressing. You be the judge. The dressing keeps for 5–6 days. If you don't have a food processor and need to whisk by hand, then use finely minced garlic instead of the peeled cloves. Great with the Homemade Croutons on page 62.

For Dressing In a food processor, place the mayonnaise, garlic, Worcestershire sauce, lemon juice, parmesan and seasonings. Process until smooth, scraping down sides of bowl with a rubber spatula as needed. Drizzle in olive oil, a little at a time, while mixing, until all is blended. Add the milk and mix until blended and smooth. Chill until needed.

For Salad Rinse the lettuce and pat dry; place in a bowl. When close to serving time, toss with the dressing. For each 2 cups of lettuce, use 2 tablespoons of dressing (or to taste). Stir in the parmesan and croutons.

GREEK SALAD

4 Servings

Dressing

  6 tablespoons creamy Caesar salad
     dressing, purchased or homemade
     (see page 63)
2 1/4 teaspoons fresh lemon juice
  1/4 teaspoon dried oregano
  1 tablespoon finely crumbled
     feta cheese
     pinch black pepper
  1/4 teaspoon + pinch salt
  3 tablespoons olive oil

Salad

  4 cups romaine lettuce, washed,
     dried and chopped
12 tomato wedges
  1/4 cup Kalamata olives,* pitted preferred
  1/2 cup cucumber, peeled, sliced thin
  1/2 cup crumbled feta cheese
  3/4 cup croutons, preferably homemade
12 thinly sliced red onion rings

This is great with the Homemade Croutons on page 62, albeit non-traditional. The imported Kalamata olives make this salad authentic, although you can use California, ripe black olives instead, if you like a milder flavor.

For Dressing In a small bowl, whisk together the Caesar dressing, lemon juice, oregano, feta, salt and pepper. Gradually drizzle in the olive oil, while stirring, until all is added and dressing is blended and smooth.

For Salad In a large salad bowl, add the lettuce, tomato, olives, cucumber, half the feta and half the croutons. Toss with enough dressing to coat lettuce mixture. Place on serving plates and top each salad with 3 onion rings, remaining feta and croutons.

* Kalamata Olives are marinated black olives from Greece and available in most supermarkets, often located where imported foods or specialty cheeses are displayed.

MANDARIN ORANGE SALAD

4 Servings

¼ cup sliced almonds
4½ teaspoons sugar

Dressing
2 tablespoons white vinegar
2 tablespoons sugar
dash hot red pepper sauce
¼ teaspoon salt
dash black pepper
¼ cup vegetable oil

Salad
3 cups chopped iceberg lettuce
2 cups chopped romaine lettuce
½ cup chopped celery
1 green onion, chopped
½ (11-ounce) can mandarin oranges, drained

The sugared almonds with crisp lettuce and mildly sweet dressing are a winning combination. We usually add sliced strawberries along with the Mandarin oranges for added color. That is an option, but is not necessary. This salad has been a favorite among many of our students and guests.

In a small skillet over medium-high heat, cook the almonds and sugar, stirring constantly, until sugar is dissolved and almonds are golden brown (watch that it does not burn). Quickly remove from the skillet onto a plate or bowl so the nuts do not continue to darken in the hot pan. Let cool, then break up any clumps before using.

For Dressing In a medium bowl, add all dressing ingredients, except the oil. Gradually add the oil, while stirring, until blended.

In a large bowl, combine the lettuces, celery, onion and half the almonds. Just before serving, toss the salad with half the oranges and enough dressing to coat well. Garnish the top of each serving with the remaining oranges and almonds.

MARY'S SPINACH MUSHROOM SALAD

4–5 Servings

Salad

  4 cups packed spinach, trimmed,
     large leaves torn

  2 tablespoons + 1 teaspoon chopped
     green onion

  1 hard-boiled egg, chopped

  1 cup fresh mushrooms, wiped clean,
     sliced thin

 12 grape or cherry tomatoes,
     halved if large

  2 slices bacon, cooked crisp, chopped
     (optional)

Dressing

  1 tablespoon + 1 $\frac{1}{2}$ teaspoons tarragon
     vinegar (or choice of vinegar)

 $\frac{1}{4}$ teaspoon garlic powder

 $\frac{1}{8}$ teaspoon salt

 $\frac{1}{8}$ teaspoon black pepper

 $\frac{1}{8}$ teaspoon paprika

  1 tablespoon mustard

 $\frac{1}{4}$ cup olive oil

  1 tablespoon grated parmesan cheese

My boss, Mary Haggans, often serves this at her annual staff Christmas party. It is flavorful and is a nice change from the usual tossed green salad. This dressing is good on other greens as well. If you're going meatless, just leave out the bacon.

For Dressing Combine all ingredients, except the oil, in a small bowl. Drizzle in the oil very gradually while whisking, until all oil is added and dressing is blended.

Combine the spinach, onion, egg, mushrooms, tomatoes and bacon. Just before serving, toss with the dressing. Sprinkle with parmesan cheese, then toss again.

BLACK-EYED PEA SALAD

12–14 Servings

Salad

- 2 (15-ounce) cans black-eyed peas, rinsed and drained
- 6 tablespoons finely chopped onion
- ½ cup chopped water chestnuts
- 1 cup thinly sliced fresh or frozen carrots
- 1 teaspoon minced garlic
- 1 cup diced green bell pepper

Dressing

- ½ cup tomato soup, undiluted
- 6 tablespoons sugar
- 4 tablespoons + 1 teaspoon red wine vinegar
- 1 tablespoon Worcestershire sauce
- 5 tablespoons vegetable oil

This recipe was given to us by Tricia Bobbett, Cottey's Assistant to the President, and has been used many times over, particularly for picnics and other cold buffets. Occasionally we will substitute black beans in place of the black-eyed peas.

For Salad Cook the carrots until crisp-tender; drain and let cool. Mix all salad ingredients together in a large bowl.

For Dressing Combine the soup, sugar, vinegar and Worcestershire sauce, and whisk until smooth. Gradually add the oil, while stirring, until mixture is blended and smooth. Stir the dressing into the salad mixture, tossing several times to coat well. Chill for at least 2 hours. Toss again before serving.

ASIAN COLESLAW

8 Servings

Slaw Mix

1 (10-ounce) package shredded
   green cabbage
2 green onions, finely chopped
2 teaspoons butter or margarine
¼ cup slivered almonds
2 tablespoons sesame seeds

Dressing

¼ cup vegetable oil
2 tablespoons white vinegar
3 tablespoons + 1 teaspoon sugar
2 teaspoons soy sauce
   pinch salt
   pinch black pepper

½ cup chow mein noodles

For Slaw Mix Mix the cabbage and onions together in a large bowl. Melt the butter in a small skillet over medium heat. Add the almonds and sesame seeds and cook, stirring constantly, until lightly browned. Quickly remove from the skillet onto a plate or bowl so they do not continue to cook in the hot pan. Set aside to cool.

For Dressing Combine all dressing ingredients in a small bowl; whisk until smooth.

Toss the cabbage and almond mixtures together; stir in dressing until well combined. Stir in the chow mein noodles just before serving so they retain their crispness.

SUNNY BROCCOLI SALAD

5–6 Servings

  4 slices uncooked bacon, chopped
3½ cups bite-size broccoli florets
  2 tablespoons + 2 teaspoons
      finely chopped onion
¼ cup raisins
¼ cup roasted, salted sunflower kernels

Dressing
⅔ cup Miracle Whip dressing
  2 tablespoons sugar
  4 teaspoons cider vinegar
     dash salt
     dash black pepper

This recipe has been in many cooks' recipe files for years. The original recipe calls for chopping up raw broccoli florets and mixing in with the remaining ingredients. I prefer to blanch the broccoli in boiling water for 30 seconds, which brightens the color and reduces the raw taste. It does involve one more step, so I leave it up to you to make that choice. For a vegetarian version, just leave out the bacon.

Drop the broccoli into boiling water for 30 seconds. Remove to a colander to drain; place in iced water to chill. Drain well, then roll in a towel to remove all moisture; set aside.

In a skillet, cook the bacon until crisp; drain well. In a large bowl, combine the broccoli, bacon, onion, raisins and sunflower kernels.

For Dressing Whisk together all dressing ingredients, until sugar is dissolved. Pour dressing over the broccoli mixture, tossing to coat. Chill for 1 hour or so before serving.

TABBOULEH

8–10 Servings

Salad

- 1 cup bulgur wheat*
  hot water, as needed
- 1 cup diced tomatoes
- ¾ cup peeled, seeded, diced cucumber
- 3 tablespoons green onion, sliced thin
- ¼ cup finely chopped fresh mint
- ¼ cup finely chopped fresh parsley

Dressing

- ½ cup extra-virgin olive oil
- 2 tablespoons + 2 teaspoons
  fresh lemon juice
- ½ teaspoon salt
  dash black pepper

This is a popular Middle Eastern salad with a zesty mint and lemon flavor. Serve on a platter with pita bread wedges or romaine lettuce spears for dipping, or serve as a side dish with roasted chicken, pork or lamb.

For Salad Place the bulgur wheat in a medium bowl. Pour enough hot water over wheat to cover by 1 inch. Soak for 45 minutes until tender, or follow the package directions (you are softening the wheat by soaking it in hot water, or by simmering on the stove for a shorter period of time). Drain off all water, pushing with the back of a spoon to remove excess water if necessary.

In a large bowl, combine the tomatoes, cucumber, onion, mint and parsley. Stir in the wheat.

For Dressing Whisk together all the dressing ingredients. Stir into the wheat mixture. Chill for 30 minutes to develop flavors.

* Available in most supermarkets

ARTICHOKE SPINACH SALAD

3–4 Servings

Dressing

  2 ounces cream cheese, softened
  2 tablespoons mayonnaise
  2 tablespoons milk
2 1/2 teaspoons grated parmesan cheese
  1/8 teaspoon garlic salt
  1/8 teaspoon onion powder
  1/8 teaspoon salt
     pinch white pepper
  2 drops hot red pepper sauce

Salad

  1 (14-ounce) can artichoke hearts,
     rinsed, drained, squeezed dry,
     quartered
1 1/3 cups fresh spinach, cut into
     1/4-inch strips
  4 teaspoons minced red onion
  2 tablespoons small diced red
     bell pepper
  1/2 cup (4 ounces) diced fresh mozzarella
     cheese

This recipe was inspired by the popular Artichoke Spinach Dip that is in the Party Foods section of this book on page 186.

For Dressing Combine all dressing ingredients in a medium bowl. Whisk until smooth and blended; set aside.

Combine all the salad ingredients together in a large bowl. Gently stir dressing into the salad until well coated. Cover and chill until serving time.

ANGEL HAIR SALAD

8 Servings

8 ounces angel hair or capellini noodles, broken in half

Dressing

¾ cup Italian dressing

¼ cup olive oil

1 tablespoon grated parmesan cheese

1 ½ teaspoons sesame seeds

1 teaspoon poppy seeds

1 teaspoon seasoning salt

½ teaspoon paprika

¼ teaspoon garlic powder

⅛ teaspoon black pepper

⅛ teaspoon cayenne pepper

1 ½ teaspoons sugar

1 cup peeled, seeded, diced cucumber

¼ cup diced red onion

1 cup diced tomato

½ cup diced green bell pepper

Cook noodles until just tender. Drain, rinse with cold water to remove starch, then drain again. Transfer noodles to a large bowl. In a small bowl, whisk together all dressing ingredients until blended and smooth. Stir dressing into the noodles, tossing well to coat. Stir in the cucumber and onion; chill. About 30 minutes before serving, stir in the tomato and green pepper.

BREADS/ROLLS

Cheese Biscuits **V**

Creamy Chive Rings **V**

Butter Crescent Rolls **V**

Focaccia Bread **V** **V**

Oatmeal Bread **V**

Potato Dill Rolls **V**

Tomato Bread **V**

King's Hawaiian Bread **V**

Cheese Cornbread **V**

Cheddar Crackers **V**

Molasses Rolls **V**

Ham and Cheese Corn Muffins

Amish Onion Cake **V**

V Vegetarian
V Vegan

CHEESE BISCUITS

12–16 Biscuits

  4 cups Bisquick
1 ½ teaspoons baking powder
1 ¾ cups shredded sharp cheddar cheese
  1 cup cold water

Topping
  ½ cup (1 stick) butter, melted
  1 teaspoon parsley flakes
  1 teaspoon garlic powder
  ½ teaspoon dried basil
  ½ teaspoon dried oregano

To get soft and fluffy biscuits, be sure to handle the dough as little as possible. Pat out the dough no less than ¾-inch thick before cutting into biscuits.

Preheat oven to 375°F. Mix the Bisquick, baking powder and cheese briefly to combine. Add water and stir just until it forms a dough. Remove to a lightly floured work surface and gently knead just to absorb crumbs. Gently pat dough out by hand to ¾-inch thick. Cut with a 3-inch biscuit cutter, or use the rim of a cup; place biscuits on a greased baking sheet. Bake for 12–14 minutes until golden.

Combine topping ingredients in a small saucepan. Generously brush or drizzle mixture over warm biscuits. Let the butter mixture soak in, then brush them a second time 15–20 minutes later (or reserve remaining butter mixture to heat and brush again just before serving).

CREAMY CHIVE RINGS

2 Rings (about 20 slices)

Dough

  1 (.25-ounce) package active dry yeast
¼ cup warm water (110–115°F)
½ teaspoon sugar
  1 cup milk
½ cup (1 stick) butter or margarine
¼ cup instant potato flakes
⅓ cup sugar
1¼ teaspoons salt
  1 egg, beaten
3½–4½ cups all-purpose flour

Cream Filling

¾ cup heavy whipping cream
  1 egg, beaten
  4 ounces cream cheese, softened
¼ cup minced fresh chives
½ teaspoon salt

Topping

¼ cup butter, melted
¼ cup sesame seeds

If you can make time for the various risings and baking of these rings, you will find them to be tasty and impressive to look at, particularly when presented whole for guests to slice their own piece. We often serve these, sliced, in baskets on each table during formal banquets.

For Dough In a small bowl, dissolve the yeast in warm water with ½ teaspoon of sugar; set aside. In a saucepan, heat the milk and butter until butter is just melted. Add the potato flakes, sugar and salt; cool. Stir in the yeast and egg. Mix by hand in large bowl or place mixture in the bowl of a stand mixer with the paddle attachment; gradually add flour until dough is no longer sticky and pulls away from the sides of the bowl. Turn dough onto a floured work surface; knead until smooth and elastic, about 1–2 minutes, adding more flour as needed. Place dough in a greased bowl, turning once to grease top. Cover and let rise in a warm place until doubled (about 1½ hours).

For Filling Place all filling ingredients in the top of a double boiler. Cook for about 12 minutes, stirring occasionally, until mixture bubbles and thickens to the consistency of gravy (it will thicken more as it cools). Cool to room temperature.

Punch dough down. On a floured surface, divide dough in half. Roll each half into a 10-by-12-inch rectangle. Spread half the cream mixture over the dough, leaving a 1-inch border. Roll up, jelly-roll style, starting at the narrow end. Place on greased cookie sheets, seam-side down. Shape into a ring, tucking one end into the other. Using scissors, cut 1-inch slices almost through the roll. Lay each slice flat. Repeat with remaining dough and filling.

For Topping and Baking Brush rings with melted butter; sprinkle with sesame seeds. Let rings rise in a warm place until doubled, about 1 hour. Bake in a 350°F oven for 25 minutes, or until golden brown.

BUTTER CRESCENT ROLLS

16 Rolls

½ cup milk
½ cup (1 stick) butter, melted
5 tablespoons + 1 teaspoon sugar
½ teaspoon salt
1 (.25-ounce) package active dry yeast
½ cup warm water (110–115°F)
½ teaspoon sugar
1 large egg, lightly beaten
3½–4 cups all-purpose flour
3 tablespoons butter, melted

Heat the milk in a saucepan until bubbles appear around edges of the pan. Add the butter, 5 tablespoons + 1 teaspoon sugar and salt; stir well. Cool to lukewarm (100–110°F).

In a small bowl, dissolve the yeast in warm water with ½ teaspoon of sugar. Let stand until foamy, 5–6 minutes. Using a stand mixer with a dough hook attachment, add yeast mixture, egg and milk mixture to mixing bowl. On low speed, beat in 2 cups of flour until smooth. Mix in enough remaining flour until dough pulls away from the sides of the bowl.

On a floured surface, knead dough gently until smooth and elastic, 2–3 minutes. Place in a large greased bowl, turning once to grease top. Cover loosely with a damp cloth; let rise in a warm place until doubled, about 1½ hours.

Punch dough down. On a floured surface, divide dough in half. Cover with a damp cloth; let rest for 10 minutes.

Grease 2 baking sheets. Using a floured rolling pin, roll 1 dough half into a 12-inch circle. Cut circle into 8 wedges. To shape rolls, begin at wide end of wedge and roll toward point. Place, point-side down, on prepared baking sheet. Curve ends to form crescents. Repeat with remaining dough half.

Cover loosely with a slightly damp cloth; let rise in a warm place until almost doubled, 30–45 minutes.

Preheat oven to 375°F. Bake until golden, about 15–16 minutes. Brush with the melted butter; transfer to a wire rack or other cool surface. Let cool slightly, then brush again with butter.

FOCACCIA BREAD

1 Loaf

1 (.25-ounce) package active dry yeast
½ teaspoon sugar
1 ¼ cups warm water (110–115 °F)
3 – 3 ½ cups bread flour
¾ teaspoon salt, divided
4 tablespoons olive oil, divided
2 tablespoons minced garlic
2 tablespoons grated parmesan cheese
   (optional)

Dissolve the yeast in warm water with ½ teaspoon of sugar; set aside until frothy.

Using Stand Mixer Add yeast mixture to mixing bowl; attach dough hook. Turn on medium speed and add ½ teaspoon of salt and 1 tablespoon of oil, then add ¾ of the flour. Gradually add remaining flour until dough forms a ball and cleans the sides of the bowl as it mixes. Sprinkle on more water if too dry. Remove dough and finish mixing by hand briefly, if necessary, but do not overwork.

By Hand Mound flour onto work surface; make a well in the center. Pour yeast mixture, ½ teaspoon salt and 1 tablespoon of oil into the well. With your fingers, slowly mix flour into liquid until dough is formed. If too dry to hold together, sprinkle additional water over dough; mixing well.

Place dough in a greased bowl, turning once to grease top. Cover with a damp towel and allow to rise in a warm place until doubled, about 45 minutes. Punch down and set aside.

Grease a baking sheet. Place dough in center of pan and spread with fingers into round or rectangular shape. Mix remaining oil, garlic and salt together in a small bowl. Brush a generous amount of this mixture over the dough. Sprinkle top with the the parmesan, if desired. Allow dough to rise again, uncovered, for 30 minutes.

Preheat oven to 375°F. Bake until bottom of loaf is golden brown, about 35 minutes.

OATMEAL BREAD

2 Loaves

1 cup water
1 cup milk
1 cup quick oats
2 tablespoons olive oil
2 teaspoons salt
¼ cup molasses
¼ cup honey
1 (.25-ounce) package active dry yeast
½ teaspoon sugar
½ cup warm water (110–115°F)
4½–5 cups all-purpose flour
2 tablespoons butter, melted

In a saucepan, combine the water and milk; scald. Pour over oats in a large bowl. Stir in the oil, salt, molasses and honey. Let cool to lukewarm (100–110°F).

In bowl of stand mixer, dissolve the yeast and sugar in ½ cup warm water. When mixture is frothy (about 5 minutes), add cooled oats mixture and 2½ cups of flour. Using dough hook, mix on medium speed for about 2 minutes, then gradually add more flour, as much as it takes to produce a dough that clings together and pulls away from the sides of the bowl.

Turn dough onto a floured work surface; knead until smooth and elastic, 3–4 minutes. Add a little more flour if dough is too sticky to handle, although be aware that the dough will be a little tacky because of the oats. Place dough in a greased bowl, turning once to grease top. Cover with a towel and let rise in a warm place until doubled, about 2 hours.

Punch dough down. Turn onto a lightly floured work surface and knead a few times, adding flour as needed. Divide dough in half; shape into loaves, tucking in ends, and place in greased 9-by-5-inch loaf pans. Let rise in a warm place, uncovered, until doubled, about 2 hours.

Bake in a preheated 350°F oven for 30–35 minutes, until loaves sound hollow when tapped. Brush warm loaves with the melted butter.

POTATO DILL ROLLS

12–15 Rolls

⅓ cup sugar
⅓ cup vegetable shortening
½ cup mashed potatoes
1 teaspoon salt
1 teaspoon dried dill
1 egg
1 (.25-ounce) package active dry yeast
⅔ cup warm water (110–115°F), divided
½ teaspoon sugar
2¾–3¼ cups all-purpose flour
2 tablespoons butter, melted

In a large mixing bowl, beat the sugar and shortening for 1 minute or so to combine. Add the potatoes, salt, dill and egg; mix until smooth.

In a small bowl, dissolve the yeast in ⅓ cup warm water with ½ teaspoon of sugar. Let stand 5 minutes, or until frothy. Add to egg mixture. Beat in 2 cups flour and remaining water.

Either mix by hand, or use dough hook attachment on a stand mixer, to gradually stir in the remaining flour to form a soft dough. Shape into a ball, kneading only briefly. Place in a greased bowl, turning once to grease top. Cover and let rise in warm place until doubled, about 1½ hours.

Punch dough down. Shape into balls by pinching off dough pieces the size of golf balls, tucking dough under itself while smoothing the top of each ball. Arrange dough balls into a greased, 9-inch round cake pan. Cover and let rise in a warm place until doubled, about 30 minutes.

Preheat oven to 350°F. Bake for 25–30 minutes; brush with melted butter. Cool for 5–6 minutes, then remove from pan to a wire rack or other cool surface. Brush again with butter and let cool completely.

TOMATO BREAD

2 Loaves

   2 cups V-8 or tomato juice
   2 tablespoons butter
   3 tablespoons sugar
   1 teaspoon salt
   ¼ cup ketchup
   1 (.25-ounce) package active dry yeast
   ¼ cup warm water (110–115°F)
   ½ teaspoon sugar
 6–7 cups all-purpose flour

This is a unique and popular bread that we often use for grilled cheese or grilled ham and cheese sandwiches.

Heat the V-8 juice and butter together until butter is melted. Add the sugar, salt and ketchup. Let cool to lukewarm (100–110°F).

In a large mixing bowl, dissolve the yeast in warm water with ½ teaspoon of sugar. After 5 minutes, or when frothy, add the tomato mixture and 3 cups of flour. Beat in a stand mixer at medium speed, using dough hook and scraping the bowl occasionally, about 2 minutes. Or, mix by hand until smooth.

Mix in enough remaining flour, a little at a time, to make a soft dough that pulls away from the sides of the bowl. Turn onto a lightly floured work surface and knead until smooth and elastic, 8–10 minutes. Place in a lightly greased bowl; turn dough over to grease top. Cover and let rise in a warm place until doubled, about 1½ hours.

Punch dough down; divide in half. Cover and let rest 10 minutes. Shape into loaves, tucking in ends, and place in greased 9-by-5-inch loaf pans. Cover and let rise until doubled, about 1½ hours.

Preheat oven to 350°F. Bake loaves for 35–40 minutes, until loaves sound hollow when tapped.

KING'S HAWAIIAN BREAD

3 Loaves

2 (.25-ounce) packages active dry yeast
1 cup warm water (110–115°F)
½ teaspoon sugar
3 eggs
1 cup pineapple juice
¾ cup sugar
½ teaspoon dried ginger
1 teaspoon vanilla
½ cup (1 stick) margarine or butter, melted
6 cups all-purpose flour

This bread is available in our local supermarket, however, it is more economical to prepare it ourselves. If it is not available commercially in your area, try making this version. It is a soft and mildly sweet bread that our students really enjoy. Use any leftover bread for Hawaiian Bread French Toast on page 24.

In a large bowl, dissolve the yeast in warm water with ½ teaspoon of sugar. Let stand 5 minutes, or until frothy.

Add the eggs, juice, sugar, ginger, vanilla and margarine to the yeast mixture. Add 3 cups of flour; stir to blend.

Gradually add remaining 3 cups of flour. Batter will be stiff; either mix well by hand, or use dough hook attachment on a stand mixer. Add just enough flour so that dough does not stick to bottom and sides of bowl. Knead dough briefly, then place in a clean, lightly-greased bowl. Cover with a cloth and leave in a warm area to rise for 1 hour.

Remove dough from bowl. Knead dough about 10 times, adding more flour as needed until dough is no longer sticky. Divide dough into 3 equal parts and place in well-greased round cake or pie pans. Cover, place in a warm area and let rise about 1 hour. Bake at 350°F for 25–30 minutes.

CHEESE CORNBREAD

20 Servings

1 ½ cups yellow cornmeal
1 tablespoon baking powder
1 teaspoon salt
½ teaspoon onion powder
4 teaspoons sugar
1 ¾ cups shredded sharp cheddar cheese
¾ cup grated or finely chopped onion
4 eggs
½ cup vegetable oil
1 cup sour cream
1 cup creamed corn

This cornbread is moist and is a tasty alternative to the ubiquitous sweeter versions.

Preheat oven to 375°F. Stir together the cornmeal, baking powder, salt, onion powder and sugar. Stir in the cheese and onion until combined, then stir in remaining ingredients. Pour batter into a greased 9-by-13-inch baking pan.

Bake for 25–28 minutes, or until a tester inserted in center comes out clean and cornbread is a light golden color.

CHEDDAR CRACKERS

16 Crackers

¾ cup + 2 tablespoons all-purpose flour

¼ cup yellow cornmeal

¼ teaspoon baking soda

½ teaspoon salt

¼ teaspoon sugar

¼ cup butter or margarine, cold, cut into pieces

¾ cup finely shredded sharp cheddar cheese

¼ cup cold water

1 tablespoon white vinegar

Topping

½ teaspoon coarsely ground black pepper

Serve these long, crisp crackers with a salad or soup main dish or in a decorative basket on a buffet in place of bread. You can use other toppings in place of pepper, such as sesame seeds, poppyseeds, flax seeds or just grated parmesan. Roll as thin as possible, but don't worry if there are ragged edges to the dough. This is part of the appeal of the cracker.

Grease 2 large baking sheets; set aside.

In a large mixing bowl, stir together the flour, cornmeal, baking soda, salt and sugar. Use a pastry blender if mixing by hand, or use the paddle attachment of a stand mixer, to cut in the butter until mixture resembles coarse crumbs. Mix in the cheese, cold water and vinegar, just until mixture forms a soft dough. If necessary, knead briefly until smooth.

Shape the dough into a ball; wrap with plastic wrap and chill for 1 hour, or until firm enough to handle.

On a lightly-floured surface, use a floured rolling pin to roll the dough into a paper-thin round approximately 13–14 inches in diameter. Sprinkle the pepper, or topping of choice, over the dough. Lightly press in the topping with the rolling pin. Using a pizza cutter or a large knife, cut in thin wedges starting from the center of the dough.

Preheat oven to 400°F. Transfer wedges to the prepared baking sheets, 1 inch apart. Bake for 10–12 minutes, or until golden and crisp. Transfer to a wire rack or other cool surface to cool completely. Store in an airtight container (will keep for 2–3 days, tightly covered).

MOLASSES ROLLS

12–15 Rolls

  1 cup boiling water
½ cup quick cooking oats
  1 (.25-ounce) package active dry yeast
  2 tablespoons warm water (110–115°F)
½ teaspoon sugar
  1 egg, beaten
¼ cup molasses
¼ cup vegetable oil
  2 tablespoons + 2 teaspoons sugar
¼ teaspoon salt
3 – 3½ cups all-purpose flour
  2 tablespoons butter, melted

These rolls are denser than many yeast rolls because of the oats and the molasses. They have a wonderful flavor, however, that may cause them to become a favorite to someone in your family, as they have for some of our staff.

In a large mixing bowl, combine the boiling water and oats; let cool to lukewarm (100–110°F). Meanwhile, dissolve the yeast in warm water with ½ teaspoon of sugar. Stir into cooled oat mixture. Add the egg, molasses, oil, sugar and salt. Add enough flour to form a soft dough.

Turn onto a floured surface; knead for a few minutes until dough is smooth and elastic. Place in a greased bowl, turning once to grease top. Cover and let rise in a warm place until doubled, about 1½ hours.

Punch dough down. Shape into balls by pinching off dough pieces the size of golf balls, tucking dough under itself while smoothing the top of each ball. Arrange dough balls into a greased 9-inch round cake pan. Cover and let rise in a warm place until doubled, about 30 minutes.

Preheat oven to 350°F. Bake for 25–30 minutes; brush with melted butter. Cool for 5–6 minutes, then remove from pan to a wire rack or other cool surface. Brush again with butter and let cool completely.

HAM AND CHEESE CORN MUFFINS

12 Muffins

 1 large egg
¼ cup sour cream
¼ cup butter, melted, cooled
 1 cup milk
 1 cup yellow cornmeal
¾ cup all-purpose flour
 1 tablespoon + 1 teaspoon sugar
1½ teaspoons baking powder
½ teaspoon salt
 2 tablespoons finely chopped
    green onion
¾ cup finely chopped ham
 1 cup shredded cheddar cheese,
    divided

Take these to chili suppers, brunch gatherings or picnics.

Mix the egg and sour cream until smooth; stir in the butter, then the milk.

In a large bowl, stir together the cornmeal, flour, sugar, baking powder, salt, onion, ham and ¾ of the cheese. Stir in the wet ingredients until just combined. Divide among greased muffin cups. Top with remaining cheese. Bake in a preheated 400°F oven for 12–14 minutes, or until a tester inserted in center comes out clean.

AMISH ONION CAKE

16 Servings

Onion Topping

4	cups diced onion
4	tablespoons butter
1	tablespoon poppy seeds
1 1/4	teaspoons salt
1 1/2	teaspoons paprika
1/4	teaspoon black pepper

Dry Batter Mix

1	cup (2 sticks) butter, cold, cut into small pieces
3	cups all-purpose flour
6	tablespoons cornstarch
2 1/4	teaspoons baking powder
1	tablespoon + 1 1/2 teaspoons sugar
1	tablespoon + 1 1/2 teaspoons brown sugar
1/2	teaspoon salt

Wet Batter Mix

1/2	cup sour cream
2	tablespoons butter, melted, cooled
4	eggs
1/2	cup milk

This is a rich, moist batter bread with a wonderful onion topping. Serve with soup or a salad for a complete meal. You will need a 10-inch springform pan for this recipe.

For Onion Topping In a large skillet, cook the onion in the butter over medium heat for 10 minutes. Stir in the poppy seeds, salt, paprika and pepper; cook until onion is softened, about 5 minutes, stirring occasionally. Remove from the heat; set aside.

For Dry Batter Mix In a bowl, combine the flour, cornstarch, baking powder, sugars and salt. Cut in the butter until mixture resembles coarse crumbs. If using a stand mixer with the paddle attachment, this will take about 3 minutes on medium-low speed. Transfer flour mixture to a large bowl.

For Wet Batter Mix In a small bowl, combine the sour cream and melted butter, then stir in the eggs and milk until smooth. Make a well in the dry ingredients and stir in the egg mixture and 1/2 cup of the onion topping *just until* batter is moistened.

Preheat oven to 350°F. Spread batter into a greased 10-inch springform pan. Spoon remaining onion topping over the batter. Place pan on a baking sheet. Bake for 45–50 minutes, or until a tester inserted in center comes out clean. Let rest for 25–30 minutes before removing sides of the pan. Serve warm or at room temperature.

SANDWICHES

Bruschetta Cheese Toasts **V**

Broccoli Cheese Bagels **V**

Italian Vegetable Heroes **V**

Vegetable Cheese Quesadillas **V**

Veggie Tostadas **V**

Vegetable Pita Pizzas **V**

Grilled Chicken Caesar Wraps

Chicken Cordon Bleu Wraps

Italian Beef Sandwich au Jus

Chicken French Bread Pizzas

Frisco Chicken Sandwich

Mexican Hot Dogs

Jumbo Franks in Blankets

Ham and Cheese Panini

Chicken Panini

V Vegetarian
Ⅵ Vegan

BRUSCHETTA CHEESE TOASTS

4 Toasts

Bruschetta

- 2/3 cup seeded, diced roma tomatoes*
- 1 1/2 teaspoons finely chopped fresh basil
- 1/4 teaspoon minced garlic
- 1 teaspoon finely chopped green onion
- 2 1/2 teaspoons olive oil
- 1/4 teaspoon balsamic or red wine vinegar
  dash salt
  dash black pepper

- 4 garlic toasts*
- 3/4 cup shredded mozzarella cheese
- 1/4 cup shredded cheddar cheese

I was looking for another meatless lunch offering when I tried combining the popular bruschetta that we make with the extremely popular garlic toasts served with melted cheese on top. I thought we might have a winner as far as our students were concerned. This has proven to be the case. You can use mozzarella cheese only if preferred, just increase the quantity to 1 cup.

*To Seed Tomatoes Cut off the stem end, then cut tomatoes in half crosswise. Pick up each half and firmly squeeze out the seeds and juice. Discard the seeds and juice.

For Bruschetta In a medium bowl, combine all bruschetta ingredients; set aside.

Preheat oven to 350°F. Meanwhile, in a large skillet, cook the toasts for 2–3 minutes per side, or until golden brown. Place on a baking sheet. Combine the cheeses and top the toasts with the cheese blend. Bake for 7–8 minutes, or until hot and cheese is melted.

Drain the bruschetta and top each of the toasts with the mixture. Another option is to serve the bruschetta in small bowls on the side and let each person spoon on his or her own as desired.

*Available in the freezer section of many supermarkets.

BROCCOLI CHEESE BAGELS

6 Servings

Vegetable Cream Cheese

- 6 ounces light cream cheese, softened
- 2 tablespoons finely chopped celery
- 2 tablespoons finely chopped green onion
- 2 tablespoons peeled, grated carrot
  dash dried basil

Broccoli Topping

- 1 tablespoon olive oil
- 1 teaspoon minced garlic
- 2 cups mushrooms, wiped clean, sliced thin
- ¼ teaspoon dried basil
- ¼ teaspoon salt
  pinch black pepper
- ¼ teaspoon onion powder
- 1 (10-ounce) box frozen chopped broccoli, thawed

- 3 whole wheat or plain bagels, halved, toasted
- 6 thin slices tomato
- 6 thin slices provolone cheese

Combine all the vegetable cream cheese ingredients together in a bowl; set aside.

Heat the oil in a skillet over medium heat. Add the garlic; cook for a few seconds, then add the mushrooms and cook for 3 minutes, or until softened. Add the seasonings and thawed broccoli. Cook for 3 minutes, stirring often; set aside.

Spread the cream cheese mixture over each toasted bagel half. Mound broccoli mixture over each, then top with a slice of tomato and a slice of cheese.

Preheat broiler to 500°F. Broil the bagel halves until cheese is melted and bubbly, but not browned. Serve hot.

Although chopped broccoli is an unlikely topping for an open-faced sandwich, this combination of vegetable cream cheese, mushrooms, broccoli, tomato and melted provolone cheese has proven to be a winner with both vegetarians and non-vegetarians alike. We sometimes use pepper jack cheese in place of provolone to "kick up" the flavor.

ITALIAN VEGETABLE HEROES

4 Servings

Garlic Butter

  2 tablespoons butter or margarine, softened

  ½ teaspoon minced garlic
     dash garlic salt

Vegetable Topping

  1 teaspoon olive oil

  ½ cup green bell pepper, cut into thin strips

 12 thinly sliced red onion rings

  ¼ cup mushrooms, sliced thin

  1 (14-ounce) can artichoke hearts, rinsed, drained

  1 (2-ounce) jar sliced pimientos, drained

  2 tablespoons black olives, sliced

  ¼ cup finely chopped tomato

  4 teaspoons Italian dressing
     pinch salt
     pinch black pepper

  1 loaf French bread (thin baguette)

1½ cups shredded mozzarella cheese

  2 tablespoons grated parmesan cheese

If you like artichoke hearts, this makes a wonderful, open-faced vegetarian sandwich, although you can substitute any combination of vegetables to suit your taste.

For Garlic Butter In a small bowl, stir the garlic butter ingredients together; set aside.

For Vegetable Topping Heat the oil in a medium skillet. Add the green pepper, onion and mushrooms; cook for 2 minutes, stirring often, over medium heat. Transfer to a bowl large enough to hold all the vegetables. Pat artichoke hearts dry and cut into eighths; add to the mushroom mixture, then stir in the pimientos, olives, tomato, dressing, salt and pepper. Set aside.

Preheat broiler to 500°F. With a serrated knife, slice bread in half lengthwise. Trim bottoms if halves are not level on the work table. Spread cut halves evenly with the garlic butter. Toast under the broiler until lightly browned.

Cut toasted bread halves in half to make 4 pieces. Cover with the vegetable mixture, evenly dividing the various vegetables between each piece. Top with the mozzarella, then sprinkle with the parmesan. Broil the sandwiches until cheese is melted and bubbly, about 2–3 minutes. Or, bake in preheated 350°F oven for 8–10 minutes.

VEGETABLE CHEESE QUESADILLAS

3–4 Servings

Guacamole

1 ripe avocado
½ teaspoon lime juice
   dash salt
   dash black pepper

Vegetable Filling

¾ cup chopped tomato
2 tablespoons chopped green onion
2½ teaspoons minced jalapeño
4 teaspoons minced cilantro
   dash salt

4 (8-inch) flour tortillas
2 cups shredded colby-jack
   cheese blend
4 teaspoons vegetable oil
   salsa, as needed

Scoop out avocado pulp into a small bowl, mashing it with the back of a fork to a chunky yet spreadable consistency. Stir in the lime juice, salt and pepper; set aside.

In a medium bowl, combine the tomato, onion, jalapeño, cilantro and salt; set aside.

Assemble Quesadillas Lay out 2 tortillas on a work table. Spread about 1 tablespoon of guacamole onto each tortilla. Sprinkle ½ cup of the cheese on one tortilla, then ½ of the vegetable mixture, and top with another ½ cup of cheese. Place the other tortilla on top, guacamole-side down. Cover assembled quesadilla and repeat the procedure with the remaining tortillas, guacamole, cheese and vegetable mixture.

Heat 1 teaspoon of vegetable oil in a nonstick skillet over medium-high heat. When the oil is hot, carefully place 1 quesadilla in the skillet and drizzle another teaspoon of oil over the top. Cook for 1½–2 minutes, then carefully turn over and cook another 1½ minutes, or until golden brown and cheese is melted. Repeat with the other quesadilla. Cut each round into 6 wedges using a large knife. Serve 3–4 wedges per person with a bowl of salsa for dipping.

VEGGIE TOSTADAS

2 Servings

2 (5- to 6-inch) corn tortillas
2 teaspoons vegetable oil

Vegetable Topping
2 teaspoons vegetable oil
½ cup finely chopped tomato
¼ cup finely chopped onion
2 tablespoons finely chopped green
    bell pepper
½ teaspoon minced garlic
1 teaspoon minced jalapeño
1 tablespoon finely chopped
    black olives
    dash salt
    dash black pepper
    dash ground cumin
¼ teaspoon chili powder
    dash garlic powder

¼ cup refried beans
2 teaspoons salsa
½ cup shredded colby-jack cheese blend

salsa, as needed
sour cream, as needed

Heat the oil in a skillet over medium-high heat. Fry tortillas for 1–1½ minutes per side, or until light golden brown and crisp. Drain on paper towels; keep warm.

For Vegetable Topping Heat the oil in a skillet. Add all the vegetables and seasonings and cook, stirring often, for 2–3 minutes until vegetables are softened; set aside.

In a small bowl, combine the refried beans and salsa; set aside.

Assemble Tostadas Preheat broiler to 500°F. Spread about 2 tablespoons of the bean mixture onto each tortilla, leaving a ½-inch border around the edges. Top with the vegetable mixture, then sprinkle with the cheese.

Place the tostadas under the broiler until hot and cheese is melted and bubbly. Serve with salsa and sour cream on the side.

VEGETABLE PITA PIZZAS

2 (6-inch) Pizzas

Pitas

1 (6-inch) loaf white or wheat pita bread
1 teaspoon olive oil
  dash salt
½ cup shredded mozzarella cheese

Vegetables

1½ teaspoons olive oil
½ medium onion, sliced thin
½ teaspoon minced garlic
¼ medium green bell pepper,
  cut into thin strips
4–5 medium mushrooms, wiped clean,
  sliced thin
¼ teaspoon dried oregano
¼ teaspoon salt-free herb
  and spice blend (optional)
  dash salt
  dash black pepper
2 tablespoons minced fresh basil
  (or ½ teaspoon dried)

Topping

½ cup chopped tomato
½ cup shredded mozzarella cheese
2 teaspoons grated parmesan cheese

For Pita Preheat broiler to 500°F. Using a serrated knife, halve the pita loaf horizontally to make 2 thin rounds (pita should separate once the edge is cut into). Arrange the rounds, cut-side up, on a baking sheet. Drizzle ½ teaspoon of oil over each round, spreading the oil with the back of a spoon. Sprinkle each round lightly with salt. Broil the pitas for 30 seconds; sprinkle ½ cup of cheese over both rounds, then broil for 30 seconds more, or until lightly browned and crisp. Set aside, covered, so they don't dry out while you prepare the vegetables.

For Vegetables Heat the oil in a skillet over medium heat. Add the onion and cook for 2 minutes, stirring often. Add the garlic, pepper, mushrooms and spices, except fresh basil (you can add dried basil at this point, if using). Cook for 3 minutes, or until vegetables are softened, stirring often. Stir in basil and remove from heat.

For Topping Divide the vegetable mixture among the pita rounds, leaving a thin border around the edges. Top each with the tomato, then the mozzarella, and then the parmesan. Broil the pitas for 2 minutes, or until cheese is melted and bubbly. Cut each round in half or in quarters.

GRILLED CHICKEN CAESAR WRAPS

2–4 Servings

Caesar Dressing

3 tablespoons + 1½ teaspoons
  real mayonnaise

½ teaspoon minced garlic

½ teaspoon Worcestershire sauce

1¼ teaspoons lemon juice

2 teaspoons grated parmesan cheese
  dash onion powder
  dash garlic powder

½ teaspoon seasoning salt
  dash salt
  dash black pepper

2 tablespoons olive oil

Caesar Salad

4 cups chopped romaine lettuce,
  rinsed, patted dry

1 tablespoon finely chopped red onion

1 tablespoon finely chopped red bell
  pepper (optional)

2 teaspoons grated parmesan cheese
  dash black pepper

2 tablespoons + 2 teaspoons Caesar
  dressing (above)

1 (6-ounce) package grilled chicken
  breast strips*

2 (10-inch) soft wraps
  (flavored or plain)*

For Dressing Combine all dressing ingredients, except the oil, in a bowl, whisking until smooth. Gradually add the oil, while whisking, until all is incorporated.

In a salad bowl, combine the lettuce, onion, bell pepper, cheese, black pepper and the 2 tablespoons + 2 teaspoons dressing, tossing to coat lettuce evenly.

Spread the remaining dressing on the surface of both wraps. Place the salad mixture across the bottom third of each wrap. Top with the grilled chicken strips. Roll up the wraps tightly; cut off the empty ends, then cut each wrap in half. Serve 1–2 pieces per person.

* Available in many supermarkets.

These always have been very popular—a Caesar salad with chicken, wrapped in a thin tortilla. Use the convenient cooked chicken strips listed, if available, or use other cooked chicken as desired.

CHICKEN CORDON BLEU WRAPS

2–4 Servings

Dressing

3 tablespoons + 2 teaspoons
   real mayonnaise
1 tablespoon mustard
2 teaspoons honey
½ teaspoon sugar

8 thin slices deli ham
6 thin slices Swiss cheese
1 (6-ounce) package grilled chicken
   breast strips*
2 (10-inch) soft wraps
   (flavored or plain)*

**This wrap sandwich is served warm
with the cheese melted in the center.
Use the convenient cooked chicken
strips listed, if available, or use
other cooked chicken as desired.**

Combine all dressing ingredients in a small bowl, stirring
to combine and dissolve the sugar.

In a bowl, toss the chicken strips with 4 teaspoons of the
dressing. Spread the remaining dressing on the surface of both
wraps. Place 4 ham slices over the dressing across ¾ of each
wrap, leaving the top ¼ without ham. Place 3 slices of cheese
over the ham just below the middle. Top with the grilled chicken
strips in the center of the cheese slices.

Preheat oven to 350°F. Roll up the wraps tightly and cover each
one in foil, seam-side down. Bake in the oven for 10–12 minutes,
or until warm in center and the cheese is just melting. Cut off
the empty ends, then cut each wrap in half. Serve warm.

* Available in many supermarkets.

ITALIAN BEEF SANDWICH AU JUS

4 Servings

Roasted Peppers and Onions

1 green bell pepper, cut into
  ½-inch strips
1 medium onion, cut into ½-inch strips
4 teaspoons olive oil
  dash salt
  dash black pepper
  dash dried basil
  dash dried oregano

Au Jus Broth

2 (1-ounce) packages au jus gravy mix
4 large garlic cloves, chopped
¼ teaspoon dried basil
¼ teaspoon dried oregano
  dash black pepper
½ teaspoon seasoning salt
2 tablespoons water

1 pound deli roast beef, cooked rare
  to medium rare, sliced thin
4 (6-inch) sub rolls
2 cups shredded mozzarella cheese

I have fond memories of a sandwich
similar to this one from a "dive"
in Chicago when living there years
ago—a French dip sandwich with
garlic beef broth, roasted veggies
and melted mozzarella.

For Roasted Peppers and Onions Preheat oven to 350°F. Put the cut pepper and onion in a medium bowl; toss with the olive oil and all seasonings. Place mixture in a baking pan and roast, uncovered, for 40 minutes, stirring after 20 minutes or so. Cover and keep warm until needed.

For Au Jus Broth Prepare the au jus mix according to the package directions. Add the garlic, all seasonings and water. Cover tightly and simmer over very low heat for 30 minutes. Taste the broth and add a little more water if too salty. Keep warm, covered, until needed.

Preheat broiler to 500°F. Place opened sub roll halves on a baking sheet. Cook under broiler just long enough to lightly brown the rolls, about 30 seconds or less. Adjust oven back to bake mode and set at 350°F.

Assemble Sandwiches Strain out the garlic and seasonings from the heated broth. Dip the roast beef into the broth just until meat is heated through (about 30 seconds). Using tongs or slotted spoon, lift beef out of broth, draining off excess liquid; portion beef onto the bottom halves of the rolls. Top with some pepper and onion mixture, then cover each serving with ½ cup of the mozzarella. Place the rolls into the oven until the cheese is melted. Place top half of rolls over each; cut in half and serve with a portion of au jus gravy on the side for dipping.

CHICKEN FRENCH BREAD PIZZAS

4 Servings

Spread

- ¼ cup butter or margarine, softened
- ½ cup shredded cheddar cheese
- 3 tablespoons grated parmesan cheese
- ¼ teaspoon minced garlic
- dash dried basil
- dash dried oregano
- dash garlic salt
- 1 teaspoon Italian dressing

- 1 loaf French bread, preferably thin baguette-style
- 2½ cups cooked chicken, shredded
- 2 cups shredded mozzarella cheese
- 2 tablespoons finely chopped green bell pepper (optional)
- 2 teaspoons grated parmesan cheese

For Spread In a bowl, stir together all the spread ingredients; set aside.

With a serrated knife, cut ends off the bread, split lengthwise, then cut each piece in half crosswise to make 4 pieces. Lay cut-side up on a work surface, trimming bottom, if needed, to make them stable.

Preheat broiler to 500°F. Spread the butter mixture evenly over each bread piece, about 2 tablespoons for each. Place on a baking sheet and broil for about 30 seconds to lightly toast the bread. Top each with the shredded chicken, then the mozzarella cheese. Sprinkle evenly with the green pepper, then the parmesan. Broil again for 1 minute or so to heat through and melt the cheese. Cut each pizza into smaller sections as desired.

FRISCO CHICKEN SANDWICH

4 Servings

- 4 (4- to 5-ounce) boneless, skinless chicken breasts
- 1/2 cup honey dijon salad dressing
- 4 teaspoons real mayonnaise
- 1 teaspoon dijon or yellow mustard
- 1 teaspoon honey
- 4 teaspoons butter or margarine, softened
- 4 hamburger buns
- 4 slices provolone cheese, sliced thin
- 4 slices bacon, cooked crisp
- 2 leaves leaf lettuce (optional)
- 8 slices tomato, sliced thin (optional)

This chicken is more flavorful if allowed to marinate 6–8 hours, or overnight. You can use any mild-flavored cheese in place of the provolone.

Rinse chicken breasts, pat dry and place in a non-aluminum container. Pour dressing over and toss lightly to coat chicken completely. Cover and chill 6 hours, or overnight.

Drain and discard excess dressing. Cook on a charcoal or gas grill for 3–4 minutes per side, or until cooked through (or broil for about 4 minutes per side).

Meanwhile, combine the mayonnaise, mustard and honey together in a small bowl; set aside. Spread the softened butter over each bun half. Toast under the broiler just until lightly browned; set aside.

Place cooked chicken in a baking pan; top each with the mayonnaise mixture, then the sliced cheese. Place under broiler until cheese is melted and bubbly; remove from heat. Place chicken on the bun bottoms. Top each with a bacon slice, broken in half, then the lettuce, tomato and the bun tops. Serve warm.

MEXICAN HOT DOGS

2 Servings

Bacon Topping

 2 slices bacon

¼ cup diced onion

¼ cup diced tomato, drained

   dash salt

   dash black pepper

 2 hot dogs

 2 hot dog buns

 2 slices pepper jack cheese

One of our students provided this family recipe. It is a nice variation from the usual. You can use another cheese in place of pepper jack if a zesty hot flavor is not desired. Suggested additions to the bacon topping include chopped cilantro, jalapeño, salsa or avocado.

Prepare Topping Cook the bacon in a skillet until crisp. Remove bacon and chop. Reserve ½ the bacon grease in the pan and cook the onion in the grease for 3–4 minutes, or until softened. Stir in the chopped bacon; set aside to cool slightly. Stir in the tomato, salt and pepper.

Meanwhile, preheat oven to 350°F. Boil the hot dogs for 5 minutes. Place in buns and set in a lightly-oiled baking pan, propped up or snugly fit to keep them from tipping over. Portion the bacon topping over the hot dogs. Cut cheese slices in half to fit over the top. Cover with foil and bake for 10 minutes, or until hot and cheese is melted.

JUMBO FRANKS IN BLANKETS

4 Servings

1 puff pastry sheet*
4 hot dogs
4 thin slices Swiss or muenster cheese
  (optional)

**These can be served whole as a
hot sandwich, or cut in 1-inch slices
and served as a party snack with a
mustard dip.**

Remove 1 pastry sheet and thaw according to package directions.

Boil the hot dogs for 5 minutes; drain and let cool enough to handle.

Lay out the thawed pastry sheet and cut into 4 squares. Place a cheese slice in the center of each square, then a hot dog. Roll up pastry around each hot dog to enclose, dabbing the seam with some water to seal. Place, seam-side down, on a baking sheet; bake in a preheated 400°F oven for 12–15 minutes, or until puffed and golden brown. Serve hot.

* Available in the freezer section of most supermarkets.

HAM AND CHEESE PANINI

2 Servings

  1 flatbread wrap (plain or flavored)*
4–6 thin slices deli ham
2–3 thin slices provolone cheese
  2 teaspoons olive oil

While in Rome on a Cottey European trip, I was intrigued by the panini sandwiches that were available, it seemed, on almost every street corner. They were simple, yet flavorful. After returning to Missouri, I wanted to recreate for students the Roman version— in this case a grilled ham and cheese "alla Romana."

Lay the flatbread on a work surface; cut in half. Place 2 layers of ham over 1 half, cutting to fit. Top with a layer of cheese, then place the other half of wrap over the cheese to make a sandwich.

Heat the oil in a large skillet. Cook the sandwich about 2 minutes, or until bottom is golden brown. Carefully flip over and cook the other side for 2–3 minutes, or until golden and crisp and cheese is melted in the center. Cut in half to make 2 large pieces.

* Available in many supermarkets. These are the rectangular wraps with the rounded ends available in several flavors.

CHICKEN PANINI

2 Servings

  1 flatbread wrap (plain or flavored)*
  2 teaspoons spaghetti sauce
  4 thin slices (3–4 ounces) deli roasted
     chicken breast
2–3 thin slices provolone cheese
  2 teaspoons olive oil
  1 garlic clove, peeled, halved lengthwise
     dash salt

**If the deli section of your local
supermarket doesn't have the roast
chicken breast that can be sliced
thin, then substitute deli turkey
breast instead.**

Lay the flatbread on a work surface; cut in half. Spread 2 teaspoons of the sauce on one half. Top with the chicken slices, then the cheese slices. Place the other half of wrap over the cheese to make a sandwich.

Heat the oil in a skillet large enough to hold the sandwich. Add the halved garlic to the hot oil. Swirl around in the oil for 1 minute over medium heat, then discard the garlic. Cook the sandwich in the oil for about 2 minutes, or until bottom is golden brown. Carefully flip over, sprinkle the top with salt, and cook the other side for about 2 minutes, or until golden and cheese is melted. Cut in half to make 2 large pieces.

* Available in many supermarkets. These are the rectangular wraps with the rounded ends available in several flavors.

PASTA

Lorraine's Pasta Casserole

Sesame Noodles with Tofu and Broccoli

Vegetable Lo Mein

Tortelloni Mac 'n' Cheese with Broccoli V

Cajun Barbecued Shrimp with Angel Hair

Fettucine with Grilled Chicken

Ziti with Spicy Chicken, Garlic and Tomato

Beef Stroganoff

Country Chicken and Noodles

Grilled Italian Chicken with Angel Hair

Pasta with Four Cheeses and Tomato V

V Vegetarian
V Vegan

LORRAINE'S PASTA CASSEROLE

10 Servings

Beef Mixture

  1 tablespoon vegetable oil
  2 teaspoons minced garlic
  1 pound ground chuck or ground round
  ½ teaspoon salt
  ¼ teaspoon black pepper
  ½ teaspoon dried basil
1 ¼ cups spaghetti sauce
  1 (14.5-ounce) can diced tomatoes, drained well

Creamy Noodles

  3 cups penne or ziti noodles
  1 (8-ounce) package cream cheese (regular or light), softened, cut into pieces
1 ¼ cups sour cream (regular or light)
  ¼ cup chopped green onion

  2 cups shredded cheddar cheese

2 ½ cups spaghetti sauce, heated

This recipe was given to my wife, Lorraine, many years ago. Our family has enjoyed it over the years, and it has become popular with students and staff as well.

For Beef Mixture Heat oil in a large skillet over medium-high heat. Add garlic; cook for 10 seconds, then add meat right away. Cook until no longer pink in center, breaking up chunks with a wooden spoon. Drain off all grease and rinse meat briefly under hot water to remove excess fat. Drain well, then return to skillet; add the salt, pepper, basil, spaghetti sauce and diced tomatoes. Simmer mixture for 15 minutes, or until thickened, stirring often. Cover until ready to use to keep from drying out.

For Creamy Noodles Meanwhile, cook noodles according to package directions. Drain and briefly rinse in hot water, then pour into a large bowl. Add the cream cheese while noodles are hot. Toss together until melted, then stir in sour cream and onion.

Preheat oven to 350°F. Grease a 9-by-13-inch pan.

Assemble Casserole Place half the noodle mixture in the prepared pan. Sprinkle half the meat mixture on top, then half the shredded cheese. Repeat with the noodles, meat mixture and remaining cheese. Cover with foil; bake for 30–35 minutes until hot and bubbly in the center. Let rest for 10 minutes or so before serving. Top each serving with a ladle of hot spaghetti sauce.

SESAME NOODLES WITH TOFU AND BROCCOLI

2–3 Servings

¾ cup firm tofu, cut into ¾-inch cubes
1 tablespoon vegetable oil
¼ (1-pound) package angel hair noodles (capellini)

Sauce

2 tablespoons soy sauce
1 tablespoon + 1 teaspoon hoisin sauce*
1½ teaspoons white vinegar (or rice wine vinegar)*
1 tablespoon dark sesame oil*
1 teaspoon minced garlic
2 teaspoons sugar
dash black pepper
1 tablespoon sesame seeds

Vegetable Mix

2 cups broccoli florets
1 tablespoon vegetable oil
¾ teaspoon minced garlic
2 tablespoons chopped green onion
3 tablespoons Honey Teriyaki with Sesame Sauce (or other thick teriyaki sauce)

Bake Tofu Preheat oven to 375°F. Pat dry the tofu cubes with paper towels to remove as much moisture as possible, then toss in the vegetable oil to coat all sides. Place coated tofu in an oil-sprayed baking pan and bake for 25 minutes. Turn over the cubes gently and bake for 12–15 minutes more, until golden brown in color. Drain on paper towels.

Cook noodles according to package directions. Drain, rinse and drain again; cover and set aside.

For Sauce Combine all sauce ingredients, except the sesame seeds, in a medium bowl; set aside.

For Vegetables Steam the broccoli until crisp-tender when pierced, 3–4 minutes; chill in ice water. Drain, then wrap in a towel; set aside. Heat the vegetable oil in a medium skillet. Add the garlic and onion, and cook for 1 minute or so over medium-high heat. Stir in the broccoli, tofu and teriyaki sauce. Turn heat to low; keep warm.

To Assemble Heat a wok or skillet over medium-high heat. Add the sesame seeds and cook, stirring constantly, until light brown. Immediately add the sauce mixture and noodles, stirring well to coat noodles evenly with sauce. Portion noodles onto serving plates. Top with the broccoli-tofu mixture and serve hot.

* Available in the Asian section of most supermarkets.

VEGETABLE LO MEIN

4 Servings

⅓ (1-pound) package linguine noodles

Sauce

1 ½ teaspoons dark sesame oil*
¾ teaspoon minced ginger
¾ teaspoon minced garlic
2 tablespoons thinly sliced green onion
5 tablespoons soy sauce
2 tablespoons + 1 ½ teaspoons water
2 tablespoons dry sherry
3 tablespoons + 1 ½ teaspoons sugar
1 ¾ teaspoons cornstarch
2 teaspoons water

Vegetables

2 teaspoons vegetable oil
¼ cup onion, cut into thin strips
2 tablespoons grated carrot
¼ cup thinly sliced celery
¼ cup red bell pepper, cut into thin strips
¼ cup fresh mung bean sprouts
16 fresh pea pods (snow peas), stemmed
12 broccoli florets
16 slices water chestnuts

This Asian-inspired dish works well as a meatless main course, or served as a side dish to grilled teriyaki chicken or fish. You can substitute other vegetables as desired.

Cook linguine until just tender. Rinse and drain; set aside.

In a saucepan, cook the pea pods in boiling water for 30 seconds, then remove with slotted spoon to ice water (this will blanch them and preserve the bright green color); drain. In the same pan of water, boil the broccoli for 2 minutes, or until crisp-tender. Drain broccoli and place in ice water; drain and wrap in a towel to absorb excess water. Set aside.

For Sauce Heat the oil in a saucepan. Add the ginger, garlic and onion and cook, stirring, for 30 seconds. Add the soy sauce, water, sherry and sugar, and bring to a boil. Mix cornstarch with 2 teaspoons of water and stir into the sauce to thicken. Remove from heat.

For Vegetables Heat the oil in a wok or skillet. Add the onion, carrot, celery, red pepper and bean sprouts. Cook, stirring often, for 2 minutes, then stir in the pea pods, broccoli and water chestnuts. Immediately stir in the sauce and noodles; toss until the sauce has coated all vegetables and noodles. Serve hot.

* Available in the Asian section of most supermarkets.

TORTELLONI MAC 'N' CHEESE WITH BROCCOLI

2–3 Servings

3 cups cheese tortelloni*
(or tortellini)
1 ½ cups broccoli florets

Cheese Sauce

2 tablespoons butter
2 tablespoons all-purpose flour
2 cups milk
1 cup shredded cheddar cheese
½ cup (4 ounces) American cheese, chopped
¼ teaspoon paprika
¼ teaspoon dry mustard
¼ teaspoon Worcestershire sauce
dash salt

Topping

½ cup shredded cheddar cheese

You might say that this is the adult version of macaroni and cheese and, by the way, our students love both versions. We offer this as a meatless main course, but this would also be good as a side dish with or without broccoli, served with grilled chicken or sausage.

Cook pasta according to package directions. Drain and rinse briefly; set aside.

Cook broccoli in boiling water until almost cooked, about 2 minutes. Place in ice water; drain and wrap in a towel to soak up all moisture; set aside.

For Cheese Sauce In a heavy-bottomed pan, melt the butter over medium-low heat. Stir in the flour and cook, stirring constantly, for 2 minutes. Stir in the milk, while whisking constantly, to avoid lumps. When mixture is smooth, stir in remaining sauce ingredients and continue stirring until cheese is melted and sauce is smooth. Remove from heat.

Assemble Dish Preheat oven to 350°F. Place pasta in an oil-sprayed 8-by-8-inch casserole dish. Place broccoli florets in and around the pasta. Pour cheese sauce over and toss gently to coat all pasta and broccoli. Sprinkle with the cheese. Oil spray a piece of foil and place, oiled-side down, over the casserole; bake until hot and bubbly, about 15 minutes.

* This recipe was tested with DiGiorno, refrigerated brand tortelloni. Tortelloni is a larger stuffed pasta compared to tortellini.

CAJUN BARBECUED SHRIMP WITH ANGEL HAIR

4–6 Servings

½ (1-pound) package angel hair noodles
   (capellini)

Sauce
¼ cup dry white wine (optional)
1 (8-ounce) bottle clam juice
1 cup chicken broth
3 tablespoons cornstarch

4 teaspoons butter
2½ teaspoons minced garlic
1 pound medium shrimp,
   peeled, deveined, rinsed
1½ teaspoons Cajun seasoning
2 teaspoons Worcestershire sauce
1 tablespoon + 1 teaspoon minced
   fresh parsley

Cook noodles according to package directions. Drain and rinse briefly; set aside.

For Sauce Add the wine (if not using wine, then add ¼ cup of another liquid such as chicken broth) to a medium saucepan and bring to a boil. Boil for 1 minute, then stir in the clam juice and chicken broth; bring to a boil. Meanwhile, combine the cornstarch in a small bowl with just enough water to make a pourable mixture; gradually whisk into boiling liquid. Boil until thickened, then remove from the heat (sauce will be thick).

Melt the butter in a large skillet over medium heat. Add the garlic, cook for 20 seconds or until fragrant, then stir in the shrimp. Cook shrimp, stirring often, until almost cooked through, about 1½ minutes. Stir in Cajun seasoning, Worcestershire sauce and 1 tablespoon of the parsley; cook for 20 seconds, or until shrimp are cooked through. Stir in the sauce and noodles, tossing well to coat the noodles evenly with sauce.

Portion noodles and shrimp onto serving plates; sprinkle remaining parsley on top. If noodles and sauce get too thick, add more chicken broth as needed.

FETTUCINE WITH GRILLED CHICKEN

4–6 Servings

Marinade

2 tablespoons sun-dried tomatoes in oil (whole or chopped)

2 medium garlic cloves, peeled

¼ cup olive oil

1 tablespoon lemon juice

¼ teaspoon dried basil

¼ teaspoon salt

¼ teaspoon black pepper

12 ounces boneless, skinless chicken breasts

½ (1-pound) package fettucine noodles

Sauce

½ teaspoon olive oil

2 slices bacon, halved lengthwise, chopped

1½ teaspoons minced garlic

2 green onions, chopped

2½ cups chicken broth

¾ cup half-and-half

2 tablespoons cornstarch

¾ cup grated parmesan cheese, divided

For Marinade Place all marinade ingredients in a blender. Process for 2 minutes, scraping down sides as needed; set aside. Rinse and trim the chicken breasts; pat dry and coat completely with marinade in non-aluminum container. Cover with plastic wrap and chill at least 2 hours, preferably overnight.

Meanwhile, cook the fettucine noodles according to package directions. Drain and rinse briefly; cover and set aside.

For Sauce Heat the oil in a saucepan, then add the bacon. Cook over medium heat until bacon is browned and fat is rendered. Drain off half the grease, then add the garlic and onion; cook for about 2 minutes. Add the broth and the half-and-half. Turn heat to medium-high and bring mixture to a boil. Mix the cornstarch with just enough water to make a pourable mixture; add to boiling broth, stirring until thickened. Turn heat to low and stir in ½ cup of the parmesan. Cover and keep warm.

Drain and discard marinade. Cook chicken on a charcoal or gas grill until cooked through, approximately 6–7 minutes per side, depending on size (chicken can be broiled instead).

Assemble Dish Slice the chicken into thin slices, then stir into the warm sauce (including any accumulated juices). Add the noodles to the sauce, tossing well to coat. Plate individually or place mixture on a platter. Top with the remaining parmesan and serve.

ZITI WITH SPICY CHICKEN, GARLIC AND TOMATO

4 Servings

1 ¾ cups ziti noodles
8 ounces chicken tenders,
   rinsed, halved lenthwise
2 cups chicken broth
   pinch salt

Sauce

1 ¼ cups chicken broth, reserved
   from above
¼ cup dry white wine (optional)
¼ teaspoon balsamic (or other) vinegar
2 ½ teaspoons cornstarch
1 ½ teaspoons water
2 ounces cream cheese
¼ cup + 2 tablespoons heavy
   whipping cream
⅛ teaspoon salt

Skillet Mixture

4 slices bacon, cut into thin strips
2 teaspoons minced red onion
½ teaspoon minced garlic
⅛ teaspoon dried basil
⅛ teaspoon dried oregano
¼ teaspoon crushed red pepper flakes
¼ cup diced roma tomato

¼ cup + 2 tablespoons grated
   parmesan cheese

Boil noodles in salted water until just cooked; drain and set aside. Meanwhile, place the chicken tenders in the broth in a saucepan. Simmer for 8–10 minutes, or until just cooked through. Remove chicken from broth; cover and set aside. Strain broth for use in sauce.

For Sauce Rinse the same saucepan and combine 1¼ cups of the reserved broth, the wine (if not using wine, then add ¼ cup more of chicken broth) and vinegar. Bring to a boil; let boil 1 minute. Combine the cornstarch and water to make a pourable mixture; gradually add to boiling broth, stirring until thickened. Remove from heat. Place cream cheese and cream in a microwave-safe bowl and heat, covered, until hot in the center but not boiling. Stir together until blended, then stir into the broth mixture with the salt. Cover and keep warm.

For Skillet Mixture In a large skillet, cook the bacon strips until just crisp, stirring frequently. Drain off the grease and add the remaining skillet ingredients. Cook, stirring, for 1 minute, then stir in the cooked chicken, sauce mixture and cooked pasta. Stir in ¼ cup of parmesan. Plate individually or place mixture on a platter. Top with the remaining parmesan and serve hot.

You can control the spicy profile by adjusting the crushed red pepper flakes. We usually go through about 120 servings of this at lunch, which reflects its strong popularity.

BEEF STROGANOFF

4 Servings

    4 cups (about 6 ounces) egg noodles

Beef Mixture

    2 tablespoons vegetable oil, divided
    4 teaspoons all-purpose flour
    1 pound sirloin steak, cut into strips
    1 tablespoon butter
    3/4 cup chopped onion
 1 1/4 teaspoons minced garlic
    2 cups sliced fresh mushrooms
    1/2 teaspoon dried thyme
    1/2 teaspoon paprika
    1/4 teaspoon salt
       dash black pepper

Sauce

    1/2 cup dry red wine
    1 cup beef broth
    1 cup heavy whipping cream
    1 cup (regular or light) sour cream

    2 teaspoons minced fresh parsley

This creamy noodle dish is a classic from a bygone era. It still satisfies, especially on a cold winter evening.

Cook egg noodles according to package directions. Drain and rinse briefly; set aside.

For Beef Mixture Heat 1 tablespoon oil in a large skillet over medium-high heat. Toss meat strips with the flour; sprinkle lightly with salt and pepper, then add to the hot skillet. Cook, stirring constantly, for 2–3 minutes, or until barely pink in center and lightly browned outside. Remove meat from the skillet (it will be cooked more later). Heat remaining oil in the skillet. Add the onion and cook for 1 minute, stirring often. Add the butter, garlic, mushrooms and spices. Cook for 2 minutes, stirring often.

For Sauce In the same skillet, turn heat to high. Pour the wine over the mushroom mixture; cook for 1 minute. Add the beef broth and cream, stirring to blend; let boil for 1½–2 minutes to reduce and thicken slightly. Turn heat to low, stir in the sour cream, and whisk until sauce is smooth and lumps are dissolved.

Stir in browned beef strips and let simmer in sauce for 2–3 minutes to thicken sauce further and finish cooking the meat. Be careful not to overcook the meat as it will toughen (test one piece for doneness). Stir in the noodles and parsley, tossing well to coat noodles in sauce mixture. Serve hot.

COUNTRY CHICKEN AND NOODLES

4 Servings

3 cups frozen egg noodles*
8 ounces chicken breasts, cut into thin strips
2 cups chicken broth

Gravy

2 tablespoons butter
¼ teaspoon minced garlic
¼ cup small-diced onion
4 teaspoons small-diced celery
4 teaspoons small-diced carrot
5 teaspoons all-purpose flour
   pinch dried thyme
   pinch dried marjoram
¼ teaspoon onion powder
   pinch salt
   pinch black pepper

¼ teaspoon minced fresh parsley
   (or pinch dried parsley)

This recipe uses frozen egg noodles, which have a pleasant chewiness resembling the texture of a dumpling. This dish is much like one that would be served in an Amish home or other rural American home, although the noodles most likely would be homemade.

Cook noodles according to package directions. Drain and rinse briefly; cover and set aside.

Heat the chicken broth in a saucepan and add the chicken strips. Cover and simmer for 7–8 minutes, or until chicken is just cooked. Remove chicken from broth, reserving broth to make gravy.

For Gravy Heat the butter in the same pot in which the noodles were cooked. Add the garlic, onion, celery and carrot; cook over medium heat for 5 minutes, stirring frequently. Stir in the flour and all spices. Cook for 2 minutes, then gradually stir in reserved broth, whisking to make a smooth gravy consistency. Turn heat to low and cook, covered, for 10 minutes to finish cooking the vegetables.

Stir in the minced parsley and chicken. Continue cooking on low for 2 minutes, then stir in the noodles. Toss gently to coat noodles with gravy. Serve immediately.

* Available in the freezer section of most supermarkets.

GRILLED ITALIAN CHICKEN WITH ANGEL HAIR

4–6 Servings

Marinade

4 tablespoons olive oil
1 tablespoon lemon juice
¾ teaspoon minced garlic
¼ teaspoon dried basil
⅛ teaspoon dried oregano
¼ teaspoon salt
⅛ teaspoon black pepper

1 pound boneless, skinless chicken breasts
½ (1-pound) package angel hair noodles (capellini)

Sun-Dried Tomato Pesto

3 tablespoons sun-dried tomatoes in oil
1 tablespoon + 2 teaspoons chopped red onion
¼ teaspoon minced garlic
1½ teaspoons balsamic or red wine vinegar
⅛ teaspoon salt
⅛ teaspoon black pepper
½ cup chicken broth

Sauce

2½ cups chicken broth
2 tablespoons + 1½ teaspoons cornstarch
4 teaspoons minced fresh basil
⅛ teaspoon salt
⅛ teaspoon black pepper
2 tablespoons butter

½ cup grated parmesan cheese

Marinate Chicken Place all marinade ingredients in a bowl; whisk to combine. Rinse and trim chicken breasts, then add to marinade, turning to coat all sides of chicken. Cover with plastic wrap and chill at least 2 hours, preferably overnight.

Cook noodles according to package directions; drain and set aside.

For Pesto Place all pesto ingredients in blender. Process for 1–2 minutes, or until mixture is smooth; set aside.

For Sauce In a saucepan, bring the broth to a boil. Mix the cornstarch with enough water to make a pourable mixture; gradually add to boiling broth, stirring until thickened. Turn heat down to medium and add the basil, salt, pepper and butter. Stir until butter is melted, then stir in pesto mixture. Keep warm.

Grill Chicken Drain and discard marinade. Cook chicken on a charcoal or gas grill until cooked through (broiling the chicken is an acceptable alternative if time is limited). Cool slightly.

Assemble Dish Combine the sauce and noodles, tossing to coat the noodles completely. Slice the chicken thinly and stir into the noodle mixture. Plate mixture individually or on a platter; sprinkle generously with the parmesan. Serve hot.

PASTA WITH FOUR CHEESES AND TOMATO

4–6 Servings

    2 cups penne or ziti noodles

Vegetables

    1 tablespoon butter
    1 teaspoon olive oil
    1 teaspoon minced garlic
    ¼ cup chopped green onions
    ½ cup diced roma tomato
    ¼ teaspoon crushed red pepper flakes

Sauce

    ¼ cup milk
    1 ¼ cups heavy whipping cream
    ½ cup ricotta cheese
    1 cup grated parmesan cheese
    ¾ cup shredded mozzarella cheese
    ¼ teaspoon salt
      pinch dried basil
      pinch dried oregano

    ¾ cup shredded cheddar cheese
    1 teaspoon minced fresh parsley
      (optional)

Cook noodles according to package directions. Drain and rinse briefly; set aside.

For Sauce In a saucepan, heat the milk and cream until warm. Transfer 1 cup of the mixture to a blender. Add the ricotta and blend until very smooth, about 1 minute. Transfer blender mixture back into the saucepan. Heat until simmering, then stir in the parmesan until smooth. Stir in the mozzarella and all spices; cook over medium heat until cheese is melted. Cover and keep warm.

In a large skillet, heat the butter and oil until butter is melted. Add the garlic, onion, tomato and crushed red pepper. Cook for 1 minute, stirring often; stir in the noodles. Stir in the sauce, then transfer the mixture to an oil-sprayed 8-by-8-inch (or similar size) pan. Sprinkle evenly with the cheddar cheese.

Preheat oven to 350°F. Bake for 15–17 minutes, or until mixture is hot and bubbly. Garnish top with parsley, if desired.

MEATS

Beef Burrito Supreme

Carne Asada

Sesame Beef Stir-Fry

Cottey Meatloaf

Italian Meatballs with Marinara Sauce

Tater Taco Casserole

Holiday Cornbread Dressing

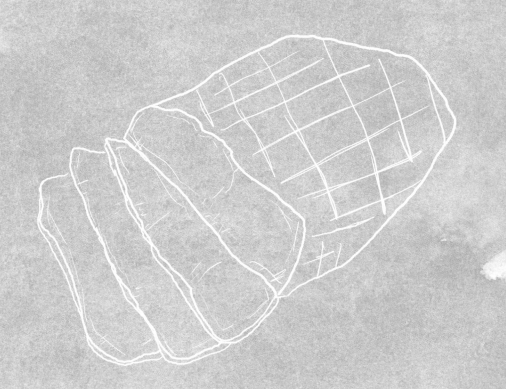

BEEF BURRITO SUPREME

4 Servings

Beef Mixture

1 1/2 teaspoons vegetable oil
1/4 cup finely chopped onion
1/2 pound ground beef
1/2 teaspoon chili powder
1/4 teaspoon salt
1/8 teaspoon onion powder
1/8 teaspoon ground cumin
1/4 teaspoon paprika
1/8 teaspoon garlic powder

4 (8-inch) flour tortillas
1/2 cup refried beans
3 tablespoons ranch dressing
5 tablespoons salsa, divided
1/2 cup shredded cheddar cheese
1/4 cup diced fresh tomato

For Beef Mixture Heat the oil in a large skillet. Add the onion and cook over medium-high heat for 3 minutes, stirring often. Add the beef and cook with the onions, breaking up large chunks, until no longer pink. Drain off all grease and rinse meat briefly under hot water to remove excess fat. Drain well, then return to skillet; turn heat to medium. Stir in all seasonings, mixing well to blend evenly into the meat; cook for 2 minutes. Remove from heat.

Wrap tortillas in foil and heat in the oven just until warm and pliable. Heat the refried beans in the microwave, or on the stove, until warmed through.

Assemble Burritos Place warm tortillas on a work surface and, for each one, spread with 2 tablespoons of refried beans. Combine the ranch dressing and 1 tablespoon of salsa together in a small bowl. Spread 1 tablespoon of this mixture over the beans. Top with 4 tablespoons of meat mixture in a neat row about 3 inches from the edge nearest you. Top with 2 tablespoons of cheese, then 1 tablespoon of tomato and 1 tablespoon of remaining salsa. Fold in the ends about an inch or so and roll up, tightly, away from you. Place, seam-side down, in an oil-sprayed baking pan. Cover with foil and bake until burritos are heated through.

Serve with salsa, sour cream and guacamole, if desired.

CARNE ASADA

4 Servings

1 pound top sirloin steak (can substitute
   skirt steak, ribeye or strip steak)

Marinade
¼ cup vegetable oil
4 teaspoons soy sauce
1½ teaspoons lime juice
1½ teaspoons minced garlic
¼ teaspoon ground cumin
1 tablespoon minced cilantro
1 tablespoon minced jalapeño
2 tablespoons salsa
   pinch salt
   pinch black pepper

8 flour tortillas (any size), warm

Topping (optional)
1 tablespoon vegetable oil
1 large onion

This is a fun way to jazz up a steak
when you want a change from the
usual. If you like it spicy hot, just
add more jalapeños. Use Miguel's
Salsa recipe, in the Party Foods
section on page 189, or use your
favorite salsa to serve with it.

Marinate Beef Combine all marinade ingredients together
in a small bowl. Place meat in a non-aluminum container; pour
marinade over meat, turning over to coat both sides completely.
Cover and chill overnight.

For Topping If using, peel the onion and slice into thick rings.
Separate out 12 rings, reserving the rest for another use. Coat the
rings with the oil, then sprinkle with salt and pepper; set aside.

Drain and discard marinade. Cook steak on a charcoal or gas
grill on both sides until desired doneness is reached; remove,
cover and keep warm. Place onion rings on the grill and cook
until tender and lightly charred on both sides; keep warm. Slice
the steak thinly and serve with the grilled onion, accompanied
by the warm flour tortillas.

Serve with one or more of the following as desired: salsa,
guacamole, jalapeño slices, pico de gallo, shredded cheese
and sour cream.

SESAME BEEF STIR-FRY

4 Servings

Stir-Fry Sauce

1 ½ teaspoons dark sesame oil*
¾ teaspoon minced garlic
¾ teaspoon minced ginger
2 tablespoons dry sherry
1 ¼ cups chicken broth
1 tablespoon hoisin sauce*
1 tablespoon oyster sauce*
4 teaspoons soy sauce
  pinch black pepper
  pinch crushed red pepper flakes
1 tablespoon + ½ teaspoon cornstarch
2 teaspoons water

1 ½ teaspoons sesame seeds
  pinch salt
4 teaspoons + 1 ½ teaspoons vegetable oil, divided
1 pound top sirloin steak, trimmed, cut into strips
¼ onion, cut into thin strips
½ red bell pepper, cut into thin strips
8 broccoli florets
12 fresh pea pods (snow peas), stemmed

1 ½–2 cups long-grain white rice

This is an Asian-inspired stir-fry that is popular on campus. Steam the rice about 20 minutes before you expect to serve this dish.

For Sauce Heat the oil in a skillet or wok. Add the garlic and ginger and cook for 30 seconds; add remaining ingredients, except cornstarch and water. Simmer for 6–7 minutes over low heat. Combine the cornstarch and water in small bowl, stirring until smooth. Turn heat to high and stir in cornstarch mixture; boil until thickened. Remove from heat; set aside.

Par-Cook Vegetables In a medium saucepan, boil the broccoli for 2 minutes; add the pea pods and boil another 15 seconds or so. Drain; place vegetables in ice water to stop the cooking and retain their color. Let chill briefly, then drain and wrap in a towel to absorb all moisture; set aside.

Toast Seeds Heat a large skillet. Add the sesame seeds and a pinch of salt. Toast until golden brown, stirring, or shaking pan constantly. Remove the seeds from the skillet to a small plate or bowl to cool.

Brown Beef In the same skillet, heat 4 teaspoons of oil, then add the beef strips. Cook for 1½ minutes per side, or until browned and just cooked through. Transfer meat to a plate while you continue with the recipe.

Assemble Dish Wipe the skillet clean, then heat the remaining oil. Add the onion and pepper strips; cook for 2–3 minutes to soften. Add the beef, sauce, sesame seeds, broccoli and pea pods, stirring well to combine. Cook for 2 minutes, or until heated through. Serve hot with steamed rice.

* Available in the Asian foods section of most supermarkets.

COTTEY MEATLOAF

10 Slices

2 1/2 pounds ground beef
1 (1-ounce) envelope onion soup mix
1/2 cup + 2 tablespoons milk
3 eggs
3/4 cup quick oats
1/2 teaspoon salt
1/4 teaspoon black pepper

Topping

1/3 cup ketchup
1/3 cup packed brown sugar
1 tablespoon + 1 1/2 teaspoons
yellow mustard
1 tablespoon plain horseradish
(or 5 teaspoons creamy
horseradish sauce)

With all the food choices available
in our world, sometimes the sim-
plest ones are the ones we crave.
This meatloaf seems to draw people
out of the woodwork. We prepare
more servings of this than anything
else in our kitchen. The horseradish
in the topping is a critical addition,
which foils the richness of the meat
very well.

In a large bowl, mix the beef, onion soup mix, milk, eggs and
oats. Form into a loaf shape in the center of a large oil-sprayed,
deep baking pan. Chill for 30 minutes to allow the oats and the
soup mix to soften and the flavors to blend.

Bake, uncovered, for 35 minutes in a preheated 350°F oven.
Meanwhile, combine the ketchup, sugar, mustard and
horseradish in a small bowl. Remove the meatloaf from the
oven, and spread the top evenly with the ketchup mixture.
Cover and bake for 35 minutes more, or until hot in center
and cooked through. Cut into serving slices.

ITALIAN MEATBALLS WITH MARINARA SAUCE

4 Servings

Meatballs

- ¾ pound ground beef
- 1 egg
- 1 tablespoon + ¾ teaspoon minced fresh parsley
- ½ teaspoon minced garlic
- 1 slice white bread, crust removed
- ¼ cup milk
- ½ teaspoon salt
- ⅛ teaspoon black pepper
- ¼ teaspoon dried basil
- ¼ teaspoon dried oregano
- ¼ teaspoon garlic powder
- ¼ teaspoon onion powder
- 1 tablespoon + 1½ teaspoons grated parmesan cheese

Marinara Sauce

- 1 (28-ounce) can whole peeled tomatoes
- 4 tablespoons olive oil
- 2 teaspoons minced garlic
- ¼ teaspoon dried basil
- ¼ teaspoon dried oregano
- ½ teaspoon salt
- ¼ teaspoon black pepper

For Meatballs In a large bowl, mix the beef, egg, parsley and garlic. Soak the bread in the milk, then gently squeeze the milk from the bread and shred it as you add it to the meat mixture. Stir in all the spices, mixing well. Stir in the parmesan, mixing well to blend evenly throughout meat. Cover and chill beef mixture for 30 minutes. Form the mixture into 12 meatballs. Place on an oil-sprayed baking sheet. Bake in a preheated 350°F oven for 20–25 minutes, or until browned and cooked through. Place on paper towels to soak up excess grease, then keep warm.

For Sauce Place the canned tomatoes and juice in a food processor. Process until smooth; set aside. Heat the oil in a saucepot. Add the garlic, basil and oregano; cook for 30 seconds or so. Add the tomatoes just before the garlic gets browned in the oil. Stir well to incorporate the oil into the sauce; add salt and pepper. Cook, uncovered, over a low simmer for 25 minutes, stirring often.

Serve with spaghetti for a comforting pasta dish, or serve alone with the meatballs on top of the sauce as part of a dinner buffet. This marinara sauce is the same one I prepared when chef of a popular Italian restaurant in Dallas, called Alessio's.

TATER TACO CASSEROLE

4–6 Servings

Cheese Sauce

- 3 tablespoons butter
- 3 tablespoons all-purpose flour
- 1½ cups milk
- 1 (8-ounce) package processed cheese spread, cut into pieces

Beef Mixture

- 1½ teaspoons vegetable oil
- 1¼ pounds ground beef
- ¾ cup tomato sauce
- ¼ cup chopped green chiles, drained
- 1 teaspoon chili powder
- ½ teaspoon ground cumin
- 1 teaspoon garlic salt

- 16 ounces (1 pound) tater puffs, thawed

A south-of-the-border variation on the classic casserole.

For Cheese Sauce Melt the butter in a saucepan over medium heat. Stir in the flour and cook for 2 minutes, stirring almost constantly. Stir in the milk; heat until thickened, then stir in the cheese. Continue to stir frequently over low heat until melted and smooth (be careful not to burn the sauce on the bottom); keep warm.

For Beef Mixture Heat the oil in a large skillet. Add the beef and cook until no longer pink in center, breaking up chunks. Drain off all grease and rinse with hot water to remove excess fat. Drain well, then return to the skillet over medium heat. Stir in tomato sauce, chiles and seasonings; cook for 1–2 minutes until heated through. Turn heat to low and stir in cheese sauce. Let cook for 1 minute, then pour into an oil-sprayed 8-by-8-inch baking pan.

Top beef mixture with an even layer of tater puffs. Bake in a preheated 350°F oven for 25–30 minutes, or until center is hot and potatoes are golden brown.

HOLIDAY CORNBREAD DRESSING

6–8 Servings

    1 (6-ounce) box cornbread stuffing mix
    3 slices uncooked bacon, diced
    2 teaspoons olive oil
    1 tablespoon butter
  1/3 cup diced onion
  1/4 cup thinly sliced green onion
  1/4 cup diced celery
    2 teaspoons minced garlic
  1/3 cup small-diced ham
  1/8 teaspoon (or to taste) salt
  1/4 teaspoon black pepper
  1/4 teaspoon dried thyme
  1/4 teaspoon onion powder
  1/4 teaspoon garlic powder
 2–4 tablespoons chicken broth (or water)

A deluxe cornbread recipe, this is often served as part of the "Hanging of the Greens" dinner buffet. A variation of this recipe adds 1 cup of sliced, fresh mushrooms to the onions and celery when cooking in the skillet, which is particularly good when serving with roast beef. This recipe can be served not only with turkey, but also roast chicken or pork.

Prepare cornbread stuffing according to package directions, except reduce by half the amount of butter (or margarine) called for; cover and set aside.

In a large skillet, cook the bacon until crisp; remove from pan and drain off the grease. To the same pan add the oil and butter. When the butter is melted, add the onion, green onion and celery; cook for 3 minutes, or until onions are softened. Stir in the garlic and cook for 1 minute. Stir in the ham, cooked bacon and all seasonings, and cook until heated through.

Stir stuffing into skillet mixture, combining all ingredients well. Add chicken broth (or water), as needed, to moisten mixture before serving.

CHICKEN

Cheesy Baked Chicken Pie

Grilled Chicken Alfredo with Bruschetta Topping

Chicken Divan

Grilled Chicken Provencal

Chicken Teriyaki Stir-Fry

Creamy Chicken Enchiladas

General Tso's Chicken

Grilled Chicken Provolone with Lemon Basil

Grilled Chicken with Honey Garlic Sauce

Honey Dijon Chicken

Regatta Chicken

Kung Pao Chicken

Planet Hollywood Chicken Crunch

CHEESY BAKED CHICKEN PIE

1 Pie (8 Servings)

Filling

 2 cups cooked, diced chicken
   (white or dark)
 1 tablespoon minced onion
 ¼ cup diced celery
 ⅓ cup diced water chestnuts
 ½ cup canned fried onions, chopped
 1 cup shredded cheddar cheese
 1 cup mayonnaise
 1 teaspoon lemon juice
 ½ teaspoon salt

 1 (9-inch) pie shell

Topping

 ¼ cup shredded cheddar cheese
 ¼ cup canned fried onions, chopped

You can omit the pie crust, if desired, and just bake the chicken filling in a lightly-oiled casserole dish, topped with the shredded cheese and fried onion.

Bake pie shell in a preheated 350°F oven for 10 minutes; cool.

In a large bowl, stir together the chicken, onion, celery, water chestnuts, fried onions and cheese. In a separate bowl, combine the mayonnaise, lemon juice and salt. Stir the mayonnaise mixture into the chicken mixture; combine thoroughly to blend.

Fill the pie shell with the chicken mixture, slightly packing it in the shell. Bake for 15 minutes. Sprinkle the cheese over the top, then the fried onions. Bake for 8–10 minutes more, or until hot in the center and cheese is melted. Cut into wedges.

GRILLED CHICKEN ALFREDO WITH BRUSCHETTA TOPPING

4 Servings

- 4 (4-ounce) boneless, skinless chicken breasts (1 pound)
- ½ cup Italian dressing
- ¼ cup olive oil

Sauce

- ½ teaspoon olive oil
- ¼ teaspoon minced garlic
- ½ cup heavy whipping cream
- ½ teaspoon lemon juice
- ½ cup grated parmesan cheese
- 1 teaspoon butter

Bruschetta

- ¼ cup seeded, diced roma tomato*
- 1 ½ teaspoons minced fresh basil
- ¼ teaspoon minced garlic
- ¾ teaspoon olive oil
- ¼ teaspoon balsamic or red wine vinegar
  dash salt
  dash black pepper

- ¼ cup shredded mozzarella cheese
- 1 teaspoon grated parmesan cheese

The sauce can be made the day before, although you may have to add a touch more cream. The bruschetta can be made several hours ahead. This dish is well worth the effort and a great choice when guests are coming.

Marinate Chicken Rinse and trim chicken; pat dry. In a small bowl, combine the dressing and oil. Place the chicken in a non-aluminum container. Pour dressing over the chicken, turning to coat both sides; cover and chill for 3–4 hours, or overnight.

For Sauce Heat the oil in a small saucepan. Add the garlic and cook for 30–45 seconds; immediately add the cream, then the lemon juice. Cook until hot and bubbly, then stir in the cheese until melted and smooth. Remove from heat, and stir in the butter; cover and keep warm.

*To Seed Tomatoes Cut off the stem and then cut tomatoes in half crosswise. Pick up each half and firmly squeeze out the seeds and juice. Discard the seeds and juice.

For Bruschetta In a small bowl, combine all bruschetta ingredients, stirring well to blend flavors. Cover and set aside at room temperature.

Drain and discard marinade. Cook chicken on a charcoal or gas grill until cooked through, about 6–7 minutes per side. Preheat oven to 350°F. Place 1 tablespoon mozzarella cheese over each breast; bake for 2 minutes, or until cheese is melted.

Assemble Dish Remove chicken from the oven. Drain the bruschetta. Top each breast with 2 tablespoons of sauce, a heaping teaspoon of the bruschetta, and ¼ teaspoon of the parmesan. Serve hot.

CHICKEN DIVAN

4 Servings

- 12 broccoli florets
- 4 teaspoons vegetable oil
- 1 pound boneless, skinless chicken breasts, cut into 1-inch strips

Sauce

- 1 (10.75-ounce) can cream of chicken soup, undiluted
- ½ cup light or regular mayonnaise
- ½ cup chicken broth
- 1 teaspoon lemon juice
- ¾ teaspoon Worcestershire sauce
- ½ teaspoon dry mustard

Topping

- ¾ cup croutons
- ¾ cup shredded cheddar cheese
- 1 tablespoon grated parmesan cheese
  dash paprika

Chicken Divan has been served in homes since the 1950s, and it is a dish that still delivers rave reviews. This recipe is a good choice for a brunch or luncheon main course. At Cottey, we use the Homemade Croutons featured in the Soups/Salads section of this book on page 62 as part of the topping, although a quality, store-bought brand will provide good results.

Steam the broccoli until crisp-tender, 2–3 minutes. Drain, chill in ice water, then drain again. Roll up in a towel to absorb excess moisture; set aside.

Heat the oil in a large skillet. Add the chicken strips and cook over medium heat for 3–4 minutes per side, or until juices run clear when pierced with a knife; set aside.

For Sauce In a large skillet or saucepan, heat the soup, mayonnaise, broth, lemon juice, Worcestershire sauce and dry mustard, whisking until smooth. Stir chicken, including the accumulated juices, into the sauce mixture.

Place the chicken mixture into an 8-by-8-inch (or similar size) pan. For a nice presentation, arrange the broccoli down 2 sides of the casserole. Top the casserole with croutons, then the cheddar cheese, and then the parmesan. Sprinkle with paprika. Bake in a preheated 350°F oven, covered, for 15–20 minutes, or until hot in the center.

GRILLED CHICKEN PROVENCAL

4 Servings

4 (4-ounce) boneless, skinless chicken breasts (1 pound)

Marinade

6 tablespoons olive oil
2 teaspoons lemon juice
1 teaspoon minced garlic
¼ teaspoon dried basil
¼ teaspoon dried oregano
¼ teaspoon salt
⅛ teaspoon black pepper

Sauce

2 tablespoons olive oil
¼ cup diced onion
1½ teaspoons minced garlic
½ cup diced mushrooms
1 tablespoon minced fresh basil
¼ cup dry white wine
2 tablespoons pitted, chopped Kalamata olives*
¾ cup chicken broth
1 cup spaghetti sauce
1 tablespoon butter

1 tablespoon grated parmesan cheese
1 teaspoon minced fresh basil

This chicken dish would go well with buttered noodles topped with parmesan cheese. You can omit the Kalamata olives, if desired. If you do, add ¼ teaspoon of salt to the sauce, since the olives add a touch of saltiness, which perks up the finished sauce.

Marinate Chicken Rinse and trim chicken; pat dry. In a small bowl, combine all marinade ingredients. Place chicken in a non-aluminum container. Pour marinade over chicken, turning to coat all sides. Cover and chill at least 3 hours, or overnight.

For Sauce Heat the oil in a saucepan; add the onion. Cook for 2 minutes; add the garlic and mushrooms, and cook for 2–3 minutes until softened. Add the basil and wine; cook until wine is reduced to almost dry. Add the olives, broth and spaghetti sauce. Cover and cook over medium-low heat for 15 minutes. Uncover and cook over low heat for 6–7 minutes, or until thickened. Swirl in the butter just before serving.

Drain and discard marinade. Cook chicken on a charcoal or gas grill until cooked through, about 6–7 minutes per side. Place chicken on plates, or a serving platter, and top each with the sauce. Sprinkle with the parmesan and basil.

* Kalamata olives are marinated black olives from Greece, which are available in most supermarkets, often located where imported foods or specialty cheeses are displayed.

CHICKEN TERIYAKI STIR-FRY

4 Servings

1 pound boneless, skinless chicken breasts or tenders, cut into strips
¼ cup teriyaki sauce

Sauce

1 ¼ cups chicken broth
5 tablespoons pineapple juice (reserved from can of chunks below)
1 tablespoon + 2 teaspoons cornstarch
2 ½ teaspoons water
3 tablespoons + 1 teaspoon teriyaki sauce
2 teaspoons hoisin sauce*
1 ½ teaspoons honey

Vegetable Mix

½ cup fresh pea pods (snow peas), stemmed
8 broccoli florets
4 teaspoons vegetable oil
1 ¼ teaspoons minced garlic
1 teaspoon minced ginger
½ cup celery, sliced thin diagonally
½ cup red bell pepper, sliced into thin strips
¾ cup fresh mung bean sprouts
1 (5.33-ounce) can pineapple chunks, drained (reserve juice for sauce)

Serve this dish with steamed or fried rice. All of the components of this recipe can be prepared a day ahead, if desired. If you marinate the chicken a day ahead, be sure to drain off the marinade after about 2 hours.

Marinate Chicken Rinse and trim chicken; pat dry. Place chicken in a non-aluminum container. Pour sauce over and chill for 2 hours. Drain and discard sauce; cover chicken and set aside.

For Sauce Bring the chicken broth and pineapple juice to a boil. In a small bowl, mix the cornstarch and water until smooth. Gradually add to boiling broth, stirring to thicken. Stir in remaining sauce ingredients; remove from heat.

Par-Cook Vegetables In a pan of boiling water, blanch the pea pods for 15 seconds. Drain; chill in ice water, then pat dry. Boil or steam the broccoli for 2 minutes, or until crisp-tender. Drain; chill in ice water, then pat dry (or wrap in a towel). Set aside.

Stir-Fry Vegetables and Chicken Heat the oil in a wok or large skillet. Add the garlic and ginger; cook for 30 seconds. Add the celery and red pepper; stir-fry for 2 minutes. In the wok, push vegetables to the side and add the chicken. Stir-fry until golden brown and cooked through (juices will run clear when pierced). Add the sprouts, pea pods and broccoli; stir-fry for 1 minute, then stir in the pineapple chunks and sauce. Simmer for 2–3 minutes, or until heated through. Serve hot with rice.

* Available in the Asian foods section of most supermarkets.

CREAMY CHICKEN ENCHILADAS

4 Servings

Filling

½ pound boneless, skinless chicken breasts or tenders, cut into thin strips

2 teaspoons cornstarch

1 tablespoon butter

1 ½ teaspoons vegetable oil

½ cup diced onion

½ teaspoon minced garlic

1 tablespoon chopped green chiles

¼ teaspoon ground cumin

¼ teaspoon garlic powder

¼ teaspoon salt

dash black pepper

6 tablespoons chicken broth

2 ounces (¼ cup) cream cheese, softened

4 (8-inch) flour tortillas

Sauce

½ cup chicken broth

¾ cup cream of chicken soup, undiluted

¼ teaspoon minced garlic

2 ¼ teaspoons chopped green chiles

¼ teaspoon onion powder

¼ teaspoon garlic powder

¼ teaspoon ground cumin

3 tablespoons sour cream

¾ cup shredded cheddar-jack cheese blend

salsa, as needed

For Filling Rinse and trim chicken; pat dry. Toss in the cornstarch to coat; set aside. Heat the butter and oil in a large skillet. Add the onion and garlic; cook over medium heat for 3–4 minutes until softened. Push onions to the side of the skillet and add the chicken strips. Cook, stirring often, for 3–4 minutes. Add the green chiles, spices and seasonings, and continue cooking until chicken is cooked in the center, about 4 minutes more. Stir in the broth and cream cheese, then remove from heat. Cover, and set aside to cool.

Divide the filling evenly between the tortillas. Roll tightly and place, seam-side down, in a lightly oil-sprayed 8-by-8-inch pan.

For Sauce In a saucepan, combine all sauce ingredients, except sour cream. Bring to a boil, then turn heat to low. Cover and simmer for 6–7 minutes. Remove from heat and stir in sour cream.

Pour sauce over the enchiladas, covering them completely. Cover with foil and bake in a preheated 350°F oven for 30 minutes, or until heated through. Remove foil and sprinkle cheese evenly over the top. Bake, uncovered, until cheese is melted and bubbly. Serve hot with salsa of choice.

GENERAL TSO'S CHICKEN

4 Servings

1 ¼ pounds boneless, skinless chicken tenders (or use chicken breasts, cut into 1-inch strips)

Marinade

3 tablespoons soy sauce
2 teaspoons sugar
½ teaspoon rice wine vinegar*
(or white vinegar)
½ teaspoon minced garlic
¼ teaspoon minced ginger
pinch crushed red pepper flakes

Sauce

1 teaspoon vegetable oil
½ teaspoon minced garlic
½ teaspoon minced ginger
½ teaspoon finely grated orange zest, (from 1 orange)
¼ teaspoon crushed red pepper flakes
1 cup chicken broth
¼ cup sugar
1 tablespoon rice wine vinegar*
(or white vinegar)
3 tablespoons soy sauce
1 tablespoon cornstarch

¼ cup cornstarch
2 tablespoons all-purpose flour
4–6 tablespoons vegetable oil

1 tablespoon chopped roasted peanuts
1 tablespoon chopped green onions

Marinate Chicken Rinse and trim chicken; pat dry. In a small bowl, combine all marinade ingredients. Place chicken in a non-aluminum pan. Pour marinade over chicken and toss gently to coat. Cover and chill for 1 hour or so.

For Sauce Heat the oil in a saucepan. Add the garlic, ginger, zest and crushed red pepper. Stir-fry for 30 seconds, then add the broth, sugar, vinegar and soy sauce. Bring mixture to a boil. Combine cornstarch with enough water to make a pourable mixture. Add to boiling sauce, while stirring. Boil until thickened, then remove from heat; cover.

Cook Chicken In a shallow container, combine the ¼ cup of cornstarch and 2 tablespoons of flour. Drain and discard marinade. Heat a thin layer of oil in a large skillet. When oil is hot, coat the chicken pieces in the cornstarch mixture and add to the skillet. Cook over medium-high heat for about 5 minutes per side, or until golden brown and cooked through. Drain on paper towels.

Wipe the skillet clean and add the sauce mixture. Simmer until heated through, then stir in the chicken. Simmer until chicken is heated through. Garnish the top of each serving with the peanuts and onion.

* Available in the Asian foods section of most supermarkets.

This is lighter than the original, deep-fried version. If you are an avid fan of Chinese food, this may become a favorite. Serve with steamed rice.

GRILLED CHICKEN PROVOLONE WITH LEMON BASIL

2 Servings

- 2 (4- to 5-ounce) boneless, skinless chicken breasts

Marinade

- ¼ cup Italian dressing
- 2 tablespoons olive oil
- ½ teaspoon minced garlic
- ¼ teaspoon garlic powder
- ¼ teaspoon onion powder
- ¼ teaspoon dried basil
- ¼ teaspoon dried oregano

Lemon Basil Sauce

- 1½ teaspoons olive oil
- 1½ teaspoons minced shallots or red onion
- 1 teaspoon minced garlic
- ¼ cup dry white wine
- ½ cup chicken broth
- 4 teaspoons fresh lemon juice (from ½ lemon)
- ¼ teaspoon salt
  dash black pepper
- 1½ teaspoons cornstarch
- 4 teaspoons butter, cut into pieces
- 1½ teaspoons minced fresh basil

- 1½ teaspoons spaghetti sauce
- 2 slices provolone cheese

Serve with buttered noodles to mop up some of the tasty sauce.

Marinate Chicken Rinse and trim chicken; pat dry. In a small bowl, combine all marinade ingredients. Place chicken in non-aluminum, shallow container; pour marinade over, turning to coat all sides. Cover and chill for at least 4 hours, preferably overnight.

For Sauce Heat the oil in a small saucepan. Add the shallots and cook for 2 minutes on medium heat. Add the garlic and cook for 30 seconds more. Add the wine and boil for 2 minutes. Add the chicken broth, lemon juice, salt and pepper. Bring to a boil, then turn heat to low; cover and simmer for 7–8 minutes. Mix cornstarch with just enough water to make a pourable mixture. Gradually add to sauce, while stirring. Boil until thickened; keep warm. Just before serving, stir in the butter and basil.

Drain and discard marinade. Cook chicken on a charcoal or gas grill about 6–7 minutes per side. Place in a shallow roasting pan. Top each breast with ¾ teaspoon of spaghetti sauce, spreading it in a thin layer over the chicken. Top with a slice of cheese. Broil for 1–2 minutes, or until cheese is just melted and bubbly. Place on serving plates and top with a generous amount of sauce.

GRILLED CHICKEN WITH HONEY GARLIC SAUCE

2 Servings

2 (4- to 5-ounce) boneless, skinless chicken breasts

Marinade

¼ cup Italian dressing
2 tablespoons vegetable oil
2 tablespoons teriyaki sauce
¼ teaspoon garlic powder

Sauce

½ cup chicken broth
2 tablespoons teriyaki sauce
1 whole garlic bulb (head)
2 teaspoons finely chopped green onions, divided
2 teaspoons cornstarch
2 teaspoons honey

Serve this dish with steamed rice to sop up some of the tasty sauce.

Marinate Chicken Rinse and trim chicken; pat dry. In a small bowl, combine marinade ingredients. Place chicken in a non-aluminum container or shallow dish. Pour marinade over chicken, and turn to coat all sides. Cover and chill for at least 4 hours, or overnight.

To Roast Garlic Wrap the garlic bulb in aluminum foil. Bake in a preheated 350°F oven for 1 hour, or until the cloves are soft when squeezed; set aside until cool enough to handle, but still warm. Turn garlic on its side and, with a sharp knife, slice ½-inch off the pointed end to expose the individual cloves. Push out the soft interior with the flat side of a large knife. Collect the roasted garlic pulp and place in a small bowl (it is ok to have some papery skin attached, as it will be strained out later).

For Sauce Heat the chicken broth in a saucepan. Add the teriyaki sauce, roasted garlic pulp and 1½ teaspoons of the onion. Cover and simmer for 10–12 minutes, then bring sauce to a boil. Combine cornstarch with just enough water to make a pourable mixture. Gradually add to sauce, while stirring. Let boil just until thickened. Strain sauce through a fine-mesh strainer. Rinse out saucepan, then add strained sauce back. Stir in the honey. Simmer sauce until heated through, then turn heat to very low; keep warm while grilling the chicken.

Drain and discard marinade. Cook chicken on a charcoal or gas grill until cooked through, about 6–7 minutes per side. Place on serving plates and top with sauce. Sprinkle the remaining onion over each breast.

HONEY DIJON CHICKEN

2 Servings

  2 (4- to 5-ounce) boneless, skinless
     chicken breasts

Marinade

  ¼ cup honey dijon salad dressing
  2 teaspoons lemon juice
1½ teaspoons honey
1½ teaspoons dijon mustard
  ½ teaspoon minced garlic
  ¼ teaspoon onion powder
  ¼ teaspoon salt
  ⅛ teaspoon black pepper

Breading

  1 cup Panko bread crumbs*
    (can substitute other bread crumbs)
1½ tablespoons grated parmesan cheese
  2 teaspoons grated red onion,
    squeezed dry
  ½ teaspoon dried parsley
  ½ teaspoon salt
  ⅛ teaspoon black pepper

  1 tablespoon butter
1½ teaspoons vegetable oil

This baked, crunchy chicken breast seems to appeal to guests of all ages, which is why it often is served as the main choice for our graduation dinner, called the "Yellow and White Dinner." For that meal, we will prepare about 450 servings of this dish.

Marinate Chicken Rinse and trim chicken; pat dry. In a small bowl, combine marinade ingredients. Place chicken in a non-aluminum container or shallow dish. Pour marinade over chicken, and turn to coat all sides. Cover and chill for at least 4 hours, preferably overnight.

For Breading In a shallow pan, combine all breading ingredients. Drain and discard marinade. Pat chicken into the bread crumb mixture to coat completely.

Heat the butter and oil in a skillet. When the pan is hot and butter is melted, cook the chicken for 2–3 minutes per side, or until golden brown. Preheat oven to 350°F. Place chicken in a roasting pan and bake until cooked through, about 18–25 minutes, depending on thickness of the chicken breasts.

* Panko bread crumbs are available in Asian markets, as well as many supermarkets. They are flaked crumbs and are preferred in this recipe for the crunchy texture.

REGATTA CHICKEN

2 Servings

  2 (4- to 5-ounce) boneless, skinless chicken breasts

Marinade

  ¼ cup plain, unsweetened yogurt
1 ½ teaspoons lemon juice
1 ½ teaspoons dijon mustard
  ½ teaspoon minced garlic
1 ½ teaspoons sugar
  ¼ teaspoon dried oregano
  ¼ teaspoon rubbed sage
  ½ teaspoon salt
  ⅛ teaspoon black pepper

Breading

  ½ cup bread crumbs
2 ½ teaspoons grated parmesan cheese
  1 teaspoon grated red onion, squeezed dry
  ½ teaspoon dried parsley
    dash salt
    dash black pepper

  1 tablespoon butter
1 ½ teaspoons vegetable oil

In some countries, yogurt is used in meat marinades for its tenderizing effect on the meat fibers. This flavorful, breaded chicken is baked not fried, and it remains very popular with students and guests.

Marinate Chicken Rinse and trim chicken; pat dry. Combine marinade ingredients in a small bowl. Place chicken in non-aluminum container or shallow dish. Pour marinade over chicken and turn to coat all sides. Cover and chill for at least 4 hours, or overnight.

For Breading Combine all breading ingredients in a shallow pan. Drain and discard marinade. Pat chicken into bread crumb mixture to coat completely.

Heat the butter and oil in a skillet. When pan is hot and butter is melted, cook the chicken for 2–3 minutes per side, or until golden brown. Preheat oven to 350°F. Place chicken in a shallow pan and bake until cooked through, about 18–25 minutes depending on thickness of the chicken breasts.

KUNG PAO CHICKEN

2 Servings

½ pound chicken tenders

Marinade

1 ½ teaspoons cornstarch
2 teaspoons soy sauce
1 ¼ teaspoons dry sherry
¼ teaspoon minced garlic
¼ teaspoon minced ginger

Sauce

4 teaspoons cornstarch
4 tablespoons soy sauce
2 tablespoons dry sherry
2 tablespoons rice wine vinegar*
2 tablespoons sugar
6 tablespoons chicken broth

Stir-Fry Blend

1 tablespoon vegetable oil
½ teaspoon minced ginger
½ teaspoon minced garlic
1 ¾ teaspoons minced fresh
   jalapeño pepper
⅓ cup green onion, cut on angle
   ½-inch long
¼ cup red bell pepper, cut into
   thin strips
¼ cup roasted, salted peanuts

   steamed rice

Marinate Chicken Rinse and trim chicken; pat dry. Combine marinade ingredients in a small bowl. Place chicken in a non-aluminum container or shallow dish. Pour marinade over chicken, and toss gently to coat all sides. Cover and chill for 1 hour.

For Sauce In a small bowl, whisk the cornstarch and soy sauce until smooth. Stir in remaining sauce ingredients; set aside.

Cook Chicken and Stir-Fry Blend Heat 2 teaspoons of the oil in a large skillet or wok. Drain and discard marinade. Pat chicken dry, then cook until browned and cooked through, about 6–8 minutes, depending on size of the tenders. Remove chicken from the pan; set aside. Add remaining oil, then add the ginger, garlic, jalapeño, onion and red pepper strips. Stir-fry for 2 minutes to soften, then add the chicken, including any accumulated juices. Stir sauce mixture to blend, then add to stir-fry. Boil until sauce is thickened, then turn heat to low; stir in the peanuts and simmer for 2 minutes to heat through. Serve with steamed rice.

* Available in the Asian foods section of most supermarkets.

PLANET HOLLYWOOD CHICKEN CRUNCH

2 Servings

½ pound chicken tenders

Breading

1½ cups Cap'n Crunch cereal
1 cup cornflakes cereal
¼ teaspoon onion powder
¼ teaspoon garlic powder
½ teaspoon salt
⅛ teaspoon black pepper

1 egg, beaten
2 tablespoons milk

¼ cup vegetable oil

I clipped this recipe from a newspaper years ago. The slightly sweet breading delights the young and young at heart. This version is not deep-fried, although you could do so for a crisper crust by adding more oil to a deep-sided skillet and frying until browned and crisp.

For Breading Process the cereals into crumbs with a food processor, or crush in a plastic bag with a rolling pin or heavy pan. Combine the crumbs and seasonings in a bowl, stirring well to distribute evenly; place in a shallow pan.

In a shallow bowl or dish, combine the beaten egg and milk. Rinse and trim chicken; pat dry. Dredge each piece in the egg mixture, then completely coat in the crumb mixture.

Add the oil to a skillet and heat over medium-high heat. Preheat oven to 350°F. When oil is hot, add the coated chicken and cook for 3 minutes per side, or until golden brown and crisp. Drain on paper towels, then transfer to a baking pan. Bake for 12–16 minutes, or until chicken is cooked through. Serve plain, or with honey mustard dressing for dipping.

SEAFOOD

Broiled Fish with Lemon Herb Sauce

Grilled Salmon with Asian Glaze

Cajun Fish and Shrimp

Seafood Enchiladas

Hawaiian Fish

Shrimp Stir-Fry

Crab Stuffed Mushrooms

BROILED FISH WITH LEMON HERB SAUCE

2 Servings

  2 (6- to 8-ounce) cod, orange roughy or
     tilapia fillets (or other mild fish fillets)
  1 tablespoon olive oil
  2 teaspoons fresh lemon juice
     dash paprika
     dash salt
     dash black pepper

Lemon Herb Sauce

  ¼ cup chicken broth
  ¼ cup clam broth
  ¼ teaspoon minced garlic
  ½ teaspoon minced fresh basil
  ¼ teaspoon minced fresh thyme
1½ teaspoons fresh lemon juice
  ¼ cup heavy whipping cream
  ¼ teaspoon salt
  1 teaspoon cornstarch
  1 tablespoon butter, cold

  2 lemon wedges (optional)

The chicken broth in the sauce
mellows the clam broth and
provides a nice background flavor
to this creamy, fresh herb sauce.

Combine the oil and lemon juice. Place fish in a lightly-oiled broiler pan. Drizzle the oil mixture over the fillets. Sprinkle with paprika, salt and pepper; set aside. Preheat broiler to 500°F.

For Sauce In a small saucepan, combine the chicken broth, clam broth, garlic, herbs, lemon juice, cream and salt. Bring to a boil, then turn heat to low; simmer, uncovered, for 10–12 minutes. Combine cornstarch with just enough water to make a pourable mixture; add to sauce, while stirring. Let boil until thickened. Remove from heat, then swirl in the butter until blended. Keep warm, covered.

Broil the fish fillets until cooked through. Plate each serving, then top generously with the sauce. Serve with lemon wedges, if desired.

GRILLED SALMON WITH ASIAN GLAZE

2 Servings

  2 (6- to 8-ounce) salmon fillets, skinless
1½ teaspoons vegetable oil
    dash salt
    dash black pepper

Glaze

  2 tablespoons + 1½ teaspoons
    Kikkoman teriyaki baste and glaze*
½ teaspoon dark sesame oil*
¼ teaspoon minced garlic
½ teaspoon minced ginger
1½ teaspoons dry sherry

  1 teaspoon sesame seeds
½ teaspoon minced green onion,
    green part only

I am suggesting skinless salmon fillets. If unavailable, then just grill the fish with the skin on. Once grilled, the skin is much easier to peel off.

For Glaze Combine all glaze ingredients in a small bowl; set aside.

Toast Sesame Seeds In a small skillet, heat the sesame seeds, stirring constantly over medium-high heat until golden brown. Remove from skillet to a small plate or bowl to cool.

Coat salmon with the oil. Sprinkle lightly with salt and pepper. Preheat oven to 350°F.

Cook the salmon on a charcoal or gas grill on both sides, but remove when still under-cooked. Place in roasting pan and brush with the glaze, saving some for later (baking with the glaze on top helps keep the fish moist, as well as heightens the flavor). Bake a few minutes until cooked to your preference. Remove from oven and brush with more glaze.

Portion onto serving plates. Sprinkle with sesame seeds and onion.

* Available in the Asian foods section of most supermarkets.

CAJUN FISH AND SHRIMP

2 Servings

Seasoning Mix:
- ¼ teaspoon cayenne pepper
- ⅛ teaspoon black pepper
- ¼ teaspoon salt
- ⅛ teaspoon dried thyme
- ⅛ teaspoon dried oregano
- ¼ teaspoon onion powder
- ⅛ teaspoon garlic powder

Sauce
- ¼ cup clam broth
- ¼ cup chicken broth
- ¼ cup heavy whipping cream
- 2 tablespoons dry white wine (optional)
- 1 ¼ teaspoons cornstarch

Shrimp
- 1 tablespoon butter
- ¾ teaspoon minced garlic
- 18–20 pieces raw medium shrimp, peeled, tails removed
- 1 ¼ teaspoons Worcestershire sauce

Fish Fillets
- 1 teaspoon olive oil
- 2 (5- to 6-ounce) cod, red snapper or tilapia fillets (or other mild fish fillets)
- ½ teaspoon minced fresh parsley (optional)

Serve with steamed rice to soak up the sauce. If you don't use the wine, just add 2 more tablespoons of chicken broth.

For Seasoning Mix Combine all seasonings in a small bowl. Divide roughly in half and keep separate. Half is for the shrimp and half for the fish fillets.

For Sauce Simmer the clam broth, chicken broth, cream and wine for 10 minutes. Combine cornstarch with just enough water to make a pourable mixture; add to simmering sauce, while stirring. Let boil until thickened, then remove from heat.

For Shrimp Melt the butter in a large skillet. Add the garlic and cook for 20 seconds or so, then immediately add the shrimp and half the seasoning mix. Cook for 2 minutes, or until shrimp are just cooked; stir in the Worcestershire sauce and cook for 20 seconds or so. Stir shrimp into the sauce mixture; keep warm.

For Fish Heat the oil in the same skillet. Sprinkle the remaining seasoning mix on both sides of the fish fillets. Cook on both sides until just cooked through. Place the fish on serving plates, and top generously with the shrimp sauce. Sprinkle parsley on top, if desired.

SEAFOOD ENCHILADAS

4 Servings

Filling

- 2 teaspoons vegetable oil
- ¼ cup finely chopped onion
- 2 tablespoons finely chopped celery
- ½ teaspoon minced garlic
- ¾ cup (6.5 ounces) raw shrimp, peeled, chopped
- ¾ teaspoon Cajun seasoning
- ¼ teaspoon salt
- 1½ teaspoons all-purpose flour
- 2 tablespoons chicken broth
- 2 tablespoons + 1 teaspoon sour cream
- ½ cup (3 ounces) crabmeat (or imitation crab)

- 4 (8-inch) flour tortillas

Sauce

- ¾ cup chicken broth
- 2 teaspoons cornstarch
  dash salt
- 5 tablespoons sour cream

- 1 cup shredded pepper jack cheese (can substitute monterey jack or other cheese)

This is reminiscent of a seafood dish that I once had when traveling along the Pacific coast of Mexico, near Mazatlan. Serve with guacamole, salsa and sour cream on the side.

For Filling Heat the oil in a large skillet. Add the onion and celery; cook for 3–4 minutes until softened. Add the garlic; cook for 1 minute, then stir in the shrimp, Cajun seasoning, salt and flour. Cook for 3–4 minutes, or until shrimp are cooked through, stirring often. Stir in the broth and sour cream, then stir in the crabmeat. Remove from heat (filling should be thick).

Warm the tortillas, covered, until softened and pliable, about 5 minutes. Divide the filling equally among the 4 tortillas. Fold up to enclose filling and place, seam-side down, in a lightly-oiled baking pan; set aside.

For Sauce Bring the chicken broth to a boil in a small saucepan. Combine the cornstarch with just enough water to make a pourable mixture; gradually add to broth, while stirring, and boil until thickened. Remove from heat. Add a dash of salt and stir in the sour cream until smooth.

Preheat oven to 350°F. Pour sauce over enchiladas to cover. Top with the shredded cheese. Bake, uncovered, for 20 minutes, or until hot in center and cheese is melted and bubbly.

HAWAIIAN FISH

2 Servings

  2 (4- to 5-ounce) cod, tilapia or
     orange roughy fillets (or other
     mild fish fillets)
½ cup all-purpose flour

Batter

  1 egg
¼ cup water
¼ teaspoon salt
¼ teaspoon baking powder
  5 tablespoons all-purpose flour

Almond Coating

  5 tablespoons all-purpose flour
  5 tablespoons flaked coconut
  5 tablespoons sliced almonds
¼ teaspoon salt

½ cup vegetable oil

While the Cottey version is deep-fried, this recipe uses a lot less oil to achieve similar results, with less clean up. However, you can add more oil to the skillet and deep-fry the fillets if you choose. The original recipe came from a local restaurant which is no longer in operation.

Place flour in a shallow container or pan.

For Batter Whisk all batter ingredients together until smooth (process in a blender if lumpy). Place in a shallow container or pan.

For Almond Coating Mix the flour, coconut, almonds and salt together to combine well. Place in a shallow container or pan.

Rinse the fish fillets and pat dry. Dredge the fillets in the flour on both sides. Dip in the batter to coat completely, then in the almond coating mixture. Lay out the fillets so that they are not touching each other, and will dry out a little before frying.

Heat the oil in a large skillet. When the oil is hot, cook the fillets over medium-high heat for about 3 minutes per side, or until golden and crisp and cooked in the center (if the fillets are very thick and need more cooking, then bake after frying in a 350°F oven until cooked through).

SHRIMP STIR-FRY

2 Servings

Sauce

1 ½ teaspoons soy sauce

  2 tablespoons + 1 teaspoon Kikkoman
    teriyaki baste and glaze*

  1 tablespoon + 1 teaspoon
    hoisin sauce*

  ½ cup chicken broth
    pinch crushed red pepper flakes

  1 teaspoon cornstarch

Stir-Fry

  8 broccoli florets

  8 fresh pea pods (snow peas), stemmed

  2 teaspoons vegetable oil

  1 teaspoon minced garlic

1 ¼ teaspoons minced ginger

  ¼ cup green onion, sliced on angle
    ½-inch long

20–24 pieces (about 6 ounces)
    raw medium shrimp, peeled

  ¼ cup mushrooms, cleaned, sliced thin
    (optional)

  ¼ cup red bell pepper, cut into thin strips

  ¾ cup fresh mung bean sprouts

Serve with steamed rice.

For Sauce In a small saucepan, combine the soy sauce, teriyaki glaze, hoisin sauce, chicken broth and crushed red pepper. Bring to a boil. Combine cornstarch with just enough water to make a pourable mixture; gradually add to sauce, while stirring. Boil until thickened, then remove from heat.

For Stir-Fry In a small saucepan, boil the broccoli for 2 minutes, then add the pea pods and boil for 15 seconds more. Drain, then place in ice water, drain again and wrap in a towel to remove excess moisture; set aside. Heat the oil in a wok or skillet. Add the garlic, ginger and onion. Cook for 30 seconds over medium-high heat, then add the shrimp. Stir-fry for 2 minutes, or until just cooked, then add the mushrooms, red bell pepper and bean sprouts. Stir-fry for 1 minute, then add the sauce, broccoli and pea pods; cook 1–2 minutes more, or until heated through.

* Available in the Asian section of most supermarkets.

CRAB STUFFED MUSHROOMS

2 Servings

   4 jumbo mushrooms,
      stemmed, wiped clean

Filling

   1 cup crabmeat, chopped, squeezed dry
   4 ounces cream cheese, softened
1 ¼ teaspoons grated parmesan cheese
  ¼ cup finely shredded mozzarella cheese
1 ½ teaspoons minced green onion,
      green part only
  ¼ teaspoon salt
  ¼ teaspoon hot red pepper sauce

Topping

   2 tablespoons finely shredded
      mozzarella cheese
2–3 round butter crackers, crushed
      into crumbs
   2 tablespoons butter, melted

We often have served these for our annual "Hanging of the Greens" Christmas dinner and typically prepare about 500. Use whichever variety of crab is available to you. We usually use a combination of real lump crabmeat and the imitation meat to make it affordable.

For Filling Combine all filling ingredients in a medium bowl. Generously fill the mushroom caps. Place mushrooms in a lightly oil-sprayed baking pan.

For Topping Sprinkle the cheese evenly over the filled mushrooms. Top with the cracker crumbs. Drizzle butter over the top and down the sides to moisten the mushrooms.

Preheat oven to 350°F. Bake, uncovered, for 18–20 minutes until mushrooms are tender and filling is hot in the center.

VEGETARIAN ENTREES

Cheese Enchiladas **V**

Broccoli Cheddar Almond Casserole **V**

Cheese Stuffed Mushrooms **V**

Italian Rice Stuffed Peppers **V**

Cheese Stuffed Phyllo Crisps **V**

Mushroom Cakes **V**

Meatless Taco Casserole **V**

Cheese Polenta with Vegetables and Tomato Sauce **V**

Zucchini Parmesan **V**

V Vegetarian

CHEESE ENCHILADAS

2 Servings

¼ cup salsa
2 (8-inch) flour tortillas
1 ¼ cups shredded cheddar-jack blend, divided

Sauce

½ cup half-and-half
¼ teaspoon ground cumin
¼ teaspoon chili powder
¼ teaspoon garlic powder
¼ teaspoon onion powder
½ teaspoon salt
½ teaspoon cornstarch

Pico de Gallo (optional)

½ cup diced tomato
1 tablespoon finely chopped onion
1 teaspoon minced jalapeño
1 ½ teaspoons minced cilantro
1 teaspoon lime juice
dash salt
dash black pepper

The pico de gallo recipe makes a wonderful topping for this dish, or serve instead with your favorite salsa and, perhaps, guacamole and sour cream.

Place salsa on the bottom of an 8-by-8-inch baking pan. Heat the tortillas, covered, until warm and pliable. Place ½ cup of the cheese blend on each tortilla. Roll up to enclose cheese, then lay, seam-side down, on top of the salsa.

For Sauce Heat the half-and-half in a small saucepan; stir in all the seasonings to blend. Bring to a boil. Combine cornstarch with just enough water to make a pourable mixture; gradually add to the sauce, while stirring. Boil until thickened, then remove from heat.

Pour sauce over the tortillas in the pan to cover completely. Top with the remaining cheese. Oil-spray a piece of foil and lay, oil-side down, over the pan. Bake in a preheated 350°F oven for 20 minutes, or until hot in center.

For Pico de Gallo Combine all ingredients in a small bowl. Plate the cheese enchiladas, then top each serving with the pico de gallo.

BROCCOLI CHEDDAR ALMOND CASSEROLE

4 Servings

3 ½ cups (8 ounces) broccoli,
    cut into florets

Sauce

  ¾ cup milk
  ¾ cup half-and-half
  ¾ teaspoon minced garlic
1 ½ teaspoons lemon juice
  ½ teaspoon onion powder
  ¼ teaspoon garlic powder
1 ½ teaspoons seasoning salt
    dash white pepper
2 ½ teaspoons cornstarch
  3 tablespoons grated parmesan cheese

  ¾ teaspoon vegetable oil
  2 tablespoons finely chopped onion
  1 tablespoon finely chopped
    red bell pepper

  ¾ cup shredded cheddar cheese
  2 tablespoons sliced almonds

Serve this with a salad for a vegetarian main course, or as a side dish for a meat-based meal.

Steam broccoli for 2–3 minutes, until crisp-tender; rinse with cold water, drain, then wrap in a towel to absorb excess water. Place broccoli in 1 layer in an 8-by-8-inch baking pan.

For Sauce In a small saucepan, stir in all sauce ingredients, except cornstarch and parmesan. Bring to a boil. Combine cornstarch with just enough water to make a pourable mixture; gradually add to sauce, while stirring. Boil until thickened; remove from heat, then stir in the parmesan. Pour sauce evenly over broccoli.

Heat the oil in a small skillet. Cook the onion and pepper, stirring often, for 2 minutes, or until softened. Sprinkle evenly over the sauce. Top with the cheese.

Meanwhile, preheat oven to 350°F. Place the almonds on a baking sheet; bake until golden and toasted, about 5 minutes. Sprinkle the almonds over the top of the casserole. Oil-spray a piece of foil and lay, oil-side down, over the pan; bake for 20 minutes. Uncover and bake for 5 minutes more. Let casserole rest for 8–10 minutes to thicken slightly before serving.

CHEESE STUFFED MUSHROOMS

2 Servings

4 jumbo mushrooms,
  stemmed, wiped clean

Filling

4 ounces cream cheese, softened

2 tablespoons + 1 teaspoon grated
  parmesan cheese

½ teaspoon garlic powder

¼ teaspoon onion powder

¼ cup + 1 tablespoon finely shredded
  mozzarella cheese

¼ teaspoon salt

⅛ teaspoon black pepper

1 teaspoon finely chopped or
  grated onion, squeezed dry

Topping

¼ cup shredded cheddar cheese

2 round butter crackers, crushed
  into crumbs

2 tablespoons butter, melted

This cheese filling has proven to be
a winner. It is the same filling used
in the **Cheese Stuffed Phyllo Crisps,**
which also are featured on page 150.

For Filling Combine all filling ingredients in a medium bowl. Fill the mushroom caps equally. Place mushrooms in a lightly-oiled baking pan.

For Topping Sprinkle the cheese evenly over the filled mushrooms. Top with the cracker crumbs. Drizzle butter over the top and down the sides to moisten the mushrooms.

Preheat oven to 350°F. Bake, uncovered, for 18–20 minutes until mushrooms are tender and filling is hot in the center.

ITALIAN RICE STUFFED PEPPERS

2–4 Servings

1 whole garlic bulb (head)

Vegetable Mixture

1 teaspoon olive oil
3 tablespoons diced onion
1 tablespoon finely chopped celery
1 tablespoon finely chopped carrot
½ teaspoon minced garlic

Seasoning

¼ teaspoon salt
⅛ teaspoon black pepper
¼ teaspoon onion powder
¼ teaspoon dried basil
¼ teaspoon dried oregano

Rice Mixture

⅓ cup long-grain white rice
1 cup water
¼ cup tomato sauce
2 tablespoons grated parmesan cheese

1 large green bell pepper, halved and seeded (for 2 servings) or quartered (for 4 smaller servings)
6 tablespoons shredded mozzarella cheese
4–6 tablespoons tomato sauce

To Roast Garlic Wrap the garlic bulb in aluminum foil. Bake in a preheated 350°F oven for 1 hour, or until cloves are soft when squeezed; set aside until cool enough to handle, but still warm. Turn garlic on its side and, with a sharp knife, slice ½-inch off the pointed end to expose the individual cloves. Push out the soft interior with the flat side of a large knife. Collect the roasted garlic pulp in a small bowl; set aside.

For Vegetables Heat the oil in small skillet and saute the onion, celery, carrot and garlic for 2–3 minutes, or until softened.

For Rice Place vegetables in a medium bowl; stir in the garlic pulp and all the seasonings. Stir in the rice, mixing well to combine flavors. Put the rice mixture in a saucepan and add the water. Cover with a tight-fitting lid and bring to a boil; turn heat to low and simmer for 18–20 minutes, until rice is cooked. Pour mixture back into the bowl; stir in the tomato sauce and parmesan.

Assemble and Bake Peppers Divide the rice mixture evenly between each pepper half (or quarter). Cover and bake in a 350°F oven for 30 minutes. Top with the cheese and bake, uncovered, for 10 minutes more, or until peppers are tender and cheese is melted and bubbly. Heat the tomato sauce and ladle 2–3 tablespoons over each serving. Serve with more parmesan cheese at the table, if desired.

CHEESE STUFFED PHYLLO CRISPS

24 Crisps (4–6 Servings)

12 sheets phyllo dough
 1 tablespoon vegetable oil
 2 tablespoons butter, melted

Filling
 4 ounces cream cheese, softened
 2 tablespoons + 1 teaspoon grated
    parmesan cheese
½ teaspoon garlic powder
¼ teaspoon onion powder
¼ cup + 1 tablespoon finely shredded
    mozzarella cheese
¼ teaspoon salt
⅛ teaspoon black pepper
 1 teaspoon finely chopped or
    grated onion, squeezed dry

This is the same filling that is used in the Cheese Stuffed Mushrooms on page 148. You can double or triple this recipe and freeze the uncooked crisps for future meals.

For Filling Combine all filling ingredients in a bowl; set aside.

To Assemble Lay out phyllo sheets on one side of a work table; cover with a slightly damp towel to keep dough from drying out. Carefully take 1 sheet and place in front of you with 1 of the shorter ends facing you. Combine the melted butter and oil in a small bowl. Brush or dab a thin layer of the butter mixture over the dough. Top with another sheet and lightly, but completely, butter it. With a sharp knife, cut the sheet from top to bottom into 4 equal strips. Place slightly less than 1 tablespoon of filling in the lower corner of each strip, about 1 inch from the bottom. Fold a corner diagonally across the filling, forming a triangle. Continue folding, corner to corner (like folding a flag). Do not fold too tightly as the filling expands when baking. Dab or brush each top and seam with butter mixture to seal the edges. Continue making triangles with remaining filling and dough.

Place crisps on a lightly buttered baking sheet, at least 1 inch apart. Bake in a preheated 375°F oven for 12–16 minutes, or until golden brown and crisp. Serve warm.

MUSHROOM CAKES

4 Patties

- 1 tablespoon olive oil
- ¾ teaspoon minced garlic
- ¼ cup finely chopped onion
- 2 tablespoons finely chopped celery
- 2 tablespoons finely chopped green bell pepper
- 1 tablespoon finely chopped carrot
- 2 cups mushrooms, wiped clean, thinly sliced
- ½ teaspoon fresh minced thyme (or ¼ teaspoon dried)
- 1 teaspoon minced fresh chives (or ½ teaspoon dried)
- ¼ teaspoon + pinch salt
- ⅛ teaspoon black pepper
- 1 teaspoon lemon juice
- 1 tablespoon sour cream
- 2 tablespoons beaten egg
- ¼ cup bread crumbs
- ¼ cup finely shredded mozzarella cheese

- 2 teaspoons olive oil
  sour cream, as needed
  minced chives, as needed

Serve these as part of a vegetarian main course, or as a side vegetable to a meat-based meal. You also could melt a slice of cheese over the cakes and serve on toasted hamburger buns for a meatless cheeseburger.

Heat the 1 tablespoon of oil in a large skillet. Add the garlic, onion, celery, green pepper and carrot and saute over medium-high heat for 4 minutes, or until softened. Add the mushrooms and saute for 4 minutes more, or until tender. Add the herbs, salt, pepper and lemon juice and continue cooking for 1–2 minutes, or until all liquid is evaporated. Cool to room temperature.

When cooled, fold in the sour cream, egg, bread crumbs and cheese. Mix well to combine, then form into patties using a ¼-cup measure; place on a plate or shallow dish. Refrigerate for 30–40 minutes to chill and firm the cakes.

Heat the 2 teaspoons of oil in a nonstick, or well-seasoned, skillet until hot. Cook the cakes for 3 minutes per side, or until golden brown and crisp. Serve plain, or with a dollop of sour cream and a pinch of chives on top.

MEATLESS TACO CASSEROLE

4–6 Servings

Meatless Chili

- 2 teaspoons vegetable oil
- ½ cup diced onion
- 1 teaspoon minced garlic
- ½ teaspoon salt
- 1 teaspoon chili powder
- ½ teaspoon ground cumin
- 1 teaspoon onion powder
- 1½ cups meatless burger crumbles*
- ¼ cup water
- ½ cup + 2 tablespoons tomato sauce
- ½ cup + 1 tablespoon salsa
- ½ cup vegetarian refried beans (no lard)
- 2½ teaspoons white vinegar

- 3 cups corn chips, divided
- 1 cup shredded cheddar cheese
- 1 cup shredded iceberg lettuce, rinsed, patted dry
- ½ cup diced fresh tomato

Even meat lovers hardly will miss the meat in this one. Serve with sour cream and your favorite salsa on the side.

For Chili Heat the oil in a medium saucepan. Add the onion and garlic; cook for 3–4 minutes, stirring often, until softened. Stir in the seasonings and cook for 1 minute more. Stir in burger crumbles, then add remaining chili ingredients. Simmer for 10 minutes; remove from heat.

Assemble and Bake Spread 2 cups of corn chips in an even layer in an 8-by-8-inch pan. Spoon the chili evenly over the chips to cover completely. Sprinkle with the cheese. Bake, covered, in a preheated 350°F oven for 15 minutes.

To serve, portion out the chili casserole onto plates, then top each serving with lettuce, tomato and more chips.

* Heat and serve TVP (textured vegetable protein) crumbles are available in the freezer section of most supermarkets. They are a soy-based meat substitute. If only dried TVP crumbles are available, rehydrate in water according to package directions.

CHEESE POLENTA WITH VEGETABLES AND TOMATO SAUCE

4 Servings

Polenta

2 cups water
¼ teaspoon + pinch salt
½ cup yellow cornmeal
½ cup shredded mozzarella cheese
1 tablespoon grated parmesan cheese
  dash black pepper

Vegetables

1 ½ teaspoons olive oil
½ teaspoon minced garlic
¼ cup small-diced green bell pepper
¼ cup small-diced red bell pepper
¼ cup small-diced onion
¼ teaspoon salt
  dash black pepper
2 teaspoons minced fresh basil

4 teaspoons olive oil
½ cup shredded mozzarella cheese
½ cup spaghetti sauce
2 teaspoons grated parmesan cheese

For Polenta Bring the water to a boil in a saucepan; add salt. Gradually add the cornmeal, while whisking. Continue whisking until mixture returns to a boil. Reduce heat to low and cook until very thick, stirring constantly, 1–2 minutes more. Remove from heat and stir in the cheeses and pepper. Pour mixture into a lightly-oiled 8-by-8-inch pan. Tap and tilt the pan to level out the cornmeal. Cover and chill 1 hour, or more, until firm.

For Vegetables Heat 1½ teaspoons of oil in a skillet. Add the garlic and cook for 30 seconds. Add the green and red peppers and onion, and saute for 4 minutes. Add the salt, pepper and basil and cook 1 minute more. Remove from heat.

Fry Polenta Cut polenta into fourths (they should be 3½-inch squares). Carefully remove from pan. Pat dry on top and bottom. Heat the oil in a large, nonstick skillet over medium-high heat (see below*). When hot, add polenta squares and cook about 6 minutes per side, or until a golden brown crust has formed. Drain and cut the squares diagonally in half to make triangles (or you can leave as squares).

Assemble Place browned polenta triangles in a lightly-oiled casserole dish. Sprinkle a portion of the vegetables decoratively on the top of each polenta, then top with the mozzarella. Bake, uncovered, until cheese is melted. Heat the spaghetti sauce and spoon over each serving, then sprinkle with the parmesan.

* Polenta may stick to the pan if your skillet is marred with scratches. This recipe was tested successfully with a newer skillet, or as an alternate method, you can broil on both sides in an oiled pan until golden brown.

ZUCCHINI PARMESAN

4 Servings

- 1 large fresh zucchini
- ¼ cup all-purpose flour
- 2 eggs, beaten

Breading

- ¾ cup plain bread crumbs
- 2 tablespoons + 1 teaspoon grated parmesan cheese
- 2 teaspoons minced red onion
- ¼ teaspoon dried basil
- ¼ teaspoon dried oregano
- ¼ teaspoon salt
- ⅛ teaspoon black pepper

- 6 tablespoons olive oil
- ¾ cup shredded mozzarella cheese
- 1½ cups spaghetti sauce
- 2 tablespoons grated parmesan cheese

A popular alternative to Eggplant Parmesan.

Scrub the zucchini clean. Slice ¼-inch thick at a 45-degree angle to create broad, oval-shaped slices.

Combine all breading ingredients in a small bowl, then transfer to a shallow pan. Put the flour and beaten eggs in separate shallow pans and place side-by-side with the breading. Dip both sides of the zucchini slices into the flour, then into the egg, and then into the breading, coating completely.

Heat half the oil in a large skillet. Fry the breaded zucchini slices in batches until browned on both sides, adding more oil as needed. Place them in one layer into a large baking pan; top each slice with the mozzarella. Cover with foil and bake in a preheated 350°F oven for 15–20 minutes, until zucchini are just tender. Heat the spaghetti sauce. Top each serving with some sauce and sprinkle with the parmesan. Serve hot.

VEGAN ENTREES

Curried Vegetables **V**

Baked Teriyaki Tofu **V**

Falafels with Tahina Sauce **V**

Grilled Vegetable Kebobs **V**

Kung Pao Tofu **V**

Potato Samosas **V**

Spiced Vegetable Patties **V**

Stuffed Zucchini **V**

Vegetable Fried Rice **V**

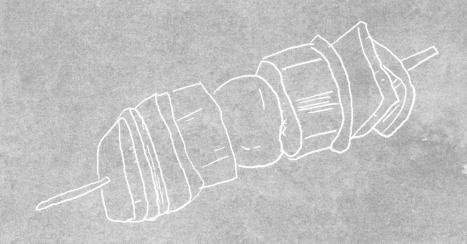

V Vegan

CURRIED VEGETABLES

2–3 Servings

Sauce

¾ cup water
    vegetable broth paste or bouillon*
    to taste
1 ½ teaspoons cornstarch
2 tablespoons raisins

Steamed Vegetables

¼ cup carrot, peeled, sliced thin
    diagonally
8 pieces cauliflower, cut into
    bite-size florets
12 pieces potato, peeled,
    cut into bite-size chunks

Seasoning Blend

½ teaspoon curry powder
¼ teaspoon ground coriander
¼ teaspoon turmeric
    dash ground cumin
¼ teaspoon salt
    dash cayenne pepper

Skillet Vegetables

1 ½ teaspoons vegetable oil
¼ cup onion, peeled, quartered
    lengthwise, sliced thin
¼ cup large-diced green bell pepper
½ cup mushrooms, wiped clean,
    sliced thick
1 teaspoon minced garlic
¼ cup frozen green peas, thawed

For Sauce Heat the water in a small saucepan. Stir in the vegetable paste or bouillon, a little at a time, until a pleasantly seasoned flavor is reached—not too bland, not too salty (or refer to package directions); bring to a boil. Combine cornstarch with just enough water to make a pourable mixture; gradually add to boiling liquid, while stirring. Boil until thickened. Stir in the raisins. Cover, and remove from heat; set aside.

For Steamed Vegetables Place the carrot, cauliflower and potato in a steamer basket over boiling water in a saucepot. Cover and steam until just tender, about 10 minutes. Uncover and rinse briefly under cold water; set aside.

For Seasoning Blend Meanwhile, combine all spices in a small bowl; set aside.

For Skillet Vegetables Heat the oil in a large skillet. Add the onion, pepper and mushrooms; cook for 2 minutes, then stir in garlic and cook for 1 minute more. Stir in seasoning blend and cook for 2 minutes, then stir in the peas, sauce and steamed vegetables; stir well to blend all flavors. Serve hot.

* Available in most supermarkets or specialty food stores.

Just follow the 4 easy steps above
for a great meatless main course or
side dish. Serve with steamed rice.

BAKED TERIYAKI TOFU

4 Servings

1 (14-ounce) package firm tofu
 (or extra-firm)

Marinade

2 tablespoons teriyaki sauce

1½ teaspoons water

1 tablespoon rice wine vinegar*
 (or white wine vinegar)

1 tablespoon sugar (or substitute 2½
 teaspoons honey or agave nectar)

¼ teaspoon minced garlic

¼ teaspoon minced ginger
 pinch crushed red pepper flakes

This recipe transforms the flavor
and texture of an otherwise bland
food into an appealing treat, especially for vegetarians trying to add
variety and more protein to their
diets. Add to stir-fry recipes or
soups, or use as a salad topper. This
tofu is the most flavorful if allowed
to marinate 6–8 hours per side.

Press Tofu Drain the tofu block and gently squeeze out excess
water, being careful not to tear or crack the block. On a cutting
board, stand the tofu on its side and cut the thickness of the
block in half lengthwise. Lay out several layers of paper towels on
a baking sheet. Place tofu pieces on top and cover with several
more layers of towels. Place another baking sheet or pan over the
covered tofu. Place a heavy weight in the middle of the sheet or
pan to press evenly (make sure the heavy weight is level and not
tilted to one side). Press for 20 minutes.

Meanwhile, combine all marinade ingredients in a small bowl;
set aside. Cut each piece of tofu in half crosswise to make 4 equal
pieces. Place in a non-aluminum pan or shallow container. Pour
marinade over tofu, turning to coat all sides. Cover and chill for
6 hours. Turn tofu over to marinate the other side. Cover and
chill for 6 hours, preferably overnight.

Drain and discard excess marinade, and pat dry the tofu pieces.
Place in a lightly-oiled baking pan. Preheat oven to 350°F and
bake for 20–25 minutes per side, or until golden brown; let cool.
Cut into cubes and add to a variety of hot or cold meals.

* Available in the Asian section of most supermarkets.

FALAFELS WITH TAHINA SAUCE

4–6 Patties

Falafels

1 ¾ teaspoons minced garlic
¼ cup chopped onion
1 (15-ounce) can garbanzo beans, drained
1 ½ teaspoons minced fresh parsley
1 ½ teaspoons lemon juice
1 slice white or wheat bread, soaked in cold water, squeezed dry
¼ teaspoon ground cumin
¼ teaspoon dried basil
¼ teaspoon ground coriander
¼ teaspoon dried thyme
¾ teaspoon salt
dash cayenne pepper
2 tablespoons + 1 ½ teaspoons plain bread crumbs

¼ cup all-purpose flour
2 tablespoons olive oil

Tahina Sauce

6 tablespoons water
6 tablespoons tahini,* stirred well
½ teaspoon minced garlic
2 teaspoons lemon juice
½ teaspoon salt
2 teaspoons minced fresh parsley

For Falafels Place all falafel ingredients in a food processor. Process to blend, scraping down the sides so that all of the mix gets processed smooth. Form into patties, adding more bread crumbs to the mix, as needed, if the mixture is too moist to make patties.

For Sauce Add the water to a blender, then add remaining sauce ingredients, except parsley. Blend until smooth, then transfer to a bowl. Stir in the parsley; set aside.

Cook Falafels Place the flour in a shallow pan or container. Dip each patty into the flour to coat all sides. Heat the oil in a large skillet. Cook the patties until golden brown and crisp, about 3 minutes per side. Serve with the sauce (sauce is served at room temperature) either on top or on the side.

* Tahini is a thick paste made of ground sesame seeds. It is available in most supermarkets and natural food stores.

Serve 2 smaller patties per person with sauce on top, or make a larger patty and serve on a bun as a veggie burger. At Cottey, we form the falafels into balls the size of golf balls and deep-fry until browned and crisp. We then serve them in pita pockets with the Tahina sauce drizzled over the top.

GRILLED VEGETABLE KEBOBS

4 Kebobs

4 (8-inch) bamboo skewers

Marinade

¼ cup vegetable oil

¼ cup olive oil

½ teaspoon lemon zest

4 teaspoons fresh lemon juice

1 ½ teaspoons minced garlic

¼ teaspoon dried thyme

¼ teaspoon dried basil

¼ teaspoon garlic powder

¼ teaspoon onion powder

¾ teaspoon salt-free seasoning blend

½ teaspoon salt

¼ teaspoon black pepper

8 pieces green bell pepper
cut into 1 ½-inch squares

8 pieces red bell pepper
cut into 1 ½-inch squares

8 pieces yellow onion, cut into
1 ½-inch squares

8 pieces zucchini, cut into 1-inch pieces
(halve or quarter if large)

4 mushrooms, whole, wiped clean

4 cherry tomatoes

**Serve with your favorite tomato
sauce and noodles, or with steamed
rice. I like to sprinkle minced fresh
basil on the kebobs just before
serving.**

Soak the wooden skewers in hot water for 1 hour (this will help prevent burning on the grill).

For Marinade Whisk together all marinade ingredients in a bowl.

To Assemble Kebobs For each kebob, thread the vegetables in the following order: green pepper, red pepper, onion, zucchini, mushroom, zucchini, onion, red pepper, green pepper (the tomatoes will be threaded on halfway through the grilling process, so leave room at the top of the skewers for them).

Place kebobs in a shallow dish, and brush or spoon marinade over them to coat all sides. Cover and chill for 2 hours, or overnight. Save the excess marinade to use for basting later when grilling.

Cook the kebobs on a charcoal or gas grill for 7–8 minutes, turning and basting with the marinade every few minutes. Remove the kebobs and thread the tomatoes at the end of each. Put back on the grill, and continue turning and basting with the marinade for 7–8 minutes more, or until vegetables are tender and just cooked through. Baste again just before serving.

KUNG PAO TOFU

2–3 Servings

1 ¼ cups firm tofu, cut into ¾-inch cubes
1 tablespoon vegetable oil

Sauce

4 tablespoons soy sauce
2 tablespoons rice wine vinegar*
2 tablespoons dry sherry
¼ cup water
2 tablespoons sugar
2 tablespoons dark sesame oil*
½ teaspoon crushed red pepper flakes

1 tablespoon cornstarch
2 tablespoons water

Vegetable Blend

1 ½ tablespoons vegetable oil
¼ cup diced onion
¼ cup diced celery
¼ cup diced carrot
½ cup diced zucchini
2 teaspoons minced garlic
¼ cup sliced green onion
¼ cup diced water chestnuts

2 tablespoons + 2 teaspoons chopped
roasted peanuts

Serve with steamed rice.

Bake Tofu Pat dry the tofu cubes with paper towels to remove as much moisture as possible, then toss in the vegetable oil to coat all sides. Place tofu in an oil-sprayed baking pan. Bake in a preheated 375°F oven for 20 minutes. Gently turn over the cubes, then bake for 12–15 minutes more, or until golden brown in color. Drain on paper towels.

For Sauce In a small bowl, combine all sauce ingredients. In a separate bowl, stir the cornstarch and 2 tablespoons of water together until smooth. Stir this mixture into the sauce mixture; set aside.

Cook Vegetables Heat the oil in a large skillet. Add the onion, celery and carrot and cook for 6 minutes, stirring often. Add the zucchini, garlic, green onion and water chestnuts and cook for 3–4 minutes more, or until softened. Add the baked tofu cubes to the skillet. Stir the sauce mixture and add it to the skillet. Cook until the sauce is boiling and thickened; remove from heat. Sprinkle chopped peanuts over each serving.

* Available in the Asian section of most supermarkets.

POTATO SAMOSAS

24–28 Pieces (4–6 Servings)

Potato Filling

1 ¼ cups peeled, diced potato
1 ½ teaspoons vegetable oil
⅓ cup diced onion
½ teaspoon minced garlic
½ teaspoon minced ginger
¾ teaspoon minced fresh jalapeño
2 teaspoons minced cilantro
½ teaspoon salt
¼ teaspoon ground coriander
¼ teaspoon curry powder
¼ teaspoon ground cumin
¼ cup frozen green peas, thawed
1 ½ teaspoons lemon juice
1 tablespoon water

12–14 sheets phyllo dough
4 tablespoons vegetable oil, approximately

Samosas are popular snacks in India. The filling in this recipe is classic Indian, although the use of phyllo dough for the crust is not. I use it in this recipe because it crisps well when baked and is readily available. The Cottey version uses egg roll skins and they are deep-fried. This baked version is lighter, yet still crisp. The samosas can be frozen, unbaked, for future meals—just thaw before baking. Serve with mango or mint chutney* for dipping.

For Filling Boil the diced potato for 8–10 minutes, or until tender. Meanwhile, heat the oil in a skillet; add the onion and cook for 3–4 minutes until golden brown. Add the garlic, ginger and jalapeño; cook for 1 minute, stirring often. Add the cilantro and all spices; cook for 1 minute, then stir in the peas, lemon juice, water and potatoes. Stir well, then remove from heat; let cool.

Assemble Samosas Lay out phyllo sheets on one side of a work table; cover with a slightly damp towel to keep dough from drying out. Carefully take 1 sheet and place in front of you with 1 of the shorter ends facing you. Brush or dab a thin layer of the oil over the dough. Top with another sheet and lightly, but completely, oil it. With a sharp knife, cut the sheet from top to bottom into 4 equal strips. Place slightly less than 1 tablespoon of filling in the lower corner of each strip, about 1 inch from the bottom. Fold a corner diagonally across the filling, forming a triangle. Continue folding, corner to corner (like folding a flag). Do not fold too tightly as the filling expands when baking. Dab or brush each top and seam with oil to seal the edges. Continue making triangles with remaining filling and dough.

Place samosas on a lightly-oiled baking sheet, at least 1 inch apart. Bake in a preheated 375°F oven for 12–16 minutes, or until golden brown and crisp. Serve warm.

* Available in most supermarkets or Asian markets.

SPICED VEGETABLE PATTIES

6 Patties

½ cup corn kernels (frozen or canned)
½ cup chopped carrot
¼ cup frozen green peas, thawed
¼ cup chopped onion

Patty Mixture

1 cup shredded hash browns, thawed, squeezed dry
¼ cup shredded spinach leaves
¼ cup diced tomato
2 tablespoons minced cilantro
1 teaspoon minced garlic
½ teaspoon minced ginger
¼ teaspoon + pinch cayenne pepper
¼ teaspoon ground cumin
½ teaspoon salt
¼ teaspoon onion powder
¼ teaspoon garlic powder
¼ teaspoon sugar
3 tablespoons all-purpose flour
¼ cup plain bread crumbs

4 teaspoons vegetable oil

These are colorful, low-fat and have lots of flavor. Serve with steamed rice.

Place the corn, carrot, peas and onion in a food processor. Process using on/off turns to finely chop, but not puree. Transfer to a large bowl and stir in patty ingredients.

Form into patties using ¼ cupful of mixture per patty. Chill patties for 30 minutes, or until firm.

Preheat oven to 350°F. Heat the oil in a large skillet. Cook patties for 3–4 minutes per side until golden brown, then transfer to a lightly-oiled baking pan. Bake for 8–10 minutes until heated through.

STUFFED ZUCCHINI

4 Servings

½ cup corn kernels (frozen or canned)
¼ cup chopped carrot
¼ cup frozen green peas, thawed
¼ cup chopped onion

Stuffing

1 cup shredded hash browns, thawed, squeezed dry
¼ cup spinach leaves, shredded
¼ cup diced tomato
1 tablespoon + ½ teaspoon minced cilantro
1 teaspoon minced garlic
1 teaspoon minced fresh basil
½ teaspoon salt
¼ teaspoon onion powder
¼ teaspoon garlic powder
2 tablespoons + 2 teaspoons plain bread crumbs

2 medium zucchini
4 teaspoons olive oil

This is a favorite among many of our vegetarian students.

Place the corn, carrot, peas and onion in a food processor. Process using on/off turns to finely chop, but not puree. Transfer to a large bowl and stir in stuffing ingredients.

Scrub, stem and halve the zucchini lengthwise. Carefully hollow out the center leaving a ¼-inch border around the edges (use a knife to cut the edges then scoop out with a spoon). Place the hollowed-out halves in an oil-sprayed baking pan.

Preheat oven to 350°F. Divide stuffing mixture evenly into each zucchini half, mounding slightly in the center. Drizzle with olive oil, then cover with foil. Bake for 35–40 minutes, or until zucchini is tender when pierced, yet still holds its shape. Uncover and bake for 5 minutes more. Serve plain, or with your favorite spaghetti sauce.

VEGETABLE FRIED RICE

4 Servings

1 cup long-grain white rice

2 tablespoons + 1 teaspoon
  vegetable oil
1 ¼ teaspoons minced garlic
1 ¼ teaspoons minced ginger
  ¼ cup green onions, ¼-inch slices
  ½ cup fresh mung bean sprouts
  ½ cup shredded cabbage
  ¼ cup shredded carrot
  ¼ cup frozen green peas, thawed
  1 tablespoon + 2 teaspoons soy sauce
1 ½ teaspoons dark sesame oil*

Rinse the rice in cool water. Drain and rinse again several times to remove starch (until water runs clear). Cook rice according to package directions. Transfer cooked rice to a large bowl or pan. Leave uncovered to let it cool slightly and dry out if still moist.

Heat the vegetable oil in a large wok or skillet. Add the garlic and ginger, and cook for 30 seconds over medium-high heat. Add the onion, bean sprouts, cabbage and carrot and stir-fry for 3 minutes. Stir in the peas, soy sauce and sesame oil. Cook for 30 seconds or so, then stir in the cooked rice, half at a time, to coat evenly with the sauce and oil. Turn to medium heat and stir-fry for 2–3 minutes more to give a pleasant chewiness to the rice. Serve hot.

* Available in the Asian section of most supermarkets.

VEGETABLES

Sesame Broccoli with Ginger Butter V

Ratatouille

Grilled Zucchini and Onion with Muhammara Sauce V

Corn Souffle V

Aztec Corn V

Onion Souffle V

Stir-Fried Vegetables V

V Vegetarian
V Vegan

SESAME BROCCOLI WITH GINGER BUTTER

4 Servings

16 pieces fresh broccoli, cut into
    2-inch florets
1 ½ teaspoons sesame seeds

Ginger Butter

3 tablespoons butter, softened
1 tablespoon minced green onion
¼ teaspoon minced garlic
1 teaspoon minced ginger
½ teaspoon dark sesame oil*
1 teaspoon soy sauce
½ teaspoon rice wine vinegar*
   (or white vinegar)

**Serve as a side dish with any Asian
main course.**

Steam the broccoli for 2 minutes, or until crisp-tender. Chill in ice water, then drain and roll in a towel to absorb all excess moisture; set aside.

Toast Sesame Seeds Place the seeds in a dry skillet and cook over medium-high heat, stirring constantly, until seeds are golden brown. Remove to a small plate or bowl to cool.

For Ginger Butter Whisk together all butter ingredients until mixture is smooth and blended.

Heat a saucepan or skillet large enough to hold the broccoli. Add the ginger butter to the pan. When melted, cook for 30 seconds then stir in the broccoli, tossing to coat well with the butter mixture. Sprinkle with the sesame seeds and toss to coat all sides. Serve hot.

* Available in the Asian foods section of most supermarkets.

RATATOUILLE

4 Servings

- 2 teaspoons olive oil
- 2 teaspoons butter
- 1 teaspoon minced garlic
- ¼ cup onion, quartered lengthwise, sliced ¼-inch thick
- ¾ cup sliced mushrooms
- 1 cup eggplant, quartered lengthwise, sliced ¼-inch thick
- 1 ¼ cups zucchini, halved lengthwise, sliced ¼-inch thick
- 3 tablespoons water
- 6 cherry or grape tomatoes, halved lengthwise
- 1 teaspoon minced fresh basil (or ¼ teaspoon dried)
- ½ teaspoon minced fresh thyme (or ¼ teaspoon dried)
- ¼ teaspoon salt
- ⅛ teaspoon black pepper
- ¼ cup spaghetti sauce

- ½ teaspoon minced fresh parsley (optional)

This is my version of a popular vegetable dish originating from the French region of Provence. Many young people can now pronounce this dish perfectly, thanks to the animated Disney movie of the same name.

Heat the oil and butter in a large skillet. Add the garlic and onion; cook for 2 minutes. Add the mushrooms and eggplant; cook for 2 minutes, then stir in the zucchini and cook for 3–4 minutes more, until vegetables are softened.

Stir in the water, tomatoes, seasonings and herbs. Cook, stirring often, for 1 minute or so. Stir in the spaghetti sauce, and cook for 1–2 minutes more to cook off all liquid and heat through the tomatoes. Serve hot, or at room temperature. Sprinkle parsley on top, if desired, or more fresh basil instead.

GRILLED ZUCCHINI AND ONION WITH MUHAMMARA SAUCE

4 Servings

Muhammara Sauce

- 2 tablespoons chopped walnuts
- 1 (2-ounce) jar pimientos, drained well
- 1 teaspoon minced garlic
- 1/2 teaspoon salt
- 3/4 teaspoon lemon juice
- 1/2 teaspoon ground cumin
  pinch cayenne pepper
- 2 tablespoons water
- 3 tablespoons olive oil

- 2 medium zucchini, scrubbed clean, stemmed
- 1/2 red onion, sliced and separated into 1/2-inch rings
- 2 tablespoons olive oil
  dash salt
  dash black pepper

- 1 teaspoon minced fresh parsley (optional)

Muhammara is a flavorful condiment originating in Turkey. You also could make the sauce separately and use as a dip for chicken wings, or with warm pita bread.

For Sauce Preheat oven to 450°F. Toast the walnuts on a baking sheet for 3–4 minutes, or until golden; let cool. In a blender, or mini-processor, add the nuts and remaining sauce ingredients, except the oil. Blend a few seconds; while still blending, drizzle in the oil until the mixture is smooth; set aside.

Cut zucchini lengthwise into 1/4-inch thick slices. Place zucchini slices and onion rings in a large container or tub and drizzle with the oil, salt and pepper. Toss gently to coat the vegetables, adding more oil as needed.

Cook the zucchini on a charcoal or gas grill for 3–4 minutes per side, or until lightly charred and softened. Grill the onion rings on both sides until lightly charred and softened. Let zucchini cool slightly, then cut the slices on an angle into large pieces. Place zucchini on a serving platter. Drizzle the sauce generously over the zucchini. Place the onion rings in the center of the platter over the sauce, then sprinkle with the parsley. Or, just place the warm zucchini, onions and sauce side by side and let guests serve themselves as desired. Serve hot, or at room temperature.

CORN SOUFFLE

8 Servings

1 1/2 cups frozen corn kernels, thawed
1 3/4 teaspoons baking powder
2 cups (8 ounces) shredded cheddar-jack cheese blend
2 tablespoons sugar
1 1/4 teaspoons salt
6 eggs
2 cups heavy whipping cream

This is rich, but very tasty. We serve this on occasion for banquets and special buffets.

Preheat oven to 350°F. Lightly oil an 8-by-8-inch pan.

In a food processor, process the corn using on/off turns for 20 seconds or so to finely chop. Transfer to a bowl and add the baking powder, cheese, sugar and salt; stir well. In another bowl, whisk the eggs until blended, then whisk in the cream. Add the cream mixture to the corn mixture, stirring well to combine.

Pour batter into the prepared pan. Bake, uncovered, for 45–55 minutes, or until a tester inserted in center comes out clean. Let souffle rest for 10–15 minutes before serving.

AZTEC CORN

4 Servings

  2 teaspoons butter
  2 tablespoons chopped green onion
½ teaspoon minced garlic
  1 tablespoon chopped green chiles
  1 teaspoon minced jalapeño
¼ cup diced fresh tomato
  1 cup frozen corn kernels, thawed
1¼ teaspoons minced cilantro (optional)
¼ teaspoon + pinch salt
⅛ teaspoon black pepper
½ teaspoon sugar
½ cup heavy whipping cream

If you want a good vegetable dish to go with your Mexican dinner, try this as an accompaniment. This dish is medium-spiced. Adjust the jalapeños or green chiles according to your own taste preference.

Heat the butter in a skillet. Add the onion and garlic; saute for 1 minute. Add the green chiles, jalapeño and tomato; saute for 2 minutes more. Stir in remaining ingredients; bring to a boil and boil for 2–3 minutes until cream thickens. Serve hot.

ONION SOUFFLE

8–12 Servings

- 1 cup finely chopped onion, patted dry with a towel
- 1 (8-ounce) package cream cheese, softened
- ¾ cup grated parmesan cheese
- ⅓ cup real mayonnaise

Apricot Onion Jam (makes 1 cup)

- 1 ½ cups onion, quartered lengthwise, thinly sliced
- 1 ½ tablespoons butter
- 2 tablespoons + 2 teaspoons sugar
- ¼ teaspoon salt
- ⅛ teaspoon black pepper
- pinch crushed red pepper flakes
- ¼ cup dry white wine (or water)
- 1 ¾ teaspoons red wine vinegar
- ½ cup packed dried apricots, thinly sliced

This is rich, so small servings are recommended. This dish is a favorite of President Judy Rogers and her husband, Glenn. The Apricot Onion Jam is optional, yet it provides a nice balance to the richness of the creamy souffle. The jam can be made 1–2 days ahead and brought to room temperature before serving. It is also very good with grilled or roast pork.

Preheat oven to 425°F. In a bowl, mix the onion, cream cheese, parmesan and mayonnaise, stirring well to blend. Spread mixture evenly into a lightly-oiled 8-by-8-inch pan. Bake for 15 minutes, or until golden brown on top. Cut into squares and top each serving with a teaspoon or so of jam, if desired.

For Apricot Onion Jam In a heavy skillet, add the onion, butter, sugar, salt, pepper and red pepper flakes. Cover and cook over low heat, stirring occasionally, until onion is soft, about 25 minutes. Add the wine, vinegar and apricots. Simmer, uncovered, stirring occasionally, for 20–25 minutes until thick. Serve at room temperature.

STIR-FRIED VEGETABLES

4 Servings

8	fresh pea pods (snow peas), stemmed
8	broccoli florets
¼	cup carrot, halved lengthwise, cut into thin slices
1	tablespoon vegetable oil
2	teaspoons dark sesame oil*
1 ¼	teaspoons minced garlic
1 ¼	teaspoons minced ginger
¼	cup sliced green onion
¼	cup thinly sliced celery
½	cup mushrooms, wiped clean, sliced thin
1	cup fresh mung bean sprouts
8	whole baby corn,* drained (optional)
1	tablespoon soy sauce

Use any fresh and colorful assortment of vegetables. You may use water chestnuts in place of the baby corn, or omit altogether. Boiling some of the longer-cooking vegetables in advance helps later when you begin stir-frying.

Boil the pea pods for 15 seconds; chill in ice water. Boil broccoli for about 2 minutes; chill in ice water. Boil carrot slices for about 3 minutes; chill in ice water. You want the vegetables to be crisp-tender when pierced. Drain well, then roll in paper towels to remove all moisture; set aside.

Heat the 2 oils in a large wok or skillet. Add the garlic and ginger; cook for 30 seconds. Add the onion, celery and mushrooms; stir-fry for 2 minutes. Stir in the bean sprouts, baby corn, pea pods, broccoli and carrot; stir-fry for 2 minutes more. Add the soy sauce and stir well to coat all vegetables. Serve hot.

* Available in the Asian foods section of most supermarkets.

POTATOES/RICE/ETC.

Golden Potato Casserole V

Sweet Potato Puff V

Potatoes Mykonos VI

Garlic Herb Red Potatoes VI

Potatoes au Gratin V

Twice-Baked Potatoes V

Homemade Potato Cakes V

Acapulco Rice VI

Roasted Garlic Rice Pilaf VI

Broccoli, Rice and Cheese Casserole V

Hushpuppies V

V Vegetarian
VI Vegan

GOLDEN POTATO CASSEROLE

8 Servings

- ½ cup cream of mushroom soup, undiluted
- ½ cup light sour cream
- 2 tablespoons milk
- 3 tablespoons butter, melted, divided
- 4½ teaspoons minced onion
- ¼ teaspoon + ⅛ teaspoon salt
- 2 cups shredded hash brown potatoes, thawed, patted dry
- 1 cup finely shredded cheddar cheese
- ¼ cup cornflakes, finely crushed

This potato dish is extremely popular. We often serve this for our special occasion Sunday brunches.

Preheat oven to 350°F. In a large bowl, combine the soup, sour cream, milk, 2 tablespoons of the butter, onion and salt; stir in the potatoes and cheese. Transfer to a lightly-oiled casserole pan, spreading mixture evenly.

Toss the crushed cornflakes with the remaining 1 tablespoon of butter and sprinkle over the potatoes. Bake, uncovered, for 35–40 minutes, or until heated through.

SWEET POTATO PUFF

8 Servings

2 large sweet potatoes
2 teaspoons dark molasses
1 tablespoon honey
3 tablespoons all-purpose flour
½ teaspoon salt
⅛ teaspoon ground nutmeg
½ teaspoon ground ginger
4 eggs, separated

2 cups miniature marshmallows

Bake this casserole for one of your favorite holiday meals, or any time you want the scent of holiday spices to permeate your home.

Preheat oven to 350°F. Place the potatoes in a lightly-oiled roasting pan. Bake for about 1½ hours until very soft. Split open and remove pulp to a large bowl. Add the molasses, honey, flour, salt, nutmeg, ginger and egg yolks. Mix until very smooth.

In another bowl, beat the egg whites until stiff. Gently fold into the sweet potato mixture until well blended. Pour into a lightly-oiled 8-by-8-inch pan, spreading mixture evenly. Bake for 30–35 minutes, or until a tester inserted in center comes out clean.

Place the marshmallows in one layer on top of the sweet potato mixture and continue baking for 5 minutes more, or until the marshmallows are golden brown and soft. Let rest for 15 minutes or so to firm up and cool slightly.

POTATOES MYKONOS

4 Servings

  2 cups russet or yukon gold potatoes, peeled, cut into ¾-inch cubes

Flavored Olive Oil

  2 tablespoons extra-virgin olive oil
  2 teaspoons fresh lemon juice
  ¼ teaspoon dried oregano
    (or use ½ teaspoon fresh)
  ¼ teaspoon garlic powder
  ¼ teaspoon onion powder
  ¼ teaspoon paprika
  ¼ teaspoon + ⅛ teaspoon salt
  ⅛ teaspoon black pepper

The subtle flavor of lemon and oregano in these roasted potatoes is certainly Greek-inspired. They are wonderful with all sorts of roasted or grilled meats, as well as fish.

Preheat oven to 350°F. In a large bowl, combine all ingredients for the flavored oil; whisk to blend. Toss the cubes in the oil to coat completely.

Lightly oil a roasting pan (yes, oil both the pan and the potatoes to keep them from sticking to the pan); spread the potatoes in one layer. Roast for 30 minutes. Turn over the cubes with a spatula and roast for 20–25 minutes more until golden brown and tender when pierced.

GARLIC HERB RED POTATOES

3–4 Servings

1 whole garlic bulb (head)

Marinade

3 tablespoons olive oil

1 ¼ teaspoons lemon juice

½ teaspoon minced garlic

⅛ teaspoon dried basil

¼ teaspoon salt

¼ teaspoon seasoning salt

⅛ teaspoon black pepper

½ teaspoon minced fresh thyme
  (or ⅛ teaspoon dried)

½ teaspoon minced fresh oregano
  (or ⅛ teaspoon dried)

2 ½ cups red potatoes,
  cut into 1-inch pieces

The roasted garlic pulp has a wonderful, nutty flavor and blends into the potatoes better when warm and very soft. If your timing gets interrupted and the garlic cools down, you can always reheat it before proceeding as described above.

To Roast Garlic Preheat oven to 350°F. Wrap whole garlic bulb in aluminum foil. Bake for 1 hour, or until cloves are soft when squeezed; set aside until cool enough to handle, but still warm. Turn garlic on its side and, with a sharp knife, slice ½-inch off the pointed end to expose the individual cloves; push out the soft interior with the flat side of a large knife. Collect the roasted garlic pulp and place in a small bowl.

Meanwhile, in a medium bowl, whisk together all marinade ingredients, except the thyme and oregano. Add the potato chunks and stir to coat completely. Lightly oil a roasting pan (yes, oil both the pan and the potatoes to keep them from sticking to the pan); spread the potatoes into the pan. Roast for 20 minutes. Add the warm garlic pulp, thyme and oregano to a medium bowl. Remove the potatoes from the oven; stir the hot potatoes into the warm pulp and herbs. Keep stirring until pulp is mixed evenly into the potatoes. Place potatoes back into the oven and roast for 25–30 minutes more until golden brown and tender when pierced.

POTATOES AU GRATIN

6–8 Servings

1 large, or 2 medium baking potatoes

Sauce

2 tablespoons butter
2 tablespoons all-purpose flour
2/3 cup chicken or vegetable broth
1/4 cup milk
1/2 cup heavy whipping cream
1 tablespoon + 1 1/2 teaspoons grated parmesan cheese
1/2 teaspoon seasoning salt
1/4 teaspoon onion powder
dash white pepper

1/2 cup shredded cheddar cheese
2 round butter crackers, crushed

Peel and slice potatoes 1/4-inch thick. Boil until tender when pierced, yet not so soft that they fall apart. Drain, then place in a buttered 8-by-8-inch pan.

For Sauce Melt the butter in a saucepan. Stir in the flour and cook over medium-low heat, stirring often, for 3–4 minutes to make a beige-colored thickening base (called a roux). Combine the broth, milk and heavy cream; gradually add to the flour mixture, while stirring. Stir in remaining sauce ingredients.

Preheat oven to 375°F. Pour the sauce over the potatoes. Top with the shredded cheese, then sprinkle with the crushed crackers. Bake for 18–20 minutes until heated through and golden brown on top.

TWICE-BAKED POTATOES

2 Servings

2 baking potatoes
2 tablespoons butter
¾ cup shredded cheddar cheese, divided
¼ teaspoon + ⅛ teaspoon salt
⅛ teaspoon black pepper
¼ cup half-and-half

These are favored by students for their annual suite dinners in the Centennial Room (formerly the Red Room). They are surprisingly easy to prepare.

Preheat oven to 350°F. Bake the potatoes for 1½ hours, or until soft in the center.

Set potatoes aside until cool enough to handle. With a sharp knife, cut off the top ½-inch of each potato, lengthwise. Scoop out all pulp into a bowl, being careful not to tear the jackets. Place the empty jackets in a lightly-oiled baking pan. Beat the butter and potato until smooth, then beat in ½ cup of the cheese, the salt and pepper, and then beat in the half-and-half until mixture is smooth and fluffy.

Turn oven up to 375°F. Fill each potato jacket with the filling, mounding slightly in the center. Sprinkle tops with the remaining cheese and bake for 15 minutes, or until heated through.

HOMEMADE POTATO CAKES

4 Servings

Cakes

- 2 medium baking potatoes, peeled, cut into ½-inch cube
- 2 teaspoons butter
- 1 teaspoon minced garlic
- ¼ cup finely chopped onion
- 4 teaspoons finely chopped green onion
- ¼ teaspoon hot red pepper sauce
- ¼ teaspoon + ⅛ teaspoon salt
- 2 tablespoons milk

- 1 egg, beaten
- ½ cup (1.5 ounces) potato chips, crushed
- ¼ cup crushed round butter crackers (about 6)
- 4 teaspoons vegetable oil (or rendered bacon fat)

Serve as the potato accompaniment to any meat, fish or vegetarian entree.

For Cakes Cook diced potatoes in boiling water for 10 minutes, or until soft but not falling apart. Drain in colander; let cool in colander for 5 minutes. Meanwhile, heat the butter in a small skillet; add the garlic and onion and saute for 2 minutes. Transfer to a large bowl. Stir cooked potatoes into the onion mixture. Stir in the green onion, pepper sauce and salt, then stir in the milk. Chill potato cake mixture for 15 minutes.

Place beaten egg in a medium bowl or shallow dish. Combine the crushed chips and crackers in a small bowl or shallow dish. Form potato mixture into patties. Dip them in the egg, then into the crumb mixture to coat completely.

Heat the oil in a large skillet. When hot, add the patties and cook for 3–5 minutes per side, or until golden brown and crisp.

ACAPULCO RICE

3–4 Servings

1 tablespoon vegetable oil
¼ cup chopped onion
½ cup long-grain rice
½ cup chicken or vegetable broth
½ cup V-8 or tomato juice
2 tablespoons chopped fresh tomato
½ teaspoon minced garlic
¼ teaspoon ground cumin
¼ teaspoon salt
dash white pepper

1 teaspoon minced cilantro (optional)

Serve this as an accompaniment to Mexican or other Latin American foods.

Heat the oil in a saucepan; add the onion and saute for 3 minutes. Add the rice, stirring to coat; saute in the oil for 4 minutes, stirring constantly, until rice and onion are lightly browned. Place in an oil-sprayed 8-by-8-inch pan.

Preheat oven to 350°F. In another saucepan, combine the broth, V-8 juice, tomato, garlic, cumin, salt and pepper; bring to a boil. Add broth mixture to rice mixture; stir well. Cover and bake for 25 minutes, or until rice is tender and liquid is absorbed. Stir in cilantro, if desired. Serve hot.

ROASTED GARLIC RICE PILAF

4 Servings

  2 whole garlic bulbs (heads)

Seasoning Blend

  ¼ teaspoon salt
  ⅛ teaspoon white pepper
  ¼ teaspoon garlic salt
  ¼ teaspoon onion powder
  ¼ teaspoon dill
  ¼ teaspoon tarragon

Vegetables

  4 teaspoons vegetable oil
  ¼ cup finely chopped onion
  2 tablespoons finely chopped celery
  2 tablespoons finely chopped carrot

  ½ cup long-grain rice
1 ½ cups water

This recipe may seem to have too much garlic. However, when the garlic bulbs are roasted and the pulp extracted, you will get a little more than 4 teaspoons of pulp depending on the bulb size. The garlic is mellowed when roasted and has an appealing nutty flavor.

To Roast Garlic Preheat oven to 350°F. Wrap whole garlic bulbs in aluminum foil. Bake for 1 hour, or until cloves are soft when squeezed; set aside until cool enough to handle, but still warm. Turn each head of garlic on its side and, with a sharp knife, slice ½-inch off the pointed end to expose the individual cloves; push out the soft interior with the flat side of a large knife. Collect the roasted garlic pulp and place in a small bowl, mashing the pulp to a paste. Measure and separate 4 teaspoons of the pulp. Any remaining pulp can be reserved for another use, or discarded.

For Seasoning Blend Combine all seasonings in a small bowl; set aside.

For Vegetables Heat the oil in a saucepan. Add the onion, celery and carrot; cook for 3 minutes, stirring often. Add the seasoning blend and the garlic pulp, stirring well to blend; cook for 2 minutes. Add the rice and cook, stirring constantly, for 1 minute more. Stir in the water; bring to a boil, then cover tightly and turn heat to low. Simmer for 20–22 minutes until rice is tender and liquid is absorbed.

BROCCOLI, RICE AND CHEESE CASSEROLE

4 Servings

½ cup long-grain white rice
10–12 broccoli florets
1 (10.75-ounce) can cream of
   mushroom soup, undiluted
1 (8-ounce) package processed cheese
   spread, cut into pieces

¼ cup shredded cheddar cheese
4 round butter crackers, crushed
2 teaspoons butter, melted

Bring 1 cup of water to a boil in a saucepan. Add the rice, cover with a tight-fitting lid, and simmer for 20 minutes, or until rice is tender and liquid is absorbed. Remove from heat.

Meanwhile, steam broccoli until tender, about 3 minutes; chill in ice water, then drain and wrap in a towel to absorb all moisture; set aside.

Heat the soup and cheese over very low heat (or in the microwave), stirring until melted; keep warm. In a small bowl, combine the cracker crumbs and melted butter; set aside.

In a large bowl, combine the rice, broccoli and soup mixture. Mix well, then pour into an oil-sprayed casserole pan. Top with the shredded cheese, then sprinkle the buttered crumbs over all. Bake in a preheated 350°F oven for 15 minutes, or until hot in the center.

HUSHPUPPIES

4 Servings

vegetable oil, as needed
½ cup yellow cornmeal
½ cup all-purpose flour
3 tablespoons + 1 ½ teaspoons sugar
1 teaspoon baking powder
¼ teaspoon + ⅛ teaspoon salt
¼ teaspoon baking soda
¼ teaspoon garlic powder
1 tablespoon minced onion
¼ cup buttermilk
1 egg, beaten

A Southern specialty, traditionally these are served with fried catfish. The name is said to have come from the fact that, to keep dogs from begging for food while the rest of the dinner was being prepared, cooks used to toss scraps of the fried batter to the pets with the command, "Hush, puppy!" Serve these treats with any fried, grilled or baked seafood.

Pour vegetable oil into a deep skillet or heavy saucepot to a depth of 1½ inches or so. Heat the oil to 350°F, or until oil sputters when a drop of water is added.

Meanwhile, combine remaining ingredients in a large bowl. Stir until smooth (batter should be thick but moist).

Portion out walnut-sized amounts of batter into the hot oil. Deep fry, turning often until they reach a rich brown color and batter is cooked in the center when tested. Adjust heat down if they start turning a dark brown color. Drain on paper towels and serve soon after frying.

PARTY FOODS

Artichoke Spinach Dip V

Hummus V

Sweet Fruit Dip V

Miguel's Salsa V

Boursin-Style Cheese Spread V

Bruschetta V

Chocolate Chip Cheese Ball V

Annie's Fruit Salsa with
   Cinnamon Chips V

Beef Mexi-Cali Dip

Walnut Tea Sandwiches V

Cider Wassail V

Marcie's Party Punch V

Sparkling Yellow Punch

Party Sangria Punch V

Mexican Hot Chocolate V

V Vegetarian
V Vegan

ARTICHOKE SPINACH DIP

2 Cups

1 (14-ounce) can artichoke hearts, chopped
¾ cup frozen chopped spinach
2 cups water
1 (8-ounce) package cream cheese
½ cup grated parmesan cheese
1 tablespoon finely chopped onion
¼ teaspoon onion powder
½ teaspoon garlic powder
½ teaspoon crushed red pepper flakes
¼ teaspoon salt
⅛ teaspoon black pepper
½ teaspoon lemon juice

This is a popular appetizer offered at several chain restaurants and is, therefore, a familiar favorite among our students. Try this version and see if it doesn't hold its own in comparison. It is moderately hot in spice due to the red pepper flakes. You can adjust the heat according to your own preference.

In a medium saucepan, add the artichoke hearts, spinach and water; bring to a boil. Let boil for 7 minutes. Drain in colander, pushing gently to extract all liquid.

Transfer to a large bowl. Heat cream cheese in the microwave for 1 minute or so, then add to the vegetable mixture. Stir well until mixture is smooth and creamy. Stir in remaining ingredients.

When ready to serve, heat mixture in the microwave until hot. Or, place mixture in a decorative crock or casserole dish and heat in the oven, covered, until hot in the center. Serve right away with tortilla chips, toasted French bread slices or crackers.

HUMMUS

1 ¾ Cups

- 1 (15-ounce) can garbanzo beans, drained
- ¼ cup tahini,* stirred well
- 1 ¼ teaspoons minced fresh garlic
- 2 tablespoons + 1 teaspoon olive oil
- 1 tablespoon + ½ teaspoon fresh lemon juice
- ¼ teaspoon + pinch salt
- ⅛ teaspoon cayenne pepper (optional)

A popular Middle Eastern spread, this can be used as a dip for pita bread or raw vegetables. Also it can be used as a sandwich spread layered with vegetables such as cucumber, tomato, sprouts, etc. Additional flavorings can be added to the processor when making this basic recipe, including roasted garlic cloves, roasted red peppers, imported olives, sun-dried tomatoes or salsa.

Place all ingredients in a food processor. Process until hummus is smooth, scraping down sides of the bowl as needed. Chill for 1 hour to allow flavors to blend. Add a little water if too thick. Taste and adjust seasoning.

* Tahini is a thick paste made of ground sesame seeds. It is available in most supermarkets and natural food stores.

SWEET FRUIT DIP

1 ½ Cups

1 (8-ounce) package cream cheese,
　　softened
　½ cup marshmallow creme
　½ cup whipped topping
　¼ cup powdered sugar
　¼ teaspoon vanilla
　¼ cup milk

**We serve this dip often with our
fresh fruit trays as students can't
get enough of it.**

In a stand mixer or food processor, combine all ingredients
and process until smooth. Serve with fresh cut fruit.

MIGUEL'S SALSA

3 1/2 Cups

1 (28-ounce) can diced tomatoes, drained
1 1/2 teaspoons minced garlic
3/4 cup chopped onion
1 1/2 teaspoons minced fresh jalapeño
2 tablespoons minced cilantro
1 cup medium-hot salsa
1 tablespoon white vinegar (cider or red vinegar ok)
2 1/4 teaspoons lime juice
1/2 teaspoon garlic powder
3/4 teaspoon taco seasoning mix
1/4 teaspoon salt
1/8 teaspoon black pepper

This salsa is the one I have made for my family throughout the years. We prepare it at Cottey in 3-gallon batches. It is medium-hot in spice so feel free to "kick it up" to your preference.

Place all ingredients in a food processor. Process using on/off turns just until onions are finely chopped and ingredients are well mixed, but not pureed. Stir briefly before using.

BOURSIN-STYLE CHEESE SPREAD

1 Cup

  1 (8-ounce) package cream cheese, softened

½ teaspoon garlic powder

½ teaspoon onion powder

¼ teaspoon salt

¼ teaspoon black pepper

  1 teaspoon minced fresh chives

  1 teaspoon minced fresh parsley, rinsed, patted dry

Combine all ingredients together in a medium bowl, stirring until well blended; chill. Let sit at room temperature for 30 minutes or so to soften before serving.

The popular soft, garlicky cheese spread, developed by Francois Boursin, is a favored ingredient in some Cottey recipes. However, Boursin cheese is costly and not always available in small-town supermarkets. This homemade version is similar to the commercial product and is wonderful served in a small crock or bowl with crackers on the side.

BRUSCHETTA

4 Cups

   4 cups seeded, diced roma tomatoes*
   2 tablespoons minced fresh basil
   2 teaspoons minced fresh garlic
   ¼ cup green onion, thinly sliced
   ¼ cup olive oil
   1 tablespoon + 2 teaspoons balsamic
       or red wine vinegar
   ½ teaspoon salt
   ¼ teaspoon black pepper
       pinch sugar

   1 loaf French bread, sliced thin
4 ½ teaspoons olive oil
   1 clove garlic, peeled, split lengthwise

*To Seed Tomatoes Cut off the stem end, then cut tomatoes in half crosswise. Pick up each half and firmly squeeze out the seeds and juice. Discard the seeds and juice.

In a medium bowl, combine the tomatoes, basil, garlic, onion, oil, vinegar, salt, pepper and sugar. Let marinate for at least 1 hour, preferably 2 hours. Drain well before serving.

Preheat broiler to 500°F. Place the bread slices on a baking sheet in 1 layer. Drizzle olive oil over the bread slices. Rub the slices with the cut side of garlic, then broil until lightly toasted. Serve the tomato mixture in a bowl surrounded by the toasts.

CHOCOLATE CHIP CHEESE BALL

1 Large Ball

½ cup (1 stick) butter, softened

¾ cup powdered sugar

¼ cup miniature chocolate chips

2 (8-ounce) packages cream cheese, softened

1 teaspoon vanilla

1 cup finely crushed Golden Grahams cereal

24 honey graham crackers

24 chocolate graham crackers

We receive compliments from young and old whenever we serve this sweet cheese ball. It looks attractive on a platter, especially if you use 2 kinds of graham crackers.

Mix together the butter, powdered sugar, cream cheese, chocolate chips and vanilla. Cover and chill mixture for 1 hour, or until firm enough to shape into a ball.

Meanwhile, grind the cereal in a food processor using on/off turns until cereal is the size of large granules, comparable to the size of ground nuts. Strain away the fine powder, continuing the process until you have 1 cup.

Roll the cheese ball in the ground cereal until completely coated; chill until ready to serve. Arrange cheese ball on a platter with assorted graham crackers and a small knife for spreading.

ANNIE'S FRUIT SALSA
WITH CINNAMON CHIPS

2 Cups / 30 Chips

Salsa

- 1 kiwi, peeled, diced
- 1 golden delicious apple, peeled, diced
- ½ cup frozen raspberries, thawed, drained
- 1 cup diced fresh strawberries
- 1 tablespoon sugar
- 1 tablespoon brown sugar
- 2 tablespoons strawberry or raspberry preserves

Cinnamon Chips

- 5 (8-inch) flour tortillas
- 5 teaspoons butter, melted
- 5 teaspoons sugar
- ½ teaspoon + pinch ground cinnamon

This is a unique and flavorful recipe provided by one of our students. It is a favorite on our catering menu for formal receptions, as well as casual gatherings. If pressed for time, you can use cinnamon graham crackers in place of the homemade cinnamon chips.

In a medium bowl, combine the fruit ingredients. In a small bowl, combine both sugars and the preserves, mixing with a whisk or spoon until smooth; add to the fruit mixture. Cover and chill for 30 minutes. Drain excess liquid and place in a serving bowl.

For Cinnamon Chips Preheat broiler to 500°F. Coat one side of each tortilla with 1 teaspoon melted butter and arrange on baking sheets in a single layer. Combine the sugar and cinnamon together in a small bowl, then sprinkle a generous teaspoon of cinnamon sugar over each buttered tortilla. Broil the tortillas for 1–2 minutes, or until golden brown (watch to prevent burning). Let cool slightly, then cut into wedges with a large knife (some tortillas will puff up when broiled — use or replace as desired).

Arrange chips on a platter with salsa in the center.

BEEF MEXI-CALI DIP

4½ Cups (15–20 Servings)

- 3 tablespoons butter
- 3 tablespoons all-purpose flour
- 1 ¼ cups milk
- 1 (8-ounce) package processed cheese spread (like Velveeta), cut into pieces
- 4 teaspoons vegetable oil
- ½ cup diced onion
- 1 pound ground beef
- 1 cup medium-hot salsa
- 1 (4-ounce) can chopped green chiles
- 1 ¼ teaspoons chili powder
- ¼ teaspoon ground cumin
- ½ teaspoon garlic salt

Melt the butter in a heavy-bottomed saucepan. Whisk in the flour until smooth; let mixture cook for 2 minutes over low heat, stirring constantly. Add the milk, stirring until smooth. Add the cheese and heat, stirring occasionally, until melted and smooth.

Meanwhile, heat the oil in a skillet. Add the onion and cook over medium heat, stirring often, for 5–6 minutes. Add the beef and cook until browned, breaking up chunks. Drain fat from the meat mixture, then stir in the salsa, chiles and spices. Combine the meat and cheese mixtures, stirring well.

Serve dip hot in an attractive serving bowl with tortilla chips or large corn chips.

WALNUT TEA SANDWICHES

14 Halves / 28 Quarters

Filling

  1 (8-ounce) package cream cheese, softened

  ¼ cup walnuts, toasted and ground*

2½ teaspoons finely minced green bell pepper

  1 teaspoon finely minced fresh parsley (optional)

1½ teaspoons finely minced onion

  ½ teaspoon lemon juice

  2 pinches nutmeg

  ¼ teaspoon salt

     dash black pepper

14 slices quality white or wheat bread

  2 tablespoons + 1 teaspoon unsalted butter, softened

A unique and tasty filling. Serve by themselves, or serve along with other fillings such as egg salad, ham or chicken salad to make a tea sandwich platter. Alternate white, wheat and pumpernickel breads to create eye appeal.

*For Walnuts Preheat oven to 350°F. Place the walnuts in a small baking pan, and bake for 6–7 minutes until golden and fragrant; let cool, then finely chop by hand or grind in a small processor.

Combine all filling ingredients in a medium bowl, stirring until well blended.

Spread one side of each slice of bread lightly with butter. Top half the slices with 2 tablespoons of the cream cheese mixture on each, spreading evenly. Top with the remaining bread slices, buttered-side down.

Carefully cut the crusts from each sandwich, preferably with a serrated knife. Cut the sandwiches in half diagonally, and then cut again if quarters are desired. Serve slightly chilled, or at room temperature.

CIDER WASSAIL

5–6 Servings

  1 quart unfiltered apple cider*
¾ cup orange juice
½ cup pineapple juice, stirred well
  1 cup cranberry juice
¼ teaspoon lemon juice
  6 tablespoons brown sugar
     dash ground cinnamon
     dash ground cloves
  2 cinnamon sticks
½ teaspoon vanilla

5–6 cinnamon sticks

There are many variations to the hot brew called Wassail. It was traditionally a drink consisting of ale or wine, sweetened with sugar and flavored with spices. The name evolved from a Norse saying "Ves heill," which means "be in good health." There was a recipe on file at Cottey that called for cider, spiced tea, grapefruit juice and loganberry juice. This recipe is an adaptation of that earlier version.

In a large saucepan, combine all ingredients, except the vanilla. Simmer over very low heat, covered, for 15 minutes; stir in the vanilla. Keep warm.

Before serving, taste for sweetness. If it is too sweet due to the sweetness of the cider, then add more lemon juice to adjust. Place a cinnamon stick in each cup or mug and serve hot.

* The unfiltered apple cider is widely available during the holiday season.

MARCIE'S PARTY PUNCH

1 ½ Gallons

  1 (.14-ounce) package strawberry
     Kool-Aid
  1 (.13-ounce) package cherry
     Kool-Aid
  3 quarts (12 cups) cold water
  2 cups sugar
  ½ cup orange juice concentrate, thawed
  ½ cup lemonade concentrate, thawed

  2 liters ginger ale, chilled

This recipe came to us from Marcie Hurshman, Cottey's faithful dining and catering supervisor. Students and staff often request this for their caterings.

Combine all but the ginger ale in a 1½–2 gallon container, stirring well to dissolve the sugar; chill.

When ready to serve, carefully stir in the ginger ale. The punch will foam up if the ginger ale is added too quickly. Slowly pour the ginger ale against the side of the container to minimize the foaming. Gently pour into a serving bowl. Serve chilled.

SPARKLING YELLOW PUNCH

½ Gallon

1¾ cups sparkling white grape juice
½ cup orange juice concentrate, thawed
½ cup lemonade concentrate, thawed
½ cup pineapple juice
1½ teaspoons orange gelatin powder
1 teaspoon pineapple gelatin powder
½ cup sugar

5¾ cups ginger ale, chilled
8 orange slices (optional)

This is a nice departure from the ubiquitous red punch. It is the preferred punch served at the President's House, both for its flavor and the fact that spills don't leave their mark as noticeably as others—something to consider if you have light-colored carpets.

Combine all but the ginger ale and orange slices in a ½ gallon container, stirring well to dissolve the sugar; chill. When ready to serve, carefully stir in the ginger ale. The punch will foam up if the ginger ale is added too quickly. Slowly pour the ginger ale against the side of the container to minimize the foaming. Gently pour into a serving bowl. Garnish with orange slices, if desired. Serve chilled.

PARTY SANGRIA PUNCH

1 ½ Gallons

Punch Base

1 ⅓ cups red grape juice

½ cup lemonade concentrate, thawed

4 cups lemonade

¾ cup orange juice concentrate, thawed

2 cups orange juice

½ cup grenadine syrup*

1 cup sugar

4 liters ginger ale, chilled

8 – 10 orange slices

This is a festive, non-alcoholic version of the Spanish classic, which is traditionally made with red wine, fruit juices and soda water.

Combine all but the ginger ale and orange slices in a 1½–2 gallon container, stirring well to dissolve the sugar; chill. When ready to serve, carefully stir in the ginger ale. The punch will foam up if the ginger ale is added too quickly. Slowly pour the ginger ale against the side of the container to minimize the foaming. Gently pour into a serving bowl. Garnish with orange slices, if desired. Serve chilled.

* Available in most large supermarkets, it is located near the liquors and bar mixes. It is a sweet, red, pomegranate-flavored syrup used to color and flavor drinks and desserts.

MEXICAN HOT CHOCOLATE

3–4 Servings

1 ¾ cups milk

1 ¼ cups heavy whipping cream

⅓ cup chopped milk chocolate

¼ cup semisweet chocolate chips

1 tablespoon + 1 teaspoon unsweetened baking cocoa

¾ teaspoon vanilla

⅓ cup packed brown sugar

1 ½ cups whipped topping

2 teaspoons grated chocolate

3–4 whole cinnamon sticks (optional)

This is the ultimate hot chocolate. It takes a little more effort than opening the instant cocoa packet, but it is wonderful and would be a treat to serve when friends and family visit.

Heat the milk and cream in a saucepan to a simmer. Stir in remaining ingredients; stir until chocolate is melted and mixture is smooth.

Serve in mugs or cups, topped with whipped topping and grated chocolate. Place a cinnamon stick in each cup just before serving, if desired.

DESSERTS

COOKIES

Butter Pecan Shortbread Sticks V

Caramel Cream Sandwich Cookies V

Chocolate Malted Cookies V

Chocolate Fantasy Cookies V

Chocolate Marshmallow Cookies V

English Toffee Cookies V

Gingersnaps V

German Chocolate Cookies V

Monster Cookies V

Peanut Butter Cookies
   with Reese's Cups V

Oatmeal Creme Pies V

Pecan Sandies V

Chocolate Peanut Butter
   Chip Cookies V

S'mores Cookies V

Snowy Chocolate Cookies V

Gingerbread Cookies
   with Orange Glaze V

Walnut Frosties V

Strawberry Cheesecake Cookies V

BROWNIES & BARS

Brownie Bonbons V

Brownie Cheesecake Bars V

Brownie Fudge Bars V

Chocolate Crumb Bars V

Chocolate Caramel Brownies V

Crispy Chocolate Brownies V

Chocolate Oreo Brownies V

Chocolate Streusel Bars V

Honey Graham S'mores Bars V

Multilayer Bars V

Lemon Bars V

Pecan Pie Bars V

Raspberry Oatmeal Bars V

Chocolate Hazelnut Crunch Bars

Snickers Bars V

V Vegetarian
V Vegan

DESSERTS

PIES & TARTS

Chocolate Buttercrunch Pie V

Cookies and Cream Pie V

Lemon Chiffon Pie V

Dutch Apple Butterscotch Pie V

Peanut Butter Cup Pie V

Strawberries and Cream Pie

Triple Chocolate Pudding Pie
   with Cappucino Cream V

Fruit Pizza V

Strawberry Lime Mousse Pie

CAKES

Blue Ribbon Carrot Cake V

Caramel Apple Cake V

Dirt Cake V

White Texas Sheet Cake V

Coca-Cola Cake V

French Silk Cake with
   Raspberry Cream

Pumpkin Cake Roll V

Tres Leches V

Strawberry Swirl Cheesecake V

Cinnamon Cheesecake V

Toffee Caramel Cheesecake V

Molten Chocolate Cake with
   Chocolate-Dipped Ice Cream V

MORE FAVORITES

Bread Pudding with Rum Sauce V

Flan V

Creme Brulee V

Peach Cobbler V

V Vegetarian
V Vegan

BUTTER PECAN SHORTBREAD STICKS

18 Sticks

1 ¼ cups all-purpose flour

¼ cup packed brown sugar

½ cup + 2 tablespoons butter, cold, cut into pieces

2 tablespoons + 1 teaspoon finely chopped pecans

1 teaspoon vanilla

¼ cup chopped chocolate almond bark

Preheat oven to 350°F. Place the pecan pieces on a baking sheet and bake for 5 minutes or so to lightly toast; set aside to cool. Turn oven down to 325°F.

In a mixing bowl, combine the flour and brown sugar. Beat in butter pieces until mixture resembles crumbs and starts to cling (2–3 minutes on medium speed). Stir in the pecans, then vanilla. Form dough into a ball and knead briefly until smooth.

Roll or pat dough out on a lightly floured surface into an 8-by-7-inch rectangle. Cut in half lengthwise, then crosswise into 1-inch sticks. Place onto an ungreased baking sheet at least 1 inch apart.

Bake for 10 minutes. Rotate the pan* and bake for 10 minutes more, or until bottoms just start to brown. Transfer sticks to a wire rack or other cool surface, and allow them to cool completely.

Melt the chocolate bark, then drizzle the cooled sticks with the chocolate—use a small spoon and a quick back and forth motion over the sticks. Chocolate will firm up when cool.

* Rotate the pan refers to turning the pan 180° (half a turn) to insure even browning.

CARAMEL CREAM SANDWICH COOKIES

18 Cookies

Cookie Dough

- ¾ cup packed brown sugar
- 2 sticks (1 cup) butter, softened
- 1 egg yolk
- 2 cups all-purpose flour

Frosting

- 2 tablespoons butter
- 1 ¼ cups powdered sugar
- ½ teaspoon vanilla
- 4–6 teaspoons milk

For Cookies In a mixing bowl, cream the butter and sugar until light and fluffy. Add the egg yolk; blend well, then gradually stir in the flour. Cover and chill dough for 15 minutes for easier handling.

Preheat oven to 350°F. Shape dough into 1-inch balls and place 2 inches apart onto ungreased baking sheets. Flatten each with a fork in 2 directions to create a cross-pattern. Bake for 6 minutes. Rotate the pans* and bake for 5–6 minutes more, or until a very light golden color. After 2 minutes, transfer cookies to a wire rack or other cool surface.

For Frosting In a small saucepan, heat the butter over medium-high heat until light golden brown, stirring constantly. Remove from heat to a bowl. Whisk in the sugar, vanilla and enough milk to make a spreading consistency.

Assemble Cookies Spread 1 teaspoon of frosting on the flat side of half of the cookies. Top with remaining cookies, flat-side down, to make sandwiches.

* Rotate the pans refers to turning the pans 180° (half a turn) to insure even browning.

CHOCOLATE MALTED COOKIES

30 Cookies

1 cup butter-flavored shortening

1 ¼ cups packed brown sugar

¾ cup malted milk powder

2 tablespoons chocolate syrup

1 tablespoon vanilla

1 egg

2 cups all-purpose flour

1 teaspoon baking soda

½ teaspoon salt

1 cup semisweet chocolate
    chunk morsels

1 cup milk chocolate chips

In a mixing bowl, combine the shortening, sugar, malted milk powder, chocolate syrup and vanilla; beat for 2–3 minutes. Mix in egg.

Combine the flour, baking soda and salt. Gradually add to the creamed mixture, mixing well after each addition. Stir in chocolate chunks and chips.

Preheat oven to 350°F. Shape dough into 1½-inch balls and place 2 inches apart onto ungreased baking sheets. Bake for 7 minutes. Rotate the pans* and bake for 5–6 minutes more, or until light golden in color. Carefully remove warm cookies to a wire rack or other cool surface as soon as possible.

* Rotate the pans refers to turning the pans 180° (half a turn) to insure even browning.

CHOCOLATE FANTASY COOKIES

24 Cookies

1 cup semisweet chocolate chips, premium brand preferred*
2 (1-ounce squares) unsweetened baking chocolate, chopped
2 tablespoons butter
2 eggs
2/3 cup packed brown sugar
1 tablespoon vanilla
6 tablespoons all-purpose flour
1/4 teaspoon baking powder
1 1/4 cups white chocolate chips
1/3 cup chopped walnuts (optional)

This recipe uses very little flour. The dough is sticky, yet workable, when chilled for 1–2 hours. If dough is chilled overnight, let soften at room temperature as it will harden after 3 hours of chilling time. These are popular among chocolate lovers of all ages.

Melt both chocolates and butter in the top of a double boiler over hot water. Transfer to a large bowl. Let cool for 5 minutes, then stir in the eggs, brown sugar and vanilla. Stir in the flour and baking powder. Stir in the white chocolate chips and walnuts. Chill dough for 45 minutes or so to firm up slightly.

Heat oven to 350°F. Cover baking sheets with parchment paper. Oil-spray the paper. Drop dough by rounded tablespoons 2 inches apart, using 1 spoon to scoop dough and 1 to scrape onto the baking sheets. Bake for 10–11 minutes. When still warm but firm, carefully remove cookies from the parchment paper to a wire rack or other cool surface. Store at room temperature in an airtight container.

* Premium brands such as Ghirardelli are preferred for this recipe. They can be purchased at most large supermarkets.

CHOCOLATE MARSHMALLOW COOKIES

24 Cookies

Dough

½ cup butter-flavored shortening
   (or margarine)
 1 cup sugar
 2 eggs
 1 teaspoon vanilla
1½ cups all-purpose flour
½ cup unsweetened baking cocoa
 1 teaspoon baking soda
¼ teaspoon salt

72 miniature marshmallows

Icing

 3 tablespoons unsweetened
   baking cocoa
¼ cup milk
¼ cup butter
2½ cups powdered sugar

For Dough In a mixing bowl, cream the shortening and sugar. Add the eggs and vanilla; mix until blended. In a separate bowl, combine the dry ingredients and gradually add to the egg mixture, mixing on low speed until all is incorporated and smooth.

For Icing In a saucepan, combine the milk, butter and cocoa; bring to a boil. Gradually stir in the powdered sugar until a spreading consistency is reached. Keep warm.

Preheat oven to 350°F. Form dough into 1½-inch balls. Place onto lightly oil-sprayed baking sheets. Press balls to flatten, then place 3 marshmallows in the center of each dough round. Bake for 8–10 minutes. Within a few minutes, transfer cookies to a wire rack or other cool surface. When the cookies are cooled, spread tops with the chocolate icing, covering most of the marshmallow. Store at room temperature in an airtight container.

ENGLISH TOFFEE COOKIES

36 Cookies

  1 cup (2 sticks) butter, softened
¾ cup + 1 tablespoon packed
     brown sugar
⅓ cup sugar
  1 egg
  2 teaspoons vanilla
2¼ cups all-purpose flour
  1 teaspoon baking soda
½ teaspoon salt
1½ cups (8 ounces) chocolate
     English toffee pieces

This is a favorite for many of our students and staff.

In a mixing bowl, cream together the butter and sugars. Beat in egg and vanilla. In a separate bowl, combine the flour, baking soda and salt. Gradually add to creamed mixture on low speed until incorporated and smooth. Stir in the toffee pieces.

Preheat oven to 350°F. Portion dough into 1½-inch balls and place onto ungreased baking sheets 2 inches apart. Bake for 6 minutes. Rotate the pans* and bake about 5 minutes more. After 2 minutes or so, transfer cookies to a wire rack or other cool surface. Store at room temperature in an airtight container.

* Rotate the pans refers to turning the pans 180° (half a turn) to insure even browning.

GINGERSNAPS

30 Cookies

2 ¼ cups all-purpose flour
 1 cup packed brown sugar
 ¾ cup vegetable oil
 ¼ cup molasses
 1 egg
 1 teaspoon baking soda
 1 teaspoon ground ginger
 1 teaspoon ground cinnamon
 ½ teaspoon ground cloves

 6 tablespoons sugar

These cookies have devoted fans on our campus. Unlike many store-bought versions, these are soft in texture and very flavorful, especially right out of the oven.

In a large bowl, place about half of the flour. Add the brown sugar, oil, molasses, egg, baking soda, ginger, cinnamon and cloves. Beat until thoroughly combined, scraping sides of the bowl occasionally. Stir in the remaining flour until well combined.

Preheat oven to 350°F. Shape the dough into 1¼-inch balls and roll in the sugar to coat. Place 2 inches apart onto ungreased baking sheets. Bake for 6 minutes. Rotate the pans* and bake for 4–5 minutes more. Cool cookies on the baking sheets for 1–2 minutes, then remove to a wire rack or other cool surface.

* Rotate the pans refers to turning the pans 180° (half a turn) to insure even browning.

GERMAN CHOCOLATE COOKIES

30 Cookies

Dough

- 1 cup powdered sugar
- 1 cup (2 sticks) butter, softened
- 2 teaspoons vanilla
- 2 cups all-purpose flour
- 2 tablespoons unsweetened baking cocoa
- ½ teaspoon salt

Filling

- ⅓ cup + 1 tablespoon evaporated milk
- ⅓ cup + 1 tablespoon sugar
- 1 egg yolk
- 4 tablespoons butter
- ¾ teaspoon vanilla
- ½ cup chopped pecans
- ½ cup + 2 tablespoons flaked coconut

Topping

- ¼ cup semisweet chocolate chips
- 1 tablespoon water
- 1 tablespoon butter
- ¼ cup powdered sugar

There are three short recipes to complete this cookie. Each one comes together quickly and easily. The result is a light chocolate cookie with a creamy pecan-coconut filling and a chocolate drizzle on top. They are impressive to look at and delicious.

For Dough In a large mixing bowl, combine the powdered sugar, butter and vanilla; beat until light and fluffy. In a separate bowl, combine the flour, cocoa and salt. Gradually add to the creamed mixture until well blended.

Preheat oven to 350°F. Form the dough into 1¼-inch balls. Place onto ungreased baking sheets about 2 inches apart. Make an indentation in the center of each ball with your finger. Bake for 6 minutes. Rotate the pans* and bake for 5–6 minutes more. Transfer cookies to a wire rack or other cool surface as soon as possible; let cool.

For Filling In a small saucepan, combine the evaporated milk, sugar, egg yolk and butter. Cook, stirring constantly, for 5–7 minutes, or until mixture is slightly thick and gold in color (mixture will thicken as it cools). Remove from heat and stir in the vanilla, pecans and coconut. Let cool for 15 minutes. Spoon 1 heaping teaspoon or so in the indentation in each cookie.

For Topping In a small saucepan, combine the chocolate chips, water and butter. Heat over low heat until melted and smooth. Stir in the powdered sugar until smooth. Drizzle chocolate topping over each cookie. Let cool.

* Rotate the pans refers to turning the pans 180° (half a turn) to insure even browning.

MONSTER COOKIES

36 Cookies

- 6 tablespoons butter or margarine, softened
- 2/3 cup packed brown sugar
- 2/3 cup sugar
- 2 eggs
- 4 teaspoons vanilla
- 1 cup creamy peanut butter
- 1 1/4 teaspoons baking soda
- 3 cups quick oats
- 6 tablespoons semisweet chocolate chips
- 2/3 cup chopped walnuts (optional)
- 6 tablespoons M & M candies

This recipe has been in the Cottey files for many years, and it never loses its appeal. No flour is required for this cookie. It is soft, chewy and filled with goodies.

In a mixing bowl, cream the butter and sugars. Add the eggs, vanilla and peanut butter; beat for 1–2 minutes. Add the baking soda and oats; mix well. Stir in the chips, nuts and candies. Chill dough for easier handling (dough can be used right away, if desired).

Preheat oven to 350°F. Portion dough into 1½-inch balls. Place 2 inches apart onto greased baking sheets. Bake for 6 minutes. Rotate the pans* and bake for 5–7 minutes more. Cool 1–2 minutes, then transfer cookies to a wire rack or other cool surface.

* Rotate the pans refers to turning the pans 180° (half a turn) to insure even browning.

PEANUT BUTTER COOKIES WITH REESE'S CUPS

30 Cookies

 5 (1.5-ounce) packages Reese's
   peanut butter cups candy, diced

 ½ cup sugar
 ½ cup packed brown sugar
 ½ cup creamy peanut butter
 ½ cup vegetable shortening
 1 egg
 1 teaspoon vanilla
1 ¼ cups all-purpose flour
 1 teaspoon baking soda
 ¼ teaspoon salt

Peanut butter cups candy, diced, are superior to using the Reese's Pieces. A little more work, but the diced pieces keep their shape better after baking.

Place on a baking sheet and freeze the diced peanut butter cups for 20 minutes, or until very cold and firm.

In a mixing bowl, beat the sugars, peanut butter and shortening for 2 minutes. Stir in the egg and vanilla; beat briefly to blend. In a separate bowl, combine the flour, baking soda and salt. Gradually add to the creamed mixture. Stir in the diced peanut butter cups.

Preheat oven to 350°F. Portion the dough into 1½-inch balls onto greased baking sheets. Flatten each with a fork in 2 directions to make a cross pattern. Bake for 5 minutes. Rotate the pans* and bake for 5 minutes more. Cool cookies 3–4 minutes, then transfer to a wire rack or other cool surface.

* Rotate the pans refers to turning the pans 180° (half a turn) to insure even browning.

OATMEAL CREME PIES

24 Cookies

Cookies

- 1 cup butter or margarine, softened
- ¾ cup packed brown sugar
- ½ cup sugar
- 1 tablespoon molasses
- 1 teaspoon vanilla
- 2 eggs
- 1½ cups all-purpose flour
- ½ teaspoon salt
- 1 teaspoon baking soda
- ⅛ teaspoon cinnamon
- 1½ cups quick oats

Creme Filling

- 2 teaspoons very hot water
- ¼ teaspoon salt
- 1 (7-ounce) jar marshmallow creme
- ½ cup shortening
- ⅓ cup powdered sugar
- ½ teaspoon vanilla

This is our homemade version of the convenience store favorite, the creme-filled oatmeal sandwich cookie.

For Cookies Preheat oven to 350°F. Place quick oats in a food processor and process using on/off turns just until oats are crumb-size; set aside. In a mixing bowl, cream together the butter, sugars, molasses, vanilla and eggs. In a separate bowl, combine the flour, salt, soda, cinnamon and oats. Gradually add the dry ingredients to the wet ingredients, while mixing.

Portion the dough into 1-inch balls onto greased baking sheets. Bake for 5 minutes. Rotate the pans* and bake for 3–4 minutes more, or until the cookies are just starting to darken around the edges. After 1½–2 minutes, transfer the cookies to a wire rack or other cool surface to cool completely. Cookies should be soft and chewy when cooled.

For Filling In a small bowl, dissolve the salt in the hot water; set aside to cool. Combine the marshmallow creme, shortening, powdered sugar and vanilla in a medium bowl; mix on low speed for a few seconds to combine. Mix in the salted water until combined, then mix on high speed until the filling is light and fluffy.

Assemble Cookies Spread filling on the flat side of half of the cookies. Top with the remaining cookies, flat-side down, to make sandwiches.

* Rotate the pans refers to turning the pans 180° (half a turn) to insure even browning.

PECAN SANDIES

30 Cookies

1 cup (2 sticks) butter or margarine, softened
½ cup powdered sugar
1 tablespoon water
2 teaspoons vanilla
2 cups all-purpose flour
1 cup + 2 tablespoons chopped pecans, more if needed

powdered sugar, as needed

Place chopped pecans in a food processor. Process using on/off turns just until the pecans are the size of coarse bread crumbs. Sift to remove the fine powder. Process more pecans, if needed, to make 1 cup of crumbs. Set aside.

In a mixing bowl, cream the butter and sugar. Add the water and vanilla; mix well. Gradually add the flour, while mixing, then stir in the pecan crumbs. Mix until combined.

Preheat oven to 350°F. Portion dough into 1-inch balls and place onto ungreased baking sheets. Flatten balls with fingers. Bake for 7 minutes. Rotate the pans* and bake for 7–8 minutes more. Within 1–2 minutes, transfer cookies to a wire rack or other cool surface. Let cool completely, then dust with powdered sugar.

* Rotate the pans refers to turning the pans 180° (half a turn) to insure even browning.

CHOCOLATE PEANUT BUTTER CHIP COOKIES

24 Cookies

- 1 cup all-purpose flour
- 6 tablespoons unsweetened baking cocoa
- ½ teaspoon baking soda
- ¼ teaspoon salt
- ½ cup + 2 tablespoons butter or margarine
- 1 cup sugar
- 1 egg
- 1 teaspoon vanilla
- 1 cup peanut butter chips

Preheat oven to 350°F. In a small bowl, combine the flour, cocoa, baking soda and salt; set aside.

In a mixing bowl, cream the butter and sugar until light and fluffy. Add the egg and vanilla; mix well. Gradually add the flour mixture, while beating, until combined. Stir in chips. Chill the dough for 15–20 minutes for easier handling.

Portion the dough into 1½-inch balls and place onto ungreased baking sheets. Bake for 6 minutes. Rotate the pans* and bake for 5 minutes more. Cool slightly, then transfer cookies to a wire rack or other cool surface.

* Rotate the pans refers to turning the pans 180° (half a turn) to insure even browning.

S'MORES COOKIES

24 Cookies

Cookie

  1 cup powdered sugar
  1 cup (2 sticks) butter, softened
  2 teaspoons vanilla
1 ¼ cups all-purpose flour
  1 cup finely ground graham
     cracker crumbs
  ½ teaspoon salt

 72 miniature marshmallows

Icing

  ¼ cup milk
  3 tablespoons unsweetened
     baking cocoa
  ¼ cup butter
  2 cups powdered sugar

We developed this recipe through trial and error. It is intended to be reminiscent of the campfire favorite. Much like a shortbread, this uses no egg in the dough.

For Cookies Preheat oven to 350°F. In a medium bowl, combine the graham cracker crumbs, flour and salt; set aside.

In a mixing bowl, cream the butter and sugar on low speed for 10 seconds, then increase the speed and beat until light and fluffy. Stir in vanilla, then gradually add the flour mixture, while beating.

Portion dough into 1½-inch balls onto ungreased baking sheets. Push dough flat with fingers. Press 3 marshmallows onto the center. Bake for 6 minutes. Rotate the pans* and bake for 6 minutes more. Let cool on the baking sheets.

For Icing Meanwhile, in a small saucepan, combine the milk, butter and cocoa. Bring to a boil, then lower heat and gradually stir in the powdered sugar until a spreading consistency is achieved (it will thicken as it cools). Spread or drizzle warm icing over the center of each cookie to cover the marshmallows. Let cool completely. Store cookies between layers of waxed paper in an airtight container.

* Rotate the pans refers to turning the pans 180° (half a turn) to insure even browning.

SNOWY CHOCOLATE COOKIES

30 Cookies

2 cups all-purpose flour
⅓ cup unsweetened baking cocoa
½ teaspoon baking powder
½ teaspoon salt
1 cup (2 sticks) butter, softened
½ cup sugar
1 large egg
1 teaspoon vanilla
¾ cup semisweet chocolate chips

½ cup powdered sugar,
or more if needed

In a medium bowl, whisk together the flour, cocoa, baking powder and salt until combined; set aside.

In a mixing bowl, cream the butter and sugar until light and fluffy. Add the egg and vanilla; mix well. Gradually add the flour mixture, while mixing. Stir in the chocolate chips. Cover and chill dough for 15–20 minutes to ease handling.

Preheat oven to 350°F. Place the powdered sugar in a medium bowl. Portion dough into 1½-inch balls and roll in powdered sugar. Place onto greased baking sheets about 2 inches apart. Flatten balls with fingers. Bake for 6 minutes. Rotate the pans* and bake for 5 minutes more. Transfer cookies to a wire rack or other cool surface as soon as possible. Let cool completely. Sprinkle tops with powdered sugar. Store between layers of waxed paper in an airtight container.

* Rotate the pans refers to turning the pans 180° (half a turn) to insure even browning.

GINGERBREAD COOKIES WITH ORANGE GLAZE

30 Cookies

Cookies

- ½ cup buttermilk
- 1 teaspoon baking soda
- 6 tablespoons vegetable oil
- ½ cup sugar
- ½ cup molasses
- 1 large egg
- 2¼ cups all-purpose flour
- ½ teaspoon salt
- 1 teaspoon ground cinnamon
- ½ teaspoon ground ginger
- ½ teaspoon ground nutmeg
- ¼ teaspoon ground allspice
- ¼ teaspoon ground cloves

Glaze

- 1 cup powdered sugar
- 1½ teaspoons butter, softened
- 1 teaspoon orange zest
- 2 tablespoons orange juice
- ¼ teaspoon vanilla
- pinch salt

This is an ideal cookie to serve when you want to get your friends and family in the holiday mood.

For Cookies In a small bowl, combine the buttermilk and baking soda and set aside (it will foam up). In a mixing bowl, add the oil, sugar, molasses and egg. Beat for 1 minute, or until well mixed. Add the buttermilk mixture and mix well. In a separate bowl, combine the flour, salt and all the spices. Gradually add the flour mixture to the molasses mixture, while beating. This is more of a batter than a dough. Let stand for 15 minutes.

Preheat oven to 350°F. Drop batter by heaping tablespoons onto greased baking sheets. Bake for 5 minutes. Rotate the pans* and bake for 4 minutes more. These cookies should be very soft.

For Glaze While cookies are baking, combine the glaze ingredients in a medium bowl and beat until blended and smooth.

Transfer cookies to a wire rack or other cool surface. Let cool slightly then frost each cookie with ½ teaspoon of glaze. Cool completely to allow glaze to harden.

---

* Rotate the pans refers to turning the pans 180° (half a turn) to insure even browning.

WALNUT FROSTIES

24–30 Cookies

Cookies

½ cup (1 stick) butter or margarine, softened
1 cup packed brown sugar
1 large egg
1 ½ teaspoons vanilla
2 cups all-purpose flour
½ teaspoon baking soda
¼ teaspoon salt

Topping

1 cup chopped walnuts
⅓ cup packed brown sugar
¼ cup sour cream

For Cookies In a mixing bowl, combine the butter, sugar, egg and vanilla. Beat until light and fluffy. In a separate bowl, whisk together the flour, baking soda and salt. Gradually add the flour mixture to the butter mixture until combined.

Preheat oven to 350°F. Portion dough into 1¼-inch balls and place onto ungreased baking sheets. Make an indentation in the center of each ball with your finger.

For Topping In a medium bowl, combine the walnuts, sugar and sour cream. Spoon 2 teaspoons of topping in the indentation in each cookie.

Bake for 5 minutes. Rotate the pans* and bake for 5 minutes more. Within 1–2 minutes, transfer cookies to a wire rack or other cool surface.

* Rotate the pans refers to turning the pans 180° (half a turn) to insure even browning.

STRAWBERRY CHEESECAKE COOKIES

24 Cookies

Cookies

- ¾ cup butter, softened
- 1 (3-ounce) package cream cheese, softened
- ½ cup sugar
- 1½ teaspoons vanilla
- 1½ cups all-purpose flour

Frosting

- 4 ounces cream cheese, softened
- 2 tablespoons powdered sugar
- 2 tablespoons strawberry preserves red food coloring (optional)

- 6–8 fresh strawberries, sliced
- ¼ cup powdered sugar (optional)

These are tasty and very festive looking. We like to serve them as part of an assorted cookie platter.

For Cookies In a mixing bowl, combine the butter, cream cheese and sugar. Beat until light and fluffy. Stir in the vanilla, then gradually add the flour, while mixing, until combined and dough is smooth. Chill dough for 30 minutes.

Preheat oven to 375°F. Portion dough into 1-inch balls and place onto ungreased baking sheets. Flatten balls with fingers. Bake cookies for 6 minutes. Rotate the pans* and bake for 4–5 minutes more. Let cool for 1 minute, then transfer to a wire rack or other cool surface. Let cool completely.

For Frosting Beat together the cream cheese, sugar and preserves until smooth. Add the red food color (if using), 1 drop at a time, until a light pink color is reached. Frost the cookies, then sprinkle with powdered sugar (if using) to make the edges look festive. Top each with 1–2 slices of strawberry.

* Rotate the pans refers to turning the pans 180° (half a turn) to insure even browning.

BROWNIE BONBONS

35 Bars

Brownie

- 4 (1-ounce) squares unsweetened baking chocolate
- ¾ cup (1 ½ sticks) butter or margarine
- 2 cups sugar
- 4 eggs
- 1 teaspoon vanilla
- 1 cup all-purpose flour

Fudge Filling

- 1 (3-ounce) package cream cheese, softened
- 1 teaspoon vanilla
- ¼ cup light corn syrup
- 3 (1-ounce) squares unsweetened baking chocolate, melted and cooled
- 1 cup powdered sugar

- 35 Maraschino cherries, drained

You can top the bonbons with strawberry slices, raspberries or chopped nuts instead of the Maraschino cherries, if preferred. These are rich and chocolatey, which is why we cut them into small squares. It is a great finger-food dessert for parties.

For Brownies Preheat oven to 350°F. Melt the chocolate and butter in a heavy saucepan (or melt in the microwave), stirring frequently, until completely melted. Pour into a mixing bowl and stir in the sugar, eggs and vanilla until blended. Gradually add the flour, while mixing, until combined. Spread batter into a greased 9-by-13-inch pan. Bake for 25 minutes, or until tester inserted in center comes out with some fudgy crumbs (better to slightly undercook than overcook). Let cool for 30 minutes, then cut 5 rows by 7 rows to get 35 small bars. While still warm, make ½-inch indentations in the center of each square. Let cool completely.

For Fudge Filling Beat the cream cheese and vanilla until smooth. Slowly pour in the corn syrup, beating until blended. Stir in the melted chocolate. Gradually add the powdered sugar, while beating, until mixture is blended and smooth.

Using 2 spoons, or a pastry bag with a star tip, spoon or pipe ½ teaspoon of the filling in the indentations of each brownie. Press a cherry on top.

BROWNIE CHEESECAKE BARS

24 Bars

Brownie

1 (18.25-ounce) package devil's food
   chocolate cake mix
½ cup flaked coconut
⅓ cup butter or margarine, softened
1 large egg

Filling

2 (8-ounce) packages cream cheese,
   softened
2 large eggs
¾ cup sugar
2 teaspoons vanilla

Topping

2 cups (16 ounces) sour cream
¼ cup sugar
1 tablespoon vanilla

For Brownie Preheat oven to 350°F. In a mixing bowl, combine the cake mix, coconut, butter and egg. Mix on low speed until mixture is crumbly. Press into an ungreased 9-by-13-inch pan.

For Filling Beat the cream cheese, eggs, sugar and vanilla until light and fluffy. Spread evenly over the brownie mixture. Bake for 25 minutes. Let cool for 15 minutes.

For Topping Mix the sour cream, sugar and vanilla until smooth. Spread over the filling. Refrigerate for 1–2 hours, or until chilled. Cut into bars.

BROWNIE FUDGE BARS

24 Bars

Brownies

   4 (1-ounce) squares unsweetened
      baking chocolate
   1 cup (2 sticks) butter or margarine
   2 cups sugar
   4 eggs
   1 cup all-purpose flour
   2 teaspoons vanilla

Fudge Topping

   1 cup sugar
   4 teaspoons butter or margarine
  ³⁄₄ cup evaporated milk
  ½ cup marshmallow creme
  ½ cup semisweet chocolate chips
  ½ cup milk chocolate chips
  ½ teaspoon vanilla

For Brownies Melt the chocolate and butter in a heavy saucepan (or melt in the microwave), stirring frequently, until completely melted; cool.

Preheat oven to 350°F. In a mixing bowl, beat the sugar and eggs until light and fluffy. Gradually mix in the cooled chocolate mixture. Stir in the flour and vanilla. Spread batter evenly into a greased 9-by-13-inch pan. Bake for 25–30 minutes, or until just set.

For Fudge Topping In a large saucepan, combine the sugar, butter and evaporated milk. Bring to a boil and continue boiling for 5 minutes, stirring constantly. Remove from heat and immediately add the marshmallow creme, chips and vanilla, stirring until chocolate is melted and mixture is smooth. Keep warm.

Let the brownies cool for 20 minutes or so, then pour the warm topping over and spread evenly. Chill until firm; cut into bars.

CHOCOLATE CRUMB BARS

30 Bars

  1 cup (2 sticks) butter or margarine,
     softened
1 ¾ cups all-purpose flour
  ½ cup sugar
  ¼ teaspoon salt
  2 cups (12 ounces) semisweet
     chocolate chips, divided
  1 (14-ounce) can sweetened
     condensed milk
  1 teaspoon vanilla

Preheat oven to 350°F. Grease a 9-by-13-inch pan.

In a mixing bowl, add the butter, flour, sugar and salt. Mix until crumbly. With floured fingers, press 2 cups of crumb mixture onto the bottom of the prepared pan, reserving remaining crumbs. Bake for 12–14 minutes, or until edges are golden brown.

In a small, heavy-bottomed saucepan, combine 1 cup of chips and the sweetened condensed milk. Warm over low heat, stirring until chocolate is melted and mixture is smooth. Stir in the vanilla. Spread over hot crust.

Stir remaining chips into the reserved crumb mixture. Sprinkle evenly over the chocolate filling. Bake for 25 minutes, or until golden brown and set. Let cool for 30 minutes before cutting into bars.

CHOCOLATE CARAMEL BROWNIES

24 Bars

Caramel Sauce

  5 tablespoons sugar

  1 tablespoon + 1 teaspoon water

  ¼ cup heavy whipping cream

  2 tablespoons butter

  ¼ teaspoon vanilla

Brownies

  1 (18.25-ounce) package devil's food cake mix

  ⅔ cup evaporated milk

  ½ cup (1 stick) butter, melted

  2 cups (12 ounces) semisweet chocolate chips

For Caramel Sauce Heat the sugar and water in a heavy, medium saucepan over low heat. Stir until the sugar dissolves. Increase heat and boil, without stirring, until mixture is a rich caramel color, occasionally swirling and washing down sides of pan with a brush dipped into cold water. This process will take 8–9 minutes. Remove from heat and add the cream (mixture will bubble up); stir until smooth. Mix in butter. Cool slightly; mix in vanilla. Keep warm.

For Brownies Preheat oven to 350°F. Combine the cake mix, evaporated milk and melted butter in a large bowl, stirring until blended. Spread 2 cups of brownie mixture into an ungreased 9-by-13-inch pan. Bake for 10 minutes. Remove from oven and sprinkle the chocolate chips evenly over the brownies. Drizzle the caramel sauce over the top, then drop the remaining brownie batter by heaping tablespoons over the caramel. With a spatula, gently spread out the mounds of batter to cover more area.

Bake for 18–20 minutes (it is better to underbake than overbake). Cool on a wire rack or other cool surface. When completely cool, cut into bars.

CRISPY CHOCOLATE BROWNIES

24 Bars

Brownies

- 1 cup (2 sticks) butter or margarine, softened
- 2 cups sugar
- 4 eggs
- 2 teaspoons vanilla
- 1 cup all-purpose flour
- 6 tablespoons unsweetened baking cocoa
- ½ teaspoon salt

Filling

- 1 (7-ounce) jar marshmallow creme

Topping

- 1 cup creamy peanut butter
- 2 cups (12 ounces) semisweet chocolate chips
- 3 cups crisp rice cereal

For Brownies Preheat oven to 350°F. In a mixing bowl, cream the butter and sugar until light and fluffy. Add the eggs and vanilla; mix until smooth. In a separate bowl, combine the flour, cocoa and salt. Gradually add to the egg mixture, while mixing. Spread batter into a greased 9-by-13-inch pan. Bake for 25–30 minutes, or until a tester inserted in center comes out clean.

For Filling Spread the marshmallow creme evenly over the hot brownies.

For Topping In a large saucepan, melt the peanut butter and chocolate chips over low heat, stirring constantly. Remove from heat and add the cereal. Stir well to coat cereal with the chocolate mixture. Spread over the marshmallow layer. Chill before cutting into bars. Store these brownies in the refrigerator, or in a cool place.

CHOCOLATE OREO BROWNIES

24 Bars

2 cups sugar

¾ cup unsweetened baking cocoa

½ teaspoon baking soda

¼ teaspoon salt

⅔ cup butter or margarine, melted

½ cup hot water

2 eggs

1 teaspoon vanilla

1 ⅓ cups all-purpose flour

2 cups (12 ounces) semisweet chocolate chips

2 cups chopped Oreo cookies

1 teaspoon powdered sugar

Chop the cookies into chunks with a knife instead of using a food processor, so that you have visible chunks on top of the brownies instead of crumbs.

In a large bowl, combine the sugar, cocoa, baking soda, salt, butter and hot water; stir well. Stir in the eggs and vanilla. Gradually add the flour, while mixing, until batter is smooth. Stir in the chocolate chips.

Preheat oven to 350°F. Spread batter into a greased 9-by-13-inch pan. Sprinkle the cookies evenly over the top, gently pressing into the batter. Bake for 35–40 minutes. When cool, dust lightly with powdered sugar.

CHOCOLATE STREUSEL BARS

24 Bars

1 ³/₄ cups all-purpose flour
1 ¹/₂ cups powdered sugar
  ¹/₂ cup unsweetened baking cocoa
   1 cup (2 sticks) butter or margarine,
       cold, cut into pieces
   1 (8-ounce) package cream cheese,
       softened
   1 (14-ounce) can sweetened
       condensed milk
   1 large egg
   2 teaspoons vanilla

Preheat oven to 350°F. In a mixing bowl, combine the flour, sugar and cocoa. Cut in butter, mixing until crumbly (mixture will be dry). Reserve 2 cups of crumb mixture, and press the remainder firmly on the bottom of a greased 9-by-13-inch pan. Bake for 16–18 minutes.

In a mixing bowl, beat the cream cheese until light and fluffy. Gradually beat in the sweetened condensed milk until smooth. Add the egg and vanilla; mix well. Pour over the baked crust. Sprinkle the reserved crumb mixture evenly over the cheese mixture. Bake for 25–28 minutes, or until tester inserted in center comes out clean. Cool, then chill before cutting into bars. Store in the refrigerator or in a cool place, covered, but let soften to room temperature before serving.

HONEY GRAHAM S'MORES BARS

24 Bars

  6 tablespoons butter or margarine
  1 (10.5-ounce) bag miniature
    marshmallows
1 ¼ cups semisweet chocolate chips
  2 teaspoons vanilla
  6 cups honey graham squares cereal

Melt the butter in a large (4-quart) saucepan over medium heat. Add the marshmallows and heat until almost melted, stirring constantly. Stir in the chocolate chips, and keep stirring until the mixture is melted and smooth. Remove from heat and stir in the vanilla.

Place the cereal in a very large bowl. Lightly grease a 9-by-13-inch pan. Grease the bottom of a spatula or other flat utensil. Pour the chocolate mixture over the cereal and fold together until the cereal is coated as evenly as possible (mixture will be thick). Using the greased spatula, press the cereal mixture into the prepared pan. Cut into bars while still warm. Cool at room temperature for about 1 hour before serving.

MULTILAYER BARS

24 Bars

½ cup butter or margarine, melted
1 ½ cups graham cracker crumbs
1 cup flaked coconut
1 ¼ cups miniature marshmallows
1 cup semisweet chocolate chips
1 cup butterscotch-flavored chips
1 teaspoon vanilla
1 (14-ounce) can sweetened condensed milk

These are decadent and loved by many.

Combine the butter and graham cracker crumbs in a bowl, stirring well to coat crumbs evenly. Pat crumb mixture into the bottom of a lightly-greased 9-by-13-inch baking pan.

Preheat oven to 350°F. Top crust evenly with the following, 1 layer at a time: coconut, marshmallows, chocolate chips and butterscotch chips.

Stir the vanilla into the condensed milk. Pour evenly over the chips. Bake for 20 minutes, or until top is a deep golden brown. Cool completely, then cut into bars.

LEMON BARS

24 Bars

Crust

1 cup (2 sticks) butter, softened
1 cup packed brown sugar
1 large egg yolk
1 teaspoon vanilla
2 cups all-purpose flour
¼ teaspoon salt

Topping

1 (8-ounce) package cream cheese, softened
1 ¼ cups sugar
4 eggs
2 teaspoons grated lemon zest
½ cup fresh lemon juice
⅓ cup all-purpose flour
1 ½ teaspoons baking powder

1 tablespoon powdered sugar

These are creamier than the typical lemon bars because of the addition of cream cheese in the topping.

Preheat oven to 350°F.

For Crust In a mixing bowl, beat the butter and sugar until light and fluffy. Add the egg yolk and vanilla; mix well. Combine the flour and salt and gradually add to the butter mixture, while mixing. Press into a greased 9-by-13-inch baking pan. Bake for 22–23 minutes, or until crust is a deep golden brown.

For Topping Beat the cream cheese and sugar until light and fluffy. Stir in the eggs, zest, lemon juice, flour and baking powder. Pour over the hot crust. Grease the bottom side of a piece of aluminum foil. Cover the pan with the foil, greased-side down, and bake for 25 minutes. Uncover and bake for 10 minutes more, or until springy when touched. Let cool completely, then dust with powdered sugar.

PECAN PIE BARS

24 Bars

  2 cups all-purpose flour

½ cup powdered sugar

  1 cup (2 sticks) butter or margarine, cold, cut into pieces

  1 (14-ounce) can sweetened condensed milk

  1 large egg

  1 teaspoon vanilla

  1 cup chocolate English toffee pieces

  1 cup chopped pecans

If you like pecan pie, you will like these bars. They have a buttery crust with a rich pecan topping. The toffee pieces make them unique and particularly tasty.

Preheat oven to 350°F. In a mixing bowl, combine the flour and sugar. Cut in butter pieces, mixing until crumbly. Press firmly on the bottom of a lightly-greased 9-by-13-inch baking pan. Bake for 22–24 minutes, or until golden brown.

Meanwhile, in a large bowl, stir together the condensed milk, egg and vanilla until smooth. Stir in the toffee pieces and pecans. Spread evenly over the hot crust. Bake for 20–22 minutes, or until golden brown. Cool, then cut into bars.

RASPBERRY OATMEAL BARS

24 Bars

1 (18.25-ounce) package moist yellow
   cake mix
2 1/2 cups quick-cooking oats
3/4 cup (1 1/2 sticks) butter or margarine,
   melted

1 cup raspberry or strawberry preserves
1 tablespoon water

**This recipe was given to us by a
former Cottey employee, Karen
Arnold. It is popular and provides
a nice change from the ever-present
chocolate brownie bars.**

Preheat oven to 350°F. Grease a 9-by-13-inch baking pan.

In a mixing bowl, combine the cake mix and oats. Add the melted butter and stir until crumbly. Measure half of the crumb mixture (about 2¾ cups), and press firmly on the bottom of the prepared pan. Combine the preserves and water, stirring until blended. Spread over the crumb mixture (warm it in the microwave if it is too stiff to spread). Sprinkle the remaining crumb mixture evenly over the preserves, patting firmly to make top even.

Bake for 20–24 minutes, or until top is light brown. Cool, then cut into bars.

CHOCOLATE HAZELNUT CRUNCH BARS

21 Small Bars

Bottom Layer

- 1 (7-ounce) milk chocolate candy bar, chopped
- ½ cup + 1 tablespoon Nutella* (chocolate hazelnut spread)
- 7 tablespoons vegetable oil
- 2 tablespoons heavy whipping cream
- 1½ cups butter cookies or vanilla wafers, chopped, sifted to remove fine crumbs

Top Layer

- 1¼ cups heavy whipping cream
- 3 (1.55-ounce) milk chocolate candy bars
- ¾ teaspoon unflavored gelatin
- 1 tablespoon water

Garnish

- 1 (1.55-ounce) milk chocolate candy bar, chilled, grated

After much trial and error, we settled on this version. It was served at the inaugural luncheon for incoming president, Dr. Judy Rogers. Surprisingly, it is now one of the easier recipes we prepare — a crunchy chocolate base with a chocolate mousse that works every time. No baking, just chill until set.

For Bottom Layer Grease an 8-by-8-inch pan. Melt the chocolate in the microwave, or over a double boiler; stir until smooth. Beat the Nutella with the oil until blended, then stir in the chocolate. Stir in the heavy cream, then the chopped cookies. Spread mixture evenly into pan. Chill until firm, about 30 minutes.

For Top Layer Break up the milk chocolate bars into pieces; melt in the microwave, or over a double boiler; stir until smooth, then let cool for a few minutes to lukewarm. Whip the cream to soft peaks. Fold the melted chocolate into the whipped cream until combined. Dissolve the gelatin in the water, then immediately stir into the chocolate mixture. Spread mixture evenly over chilled bottom layer. Sprinkle the grated chocolate over the top. Cover with plastic wrap; chill until firm, at least 2 hours or overnight.

* Nutella is available in most supermarkets and is packaged in 13-ounce jars.

SNICKERS BARS

20 Bars

Bottom Layer

1 (18.25-ounce) package German chocolate cake mix

1 large egg

½ cup (1 stick) margarine, melted

1 tablespoon water

Top Layer

4 (2.07-ounce) Snickers candy bars

1 (8-ounce) package cream cheese, softened

2 large eggs

½ cup powdered sugar

You will get better results by baking these in a metal pan rather than a glass (Pyrex) one. These cook on a lower temperature for a longer time than most brownie bars. They are loved by young and old for their chewy edges and soft, decadent centers.

In a mixing bowl, combine the cake mix, egg, margarine and water, stirring until smooth. Butter and flour a 9-by-13-inch metal baking pan. Spread mixture evenly into the pan.

Melt the candy bars in the microwave for about 2 minutes, or until just melted. Let cool slightly, then add to a mixing bowl. Add the softened cream cheese, eggs and powdered sugar; stir until smooth. Pour mixture over the bottom layer, spreading to the edges.

Preheat oven to 300°F. Bake for 45 minutes. Cover pan with foil; turn off the oven and partially open the oven door and let the pan sit in the oven for 10 minutes more. Remove from the oven and, while still covered with foil, let cool completely. Cut into bars.

CHOCOLATE BUTTERCRUNCH PIE

1 (9-Inch) Pie

Crust

- ¾ cup all-purpose flour
- ¼ cup packed brown sugar
- ¼ teaspoon salt
- 6 tablespoons butter, cold, cut into pieces
- ½ cup chopped walnuts
- 1 (1.55-ounce) milk chocolate candy bar, finely chopped

Filling

- 1 (3.9-ounce) package instant chocolate pudding and pie filling
- 1 (3.4-ounce) package instant vanilla pudding and pie filling
- 1 (14-ounce) can sweetened condensed milk
- 1¼ cups cold milk
- ¼ cup butter, melted, cooled
- 2 tablespoons unsweetened baking cocoa
- 1 teaspoon vanilla

Topping

- 1 cup whipped topping
- 1 (1.55-ounce) milk chocolate candy bar, cut into chocolate curls or grated

The crust makes this pie unique, with its crunchy texture from toasted nuts and chocolate bits.

For Crust Preheat oven to 350°F. Place the walnuts in a baking pan and bake for 4–5 minutes until golden brown; cool to lukewarm. Combine the flour, sugar and salt in a food processor. Add the butter; cut in, using on/off turns, until mixture resembles coarse meal. Add the nuts and chocolate; blend, using on/off turns, until nuts are finely chopped. Press onto bottom and up sides of a lightly-greased 9-inch pie pan. Bake crust until golden brown, about 20 minutes. Cool completely.

For Filling In a large bowl, combine all filling ingredients. Beat for 2 minutes, then pour into the pie crust, spreading evenly. Refrigerate until firm, about 1 hour.

For Topping Once the filling is firm, spread the whipped topping to cover. Sprinkle top with the chocolate curls or grated chocolate. Keep chilled until ready to serve.

COOKIES AND CREAM PIE

12 Servings

Crust

- 3 cups Oreo cookies, processed to crumbs (or crushed)
- 4 tablespoons butter, melted

Filling

- 2 (8-ounce) packages cream cheese, softened
- 1 (3.4-ounce) package instant vanilla pudding and pie filling
- 2 cups milk
- 4 cups whipped topping
- 1 cup Oreo cookies, chopped into $\frac{1}{2}$-inch pieces

Topping

- $\frac{3}{4}$ cup whipped topping
- 6 Oreo cookies, halved

You will need a 1-pound, 2-ounce package of Oreo cookies for this recipe. In addition, a 9-inch springform pan is used to form this deep and decadent pie.

For Crust Preheat oven to 350°F. Mix the cookie crumbs and melted butter together in a bowl. Press onto bottom of a 9-inch springform pan. Bake about 8 minutes; let cool.

For Filling In a large bowl, beat the cream cheese and pudding mix until light and fluffy; gradually beat in the milk until smooth. Fold in the whipped topping until blended, then fold in the cookie pieces. Pour mixture into the cooled crust, smoothing the top with a spatula. Chill for 3 or more hours to allow the filling to set. Remove the springform sides, then cut the pie into 12 servings.

For Topping Place a dollop of whipped topping on the wide end of each serving of pie, then place a halved cookie over the topping, flat-side down. Keep chilled until ready to serve.

LEMON CHIFFON PIE

1 (9-Inch) Pie

1 (9-inch) graham cracker pie crust

Filling

1 (14-ounce) can sweetened
condensed milk (regular or fat-free)

½ cup freshly squeezed lemon juice
(about 3 lemons)

1 (8-ounce) container whipped topping
(regular or light)

Topping (optional)

½ cup whipped topping

5–6 strawberries, sliced or quartered

This creamy pie has a light lemony
flavor—great for those who like a
lemon pie, but prefer just a hint of
lemon. It can be a low-fat dessert
by using fat-free condensed milk
and light whipped topping. If you
are a whipped topping fan, then
buy a 12-ounce container to
have for the optional garnish.

Whisk together the condensed milk and lemon juice until smooth and blended. Fold in the whipped topping, then pour into the crust. Chill for at least 2 hours before serving. Garnish each serving with a dollop of whipped topping and a slice of strawberry, if desired.

DUTCH APPLE BUTTERSCOTCH PIE

1 (9-Inch) Pie

- 1 (9-inch) pie crust
- 4 cups Gala or Fuji apples, peeled, sliced thin
- 1 cup all-purpose flour, divided
- ¼ cup sugar
- ½ teaspoon ground cinnamon
- 1⅔ cups butterscotch chips, divided
- ½ cup heavy whipping cream
- 2 tablespoons butter or margarine

This is an amazing flavor combination—apples and butterscotch! The crumb topping seals in the moist filling and the baked crust retains its crispness.

Preheat oven to 350°F. Bake the pie crust for 10 minutes, or until golden brown.

In a large bowl, toss the apples, ¼ cup flour, sugar and cinnamon; spread into the pie crust. Combine ⅔ cup of butterscotch chips and the whipping cream; microwave until melted and smooth when stirred, 1–1½ minutes. Pour mixture over the apples.

Melt remaining 1 cup chips and the butter in the microwave for 1–1½ minutes, or until smooth when stirred. Place in a large bowl and add remaining ¾ cup flour. Stir with a fork or pastry blender until the mixture is crumbly. Keep mixing until small crumbs are formed. Sprinkle crumbs over top of pie to cover completely, patting down lightly.

Place pie on a baking sheet (to catch juices during baking). Bake for 35 minutes, uncovered, then cover with foil and bake for 15 minutes more, or until apples are tender when pierced. Let cool at room temperature for at least 1 hour, or until pie is lukewarm.

PEANUT BUTTER CUP PIE

1 (9-Inch) Pie

1 (9-inch) graham cracker pie crust

Filling

½ cup creamy peanut butter

½ cup light corn syrup

¼ cup packed brown sugar

1 tablespoon + 1 ½ teaspoons
all-purpose flour

¼ teaspoon salt

3 large eggs

Glaze

3 tablespoons butter

3 tablespoons light corn syrup

3 (1.55-ounce) milk chocolate
candy bars, broken into pieces

Topping

1 ½ cups whipped topping

2 (1.5-ounce) packages peanut butter
cups candy, chopped

Preheat oven to 350°F.

For Filling In a mixing bowl, stir together the peanut butter, corn syrup, brown sugar, flour and salt until smooth. Add eggs, 1 at a time, stirring until blended. Pour mixture into the crust.

Place pie on a baking sheet (to catch juices during baking). Bake for 25 minutes. Cool completely on a wire rack or other cool surface.

For Glaze In a small saucepan, melt the butter and corn syrup. Stir in the chocolate and melt together over low heat until mixture is smooth. Spread glaze evenly over the cooled pie. Chill 30 minutes to set.

Cover the pie with whipped topping and sprinkle with the peanut butter cups.

STRAWBERRIES AND CREAM PIE

1 (9-Inch) Pie

   1 (9-inch) pie crust

Creamy Layer

   1 (8-ounce) package cream cheese,
      softened

   2 tablespoons powdered sugar

  ½ teaspoon vanilla

Strawberry Filling

   1 cup sugar

   1 tablespoon + 1 teaspoon cornstarch

   1 cup water

   2 tablespoons + ¾ teaspoon
      lemon juice

   1 (3-ounce) package strawberry
      flavored gelatin

   1 (1-pound) package fresh strawberries,
      cleaned, hulled, cut into thick slices

Preheat oven to 350°F. Prick the pie crust with a fork, then bake for 10–12 minutes, or until light golden; cool.

For Creamy Layer Beat together the cream cheese, sugar and vanilla; spread over the crust. Chill.

For Strawberry Filling In a medium saucepan, combine the sugar, cornstarch, water and lemon juice. Bring to a boil over high heat. Reduce heat; cook and stir for 5 minutes, until slightly thickened and clear. Remove from heat and stir in gelatin. Cool to room temperature. Stir in strawberries and carefully pour into the pie crust (filling will be thin until it sets). Chill for at least 4 hours, or overnight.

TRIPLE CHOCOLATE PUDDING PIE WITH CAPPUCINO CREAM

12–16 Servings

Crust

- 3 cups chocolate sandwich creme cookies, processed to crumbs (or crushed)
- 4 tablespoons butter, melted

Filling

- 1¼ cups sugar
- ½ cup unsweetened baking cocoa
- ¼ cup cornstarch
- 3½ cups half-and-half
- 4 egg yolks
- 2 (1.55-ounce) milk chocolate candy bars, chopped
- 3 (1-ounce) squares unsweetened baking chocolate, chopped
- 2 tablespoons butter
- 1 teaspoon vanilla

Topping

- 4 cups whipped topping
- 2 tablespoons + 2 teaspoons unsweetened baking cocoa
- 4 teaspoons very strong coffee, cooled (espresso would be great)
- 1 teaspoon vanilla

Garnish

- 1 (1.55-ounce) milk chocolate candy bar, grated

For Crust Preheat oven to 350°F. Combine crumbs and melted butter. Press onto the bottom and up sides of a 9-inch springform pan. Bake for about 8 minutes; cool.

For Filling In a large saucepan, whisk the sugar, cocoa and cornstarch. Gradually whisk in 1 cup of the half-and-half until smooth. Whisk in remaining 2½ cups half-and-half and the egg yolks. Cook over medium-high heat, whisking constantly, until mixture thickens and boils; continue whisking over heat for 1 minute. Remove from heat and add both chocolates and the butter. Whisk until melted and smooth, then mix in the vanilla. Pour filling into the crust. Press plastic wrap directly onto filling and chill until filling sets, at least 6 hours or overnight.

For Topping and Garnish Whisk together all topping ingredients. Spread over the chilled filling. Sprinkle with the grated chocolate; chill until serving. Remove sides of springform pan and cut into 12–16 pieces, as desired

Consider making this 1 day ahead to allow the filling to set. This is impressive to look at and a definite treat for chocolate lovers. A 9-inch springform pan is required for this recipe.

FRUIT PIZZA

10–12 Servings

1 (1-pound) package refrigerated
   sugar cookie dough

4 ounces cream cheese, softened
3 tablespoons powdered sugar
½ cup whipped topping
1–2 kiwi, sliced thin
1 banana, sliced
¾ cup Mandarin oranges, drained
½ cup red grapes, halved

Glaze

¼ cup + 1½ teaspoons orange juice
½ teaspoon lemon juice
2 tablespoons sugar
1½ teaspoons cornstarch

**You can use any combination of
fruit to decorate this sweet pizza.**

Preheat oven to 350°F. Pat cookie dough into a 10-inch round on a greased baking sheet. Bake for 10 minutes, or until golden brown; cool.

In a bowl, beat together the cream cheese and sugar until smooth. Fold in whipped topping; spread over crust. Arrange fruit decoratively on the top.

For Glaze In a small saucepan, heat the orange and lemon juice. Combine the sugar and cornstarch and stir into the juice mixture, whisking constantly, until boiling and thickened. Remove from heat and let cool to lukewarm. Brush a thin layer of glaze over the fruit. Chill until serving.

STRAWBERRY LIME MOUSSE PIE

1 (9-Inch) Pie

1 (9-inch) graham cracker pie crust

Filling

¼ cup fresh lime juice

½ teaspoon unflavored gelatin

¾ cup heavy whipping cream, divided

1 cup premium white (chocolate) morsels (or white chocolate bar, chopped)

1 teaspoon grated or minced lime zest

2 tablespoons sugar

2 tablespoons sour cream

Topping

3 cups fresh strawberries, sliced

3 tablespoons seedless strawberry jam

The creamy white chocolate and lime mousse filling is wonderful combined with the sliced berries. We often feature this dessert on our Sunday brunch menu.

For Filling Place the lime juice in a small bowl and sprinkle with the gelatin; let stand for 10 minutes to soften. In a medium saucepan, bring ¼ cup of the cream to a simmer. Reduce heat to low. Add white chocolate; stir until melted and smooth. Add gelatin mixture; stir to dissolve, then stir in the zest. Chill mixture about 40 minutes, stirring occasionally, until cold and beginning to thicken, but not set.

In a medium bowl, beat the sugar, sour cream and remaining cream to medium-stiff peaks. Fold the whipped cream mixture into the white chocolate mixture. Spoon filling into the crust. Chill until it sets, about 1½–2 hours. Can be made 1 day ahead to this point. Cover and refrigerate.

For Topping Decoratively arrange the strawberries over the filling. Heat the jam in the microwave or a small saucepan until hot. Stir well and break up any clumps. Brush or spread a thin layer of jam over the berries to form a glaze. Chill until serving time.

BLUE RIBBON CARROT CAKE

24 Servings

Cake

1 ½ cups all-purpose flour

1 ½ teaspoons baking soda

½ teaspoon salt

1 ½ teaspoons ground cinnamon

2 large eggs

½ cup + 1 tablespoon vegetable oil

½ cup + 1 tablespoon buttermilk

1 ½ cups sugar

1 ½ teaspoons vanilla

1 (8-ounce) can crushed pineapple, drained

1 ½ cups peeled, grated carrot

¾ cup flaked coconut

¾ cup chopped walnuts (optional)

Frosting

½ cup butter, softened

1 (8-ounce) package cream cheese, softened

1 teaspoon vanilla

2 cups powdered sugar

1 teaspoon grated orange zest

1 teaspoon fresh orange juice

The original recipe that we have used makes a 2-layer cake. This is a simplified version that we tend to serve more often. The cake is just as moist and the rich cream cheese frosting equally delicious.

For Cake Preheat oven to 350°F. Combine the flour, soda, salt and cinnamon; set aside. In a large mixing bowl, combine the eggs, oil, buttermilk, sugar and vanilla; beat until smooth. Gradually stir in the flour mixture. Stir in the pineapple, carrot, coconut and walnuts. Pour batter into a greased 9-by-13-inch pan.

Bake for 30 minutes, or until a tester inserted in center comes out clean. Let cool completely.

For Frosting In a medium bowl, combine the butter and cream cheese; beat until light and fluffy. Add the vanilla, powdered sugar, zest and juice; beat until smooth. Spread frosting evenly over cooled cake (there is enough to be generous with the frosting, so use as desired).

CARAMEL APPLE CAKE

16 Servings

Cake

   ¾ cup vegetable oil
   ¾ cup applesauce
1 ⅓ cups sugar
   ½ cup packed brown sugar
   3 eggs
   3 cups all-purpose flour
   2 teaspoons ground cinnamon
   ½ teaspoon ground nutmeg
   1 teaspoon baking soda
   ½ teaspoon salt
3 ½ cups apples, peeled, diced
   ¾ cup chopped walnuts (optional)
   2 teaspoons vanilla

Caramel Icing

   ½ cup packed brown sugar
   ⅓ cup half-and-half
   ¼ cup butter
      pinch salt
   1 cup powdered sugar

This is impressive looking when made in a bundt pan. The caramel icing goes well with this apple-flavored cake. It is a great dessert for a brunch or other festive occasion. If a bundt pan is not available, pour batter into a greased 9-by-13-inch pan and bake for about 30 minutes or so, then spread the icing over the cooled cake.

For Cake Preheat oven to 325°F. In a mixing bowl, combine the oil, applesauce and sugars. Add eggs, 1 at a time, beating well after each addition. Combine the dry ingredients and gradually add to the batter, while stirring. Fold in the apples, walnuts and vanilla.

Pour batter into a greased and floured bundt pan. Bake about 1 hour and 20 minutes, or until a tester inserted in center comes out clean. Cool in pan for 10 minutes, then flip over to release cake onto a wire rack or other cool surface. Let cool completely before icing.

For Icing In a small saucepan over medium-low heat, combine the brown sugar, half-and-half, butter and salt, stirring constantly until the sugar is dissolved. Cool to room temperature. Beat in the powdered sugar until smooth. Drizzle over cake.

DIRT CAKE

10–12 Servings

Cookie Mix

2¾ cups chocolate sandwich creme
    cookies, processed to crumbs
    (or crushed)
  5 tablespoons butter, melted

Cream Cheese Layer

  1 (8-ounce) package cream cheese,
    softened
  ½ cup butter or margarine, softened
  1 cup powdered sugar
  1 (8-ounce) container whipped topping

Pudding Layer

  2 (3.4-ounce) packages instant vanilla
    pudding mix
  3 cups cold milk
  ¾ teaspoon vanilla

For our special suite dinners, when
students order these for their
dessert, we layer them in clean clay
pots, stick a silk flower in the top
and add some gummy worms for
a fun look. We also include a clean
garden trowel for scooping the
"dirt." This recipe suggests a clear
2-quart bowl so guests can see the
layers within.

For Cookie Mix Combine the crushed cookies and melted butter in a medium bowl; set aside.

For Cream Cheese Layer Beat the cream cheese and butter until smooth; beat in the sugar until blended, then stir in the whipped topping until evenly mixed; set aside.

For Pudding Layer Beat the pudding mix, milk and vanilla until very smooth, 1–2 minutes; set aside.

Assemble Cake In a 2-quart bowl (preferably a clear bowl, such as a trifle bowl), press 1 cup of cookie mix evenly on the bottom. Spread the cream cheese mixture evenly over the cookie layer. Spread another cup of cookie mix evenly over cream cheese layer. Pour or spread the pudding mixture over cookie layer. Let the pudding layer set (takes just a few minutes), then top the cake with the remaining cookie mix. Chill until serving time.

WHITE TEXAS SHEET CAKE

20 Servings

Cake

1 cup (2 sticks) butter or margarine

1 cup water

2 cups all-purpose flour

2 cups sugar

2 large eggs, beaten

½ cup sour cream

1 teaspoon almond extract

1 teaspoon salt

1 teaspoon baking soda

Frosting

½ cup (1 stick) butter or margarine

6 tablespoons milk

½ teaspoon almond extract

4½ cups powdered sugar

This cake is buttery and moist with a pleasant hint of almond.

For Cake Preheat oven to 350°F. Grease a 9-by-13-inch pan; set aside. In a medium saucepan, bring the butter and water to a boil. Remove from heat and transfer the mixture to a large mixing bowl. Stir in the flour, sugar, eggs, sour cream, almond extract, salt and baking soda. Mix until batter is smooth, then pour into the prepared pan. Bake for 30–35 minutes, or until a tester inserted in center comes out clean. Cool for 20 minutes.

For Frosting In a saucepan, combine the butter and milk. Bring to a boil, then remove from heat. Let cool slightly, then transfer to a mixing bowl. Add sugar and almond extract; beat until smooth. Spread evenly over warm cake. Let cool completely.

COCA-COLA CAKE

20 Servings

Cake

   2 cups all-purpose flour
   2 cups sugar
   1 cup (2 sticks) butter
   1 cup Coca-Cola
   2 tablespoons unsweetened
      baking cocoa
   ½ cup buttermilk
   2 eggs, lightly beaten
   2 teaspoons vanilla
   1 teaspoon baking soda
   ¼ teaspoon salt
1 ½ cups miniature marshmallows

Frosting

   ½ cup (1 stick) butter
   6 tablespoons Coca-Cola
   2 tablespoons unsweetened
      baking cocoa
   4 cups powdered sugar
   1 teaspoon vanilla

Preheat oven to 350°F. Grease a 9-by-13-inch pan; set aside.

For Cake In a large mixing bowl, combine the flour and sugar. Melt the butter in a medium saucepan. Add the cola and cocoa; bring just to a boil. Remove from heat and stir into the flour mixture. Stir in the buttermilk, eggs, vanilla, baking soda and salt until well blended, then stir in the marshmallows. Pour into the prepared pan; bake for 35–40 minutes, or until a tester inserted in center comes out clean.

For Frosting Melt the butter in a medium saucepan. Add cola and cocoa; bring just to a boil. Remove from heat and transfer to a large mixing bowl. Beat in the sugar and vanilla until smooth. Spread over the hot cake. Let cool completely.

FRENCH SILK CAKE WITH RASPBERRY CREAM

12–16 Servings

Crust
    2 cups Oreo cookies, processed
    to crumbs (or crushed)
    2 tablespoons butter, melted

Mousse Filling
1½ cups (3 sticks) butter, softened
    1 cup + 2 tablespoons sugar
    3 (1-ounce) squares unsweetened
    baking chocolate
    1 tablespoon vanilla
    6 eggs, divided
    2 cups whipped topping

Chocolate Ganache
    1 cup (6 ounces) milk chocolate
    candy bars, chopped
    ½ cup heavy whipping cream

Raspberry Whipped Cream
    2 cups whipped topping
2½ teaspoons raspberry Jell-O powder
    (not sugar-free)

**This is impressive. It is a tall choco-
late mousse cake with chocolate
ganache (soft icing) and raspberry
whipped cream on top. The various
layers of this dessert come together
fairly easily, however, you'll need to
allow at least 3 hours of chilling
time for the filling to firm.**

For Crust Combine the cookie crumbs and melted butter.
Press onto the bottom of a 9-inch springform pan. Chill.

For Filling In a large mixing bowl, beat the butter and sugar
until creamy. Heat the chocolate squares in the microwave
for 1 minute or so to melt; stir into the butter mixture. Stir
in vanilla. Add 4 eggs, one at a time, while mixing, then beat
rapidly for 3 minutes. Add the last 2 eggs, one at a time, while
mixing, and beat for 2 minutes more. Fold in the whipped
topping until well combined. Pour filling into the crust,
spreading evenly. Chill for at least 3 hours until filling is firm,
or overnight.

For Ganache Heat the milk chocolate in the microwave until
just melted. Whisk in the cream until the mixture is smooth.
Pour ganache over the chilled filling, tilting pan so that ganache
covers the filling evenly; chill.

For Raspberry Cream Whisk together the whipped topping
and the Jell-O powder, stirring well to dissolve the granules.
Using a pastry bag with a decorative tip, pipe out a dollup of
cream in a ring around the top of the cake and a dollup in the
center. Or, if a pastry bag is not available, just spoon the cream
on top of each serving when plated (if cream sits and becomes
too thick, just thin with a little milk).

PUMPKIN CAKE ROLL

10–12 Servings

Cake

3	eggs
1	cup sugar
2/3	cup canned pumpkin
1	teaspoon lemon juice
3/4	cup all-purpose flour
1	teaspoon baking powder
2	teaspoons ground cinnamon
1	teaspoon ground ginger
1/2	teaspoon ground nutmeg
1/2	teaspoon salt
1	cup powdered sugar

Filling

6	ounces cream cheese, softened
1	cup powdered sugar
4	tablespoons butter, softened
1/2	teaspoon vanilla

This is a personal favorite that I would be happy to have any time of year, although it is particularly fitting to serve during the holidays.

Preheat oven to 350°F. Grease a 15-by-10-inch jelly roll pan. Line with waxed paper and grease the waxed paper.

For Cake Beat the eggs on high speed for 5 minutes. Gradually add the sugar. Stir in the pumpkin and lemon juice. In a medium bowl, stir together all dry ingredients. Gradually add to the pumpkin mixture, stirring until batter is smooth. Spread batter into the prepared pan.

Bake for 10 minutes. Rotate the pan* and bake for 10–12 minutes more, or until cake feels dry when touched and has slightly pulled away from the pan edges. Let cool for 15 minutes, then turn out onto a large towel sprinkled generously with the powdered sugar. Peel off the waxed paper and roll up from one of the long sides in the towel. Let cool completely.

For Filling In a medium bowl, beat together all filling ingredients until smooth and creamy. Set aside.

Unroll the cake and spread with the filling. Gently roll up the cake over the filling and lay seam-side down. If the cake cracks, gently pinch together as much as possible. Slide the cake onto a cookie sheet and chill. Sift more powdered sugar over the top, if desired, and slice with a sharp, serrated knife.

* Rotate the pan refers to turning the pan 180° (half a turn) to insure even browning.

TRES LECHES

20 Servings

Spongecake

  6 eggs, separated
  2 cups sugar
  2 cups all-purpose flour
  1/2 cup milk
  2 teaspoons baking powder
  1 teaspoon vanilla

Three Milks

  1 (12-ounce) can evaporated milk
  1 (14-ounce) can sweetened
    condensed milk
  1 cup heavy whipping cream

Topping

  1 (8-ounce) container whipped topping
  1/2 teaspoon vanilla

This is one version of the "three milks" cake, which is the national dessert of Nicaragua. It is also found in southern Mexico, however, this recipe came to me from a Panamanian student whose mother often prepared it. Her original version has two pureed bananas in the whipped topping, although I found that our students prefer the plain whipped topping.

For Spongecake Preheat oven to 350°F. Place the egg whites in the bowl of a stand mixer. Beat at low speed first, then increase speed to high and beat until soft peaks form. Gradually add the sugar and beat until stiff. Add the egg yolks, one at a time, beating well after each addition. Mix the flour with the baking powder; add to the mixture, alternating with the milk. Add the vanilla. Pour batter into a greased and floured 9-by-13-inch baking pan. Bake for 20 minutes. Rotate the pan* and bake for 10–12 minutes more, or until a tester inserted in center comes out clean.

For Three Milks Mix all three ingredients together until smooth. Poke holes in the warm cake all over with a fork, then pour the milk mixture, a little at a time, over the whole cake until all is absorbed. Let cool completely.

For Topping Stir the vanilla into the whipped topping, then spread a thick layer evenly over the cake. Chill until serving time.

* Rotate the pan refers to turning the pan 180° (half a turn) to insure even browning.

STRAWBERRY SWIRL CHEESECAKE

12 Servings

Strawberry Sauce

- 1 cup packed frozen strawberries, thawed
- 1 ½ teaspoons cornstarch

Crust

- 1 ¼ cups graham cracker crumbs
- ¼ cup sugar
- ⅓ cup butter or margarine, melted

Filling

- 3 (8-ounce) packages cream cheese, softened
- 1 (14-ounce) can sweetened condensed milk
- 3 large eggs
- 2 tablespoons lemon juice

For Strawberry Sauce In a food processor or blender, puree the strawberries; add the cornstarch and process until smooth. Place the mixture in a saucepan and bring to a boil. Turn heat to medium and cook, stirring constantly, for 1–2 minutes until sauce thickens slightly. Transfer the sauce to a small bowl; chill.

For Crust Grease the bottom and sides of a 9-inch springform pan. In a bowl, combine the crumbs, sugar and melted butter; mix well. Press firmly onto the bottom of the pan; set aside.

For Filling In a mixing bowl, beat the cream cheese on medium speed until light and fluffy. Gradually stir in the sweetened condensed milk; mix until smooth. Stir in the eggs and lemon juice until smooth. Pour filling over the crust. Spoon the chilled strawberry sauce over the filling. With a thin knife or spatula, gently cut through the filling to swirl in the strawberry sauce.

Preheat oven to 300°F. Bake for 60–65 minutes, or until the cake jiggles just slightly when gently shaken. Leave cake in the oven for 10 minutes more, but turn off the oven and partially open the oven door. Cool cake on a wire rack or other cool surface for 10 minutes, then run a knife around the edges to loosen the cake from the pan. Continue to cool for 30 minutes more. Remove side of pan and cool for 45–60 minutes more, or until completely cooled.

CINNAMON CHEESECAKE

16 Servings

Crust

1 ½ cups graham cracker crumbs
⅓ cup butter, melted

Cake

3 (8-ounce) packages cream cheese, softened
1 cup sugar
1 teaspoon vanilla
2 (8-ounce) cartons sour cream
3 eggs, lightly beaten
1 (10-ounce) package cinnamon chips*

This is a unique and wonderful cheesecake, which would be a great choice to serve during the holidays. This recipe was provided by my boss, Mary Haggans, several years ago and we continue to feature this on holiday buffets or for Sunday brunch.

For Crust Combine the cracker crumbs and melted butter. Press evenly onto the bottom of a greased 9-inch springform pan; set aside.

For Cake In a mixing bowl, beat the cream cheese, sugar and vanilla on medium speed until combined. Add the sour cream and beat on low speed until combined. Add the eggs and beat on low speed until just combined (do not overbeat).

Preheat oven to 300°F. Pour half the filling over the crust. Sprinkle the cinnamon chips over the filling in one layer; pat gently to level. Carefully pour the remaining filling over the chips. Place the filled springform pan in a shallow baking pan and bake for 1 hour and 15 minutes, or until cake is slightly jiggly in center. Turn the oven off and partially open the oven door. Let cake sit for 10 minutes more. Remove from oven to a wire rack or other cool surface.

Cool for 20 minutes. Use a knife to loosen cheesecake from the sides of the pan. Continue to cool for 30 minutes more. Remove side of pan and cool for 45–60 minutes more. Cover and refrigerate at least 2 hours before serving.

* Cinnamon chips are available in most supermarkets, located next to the chocolate baking chips.

TOFFEE CARAMEL CHEESECAKE

16–20 Servings

Crust

1 ½ cups graham cracker crumbs

⅓ cup butter, melted

Filling

4 (8-ounce) packages cream cheese, softened

1 ⅔ cups sugar

¼ cup cornstarch

2 teaspoons vanilla

3 eggs

⅔ cup heavy whipping cream

Caramel Sauce

10 tablespoons sugar

2 tablespoons + 2 teaspoons water

½ cup heavy whipping cream

4 tablespoons butter, cut into pieces

½ cup English toffee pieces

This is a tall, very creamy cheesecake that is excellent served with or without the caramel topping. Although it fills the pan to the brim, I never have seen it spill over when baking. Place it in a shallow baking pan, if desired, just to be safe.

For Crust Combine cracker crumbs and melted butter; mix well. Press onto the bottom of a greased 9-inch springform pan.

For Filling Place 1 (8-ounce) package of the cream cheese, ⅓ cup of the sugar and the cornstarch in a mixing bowl. Beat on low speed until creamy, about 3 minutes, then beat in the remaining cream cheese. Increase the mixer speed to high and beat in the remaining sugar, then the vanilla. Add the eggs, one at a time, beating well after each addition. Stir in the heavy cream; at this point, mix only until just blended. Be careful not to overmix.

Preheat oven to 300°F. Gently spoon filling into the prepared pan. Bake for 1 hour and 20 minutes, or until the cake barely jiggles when you shake the pan. Leave cake in the oven for 30–40 minutes more, but turn off the oven and partially open the oven door. Let cool on a wire rack or other cool surface for 45 minutes or so before carefully removing the sides of the pan.

For Caramel Sauce Heat the sugar and water in a heavy medium saucepan over medium heat, stirring until the sugar dissolves. Increase heat and boil, without stirring, until mixture is a rich caramel color, occasionally swirling and washing down the sides of the pan with a brush dipped in cold water, about 8 minutes. Remove from heat; add cream (mixture will bubble up), and stir until smooth. Stir in butter. Chill sauce for about 20 minutes, so that it is lukewarm yet still pourable. Drizzle or pour sauce over the cheesecake (place wax paper under and around the cake when drizzling sauce over for easy cleanup). Sprinkle top with the toffee pieces. Chill until serving time.

MOLTEN CHOCOLATE CAKE WITH CHOCOLATE-DIPPED ICE CREAM

4 Servings

Batter

½ cup (1 stick) butter, cut into pieces
4 ounces good quality dark chocolate,* chopped
2 eggs
3 egg yolks
1 cup powdered sugar
¾ cup all-purpose flour
1 tablespoon + 2 teaspoons cornstarch

4 scoops vanilla ice cream
½ (7.25-ounce) jar Smucker's Magic Shell chocolate topping

1 cup whipped topping, approximately
1 teaspoon grated chocolate (optional)

4 (4-inch) buttered ramekins

For Batter Combine the butter and chocolate; heat in the microwave until melted. Whisk until smooth, then transfer to a medium-to-large bowl. Whisk in the eggs and the yolks, all at once, until well incorporated. Stir in the sugar, flour and cornstarch and either whisk or beat on low speed until batter is smooth. Pour batter equally into the ramekins to about ¾ full. Lightly cover and leave at room temperature until ready to bake.

Place the scoops of ice cream on small baking sheets or trays; freeze until firm. Shake jar of topping well, according to the package directions, then pour about ½ into a medium bowl. With 2 forks, or a slotted spoon, place each scoop of ice cream into the chocolate mixture, turning to coat completely, then place back on the baking sheet or tray. Patch any exposed areas with more chocolate, if needed. Freeze the coated ice cream until firm.

Preheat oven to 400°F. Bake the cakes for 15 minutes (you want the center to be runny, but the edges to be firm). Let cool for 2–3 minutes, then top each with the chocolate coated ice cream, a dollup of whipped topping and a sprinkle of grated chocolate on top. Serve immediately.

This cake is also known as lava cake as it is a cake that is slightly underbaked to allow for the smooth and runny chocolate center to ooze out. This has been the most popular dessert chosen by students for their suite dinners since it was introduced. You can omit the dipped ice cream, if desired, although the Smucker's "Magic Shell" product makes it easy and looks impressive.

* Choose a quality chocolate such as Ghirardelli.

BREAD PUDDING WITH RUM SAUCE

8 Servings

Pudding

5 eggs

2 cups heavy whipping cream

1 cup sugar

½ cup (1 stick) butter, melted

   dash ground cinnamon

1 tablespoon vanilla

¼ cup raisins

1 cup milk

   dash nutmeg

10 slices stale French bread,
   sliced 1-inch thick

4 egg whites

½ cup sugar

Rum Sauce

1 cup milk

1 cup heavy whipping cream

¾ cup sugar

3 tablespoons cornstarch

3 tablespoons rum

In this popular version, the pudding gets baked, then broken into large pieces, folded into whipped egg whites and baked again. This creates a lighter texture to the pudding, which then is served with the delicious rum sauce. The preparation up through the first bake can be done 1 day ahead, if desired.

For Pudding In a large bowl, combine the eggs, cream, sugar, butter, cinnamon, vanilla, raisins, milk and nutmeg; mix well until sugar is dissolved. Pour into a lightly-greased 9-inch square pan. Arrange the bread slices as flat as possible in the egg mixture. Let stand for 5 minutes to soak up some of the liquid. Turn bread over and let stand for 10 minutes more. Push the bread down so most of it is covered by the custard mixture.

Preheat oven to 350°F. Set the pan into a larger pan (a 9-by-13-inch pan works well). Add hot water to come up to ¾ inch from the top. Oil-spray a piece of foil and lay, oil-side down, over the pan. Bake for 50 minutes or so. Uncover, and bake for 12–15 minutes more, or until golden brown on top. When done, the custard should be soft but not runny (this is not critical because it will bake some more).

With a large spoon, break up the pudding mixture into chunks and place in a large bowl. In another bowl, whip the egg whites until they form stiff peaks. Add ½ cup sugar and whip for another 20–30 seconds. Fold the beaten egg whites gently into the pudding mixture. Butter and sugar the 9-by-13-inch pan. Spoon the pudding mixture evenly into the pan and bake for 22–25 minutes, or until golden brown. Keep warm.

For Sauce In a saucepan, combine ½ cup of the milk, all of the cream and the sugar; bring to a simmer. In a small dish, mix the remaining ½ cup of milk and the cornstarch until dissolved. Stir this into the simmering mixture slowly, while whisking. Continue to simmer for 3–4 minutes, or until thickened and smooth. Remove from heat; stir in the rum. Serve sauce warm with the warm pudding.

FLAN

8–12 Servings

3/4 cup sugar
3 eggs
3 egg yolks
2 teaspoons vanilla
1 (14-ounce) can sweetened
condensed milk
1 3/4 cups milk
2 ounces cream cheese, softened

Optional Topping

1 cup whipped topping
8–10 medium fresh strawberries, sliced

This is one of the favorite recipes from our Mediterranean cooking class during the Vacation College program in May. It is very similar to the French Creme Caramel. This version has the ultra-rich additions of sweetened condensed milk as well as cream cheese, which negate its authenticity, but delight those who try it.

Place the sugar in a small skillet over medium heat and stir while it liquifies. Allow the sugar to boil and turn a walnut brown color, stirring occasionally. Watch it carefully so that it does not burn. Pour the caramel into the bottom of an ungreased 9-inch round cake pan and, working quickly, tilt the pan to spread the caramel across the bottom. (If the caramel hardens too soon, place in a warm oven until it liquifies and repeat the tilting process).

Preheat oven to 325°F. Place the eggs, egg yolks, vanilla, both milks and cream cheese in a blender; process for 2 minutes, or until very smooth. Pour over the caramel; place this pan into a larger baking pan which has 1½–2-inch sides. Pour boiling water halfway up the sides of the pan and bake for 1 hour and 30 minutes, or until a tester inserted in center comes out clean.

Allow flan to cool to room temperature. Cut around the edge and carefully invert onto a serving platter or plate, preferably one with a side rim to contain the thin caramel sauce. If a platter with a rim is not available, use one that is at least 12 inches in diameter or larger. Garnish the servings with sliced strawberries and whipped topping, if desired. You can also leave the flan in the pan and chill overnight, covered (the sauce will still be liquid after chilling). Invert onto a platter and garnish as desired just before serving.

CREME BRULEE

4 Servings

Custard

- 2 cups heavy whipping cream
- ½ teaspoon vanilla
-   pinch salt
- 4 egg yolks
- 7 tablespoons sugar

Topping

- ¼ cup packed brown sugar

- 4 (¾-cup) ramekins or soup cups

We've had compliments galore on this version. It is the favorite of many members of the Cottey board of trustees. Every year, I make certain that it is served at least once during their campus visits. We don't use a mini-torch to burnish the tops as some do—a preheated broiler works well, especially if you spread a paper-thin layer of brown sugar over the top.

For Custard Preheat oven to 300°F. In a medium saucepan, combine the cream, vanilla and salt. Warm over medium heat until the surface begins to shimmer, about 5 minutes. Remove from heat.

In a large bowl, stir the egg yolks and sugar with a wooden spoon until blended. Pour into the hot cream mixture and stir gently to avoid forming air bubbles. Strain the custard through a fine-mesh strainer or cheesecloth into a pitcher; skim off surface bubbles (if any).

Place ramekins in a baking pan with 1½–2-inch high sides. Pour custard into the ramekins, filling them to the rim. Pour in enough very hot water to reach halfway up the sides of the ramekins. Cover loosely with foil and bake for 1 hour and 40 minutes, or until the custard is firm around the edges (it may still be wobbly in the center, but it will firm up as it chills).

Cool for 15 minutes, then remove custards from the water bath; let cool to lukewarm. Cover and refrigerate until cold, at least 2 hours (the custards can be prepared to this point up to 2 days ahead). If small pools of liquid develop on the surfaces, blot with a paper towel before proceeding.

For Topping Preheat broiler to 500°F. Set the ramekins on a baking sheet. Sprinkle a very thin layer of brown sugar over the chilled custard, about 1 tablespoon, patting it evenly. Broil the custards as close to the heat as possible until the sugar is caramelized, about 1 minute (it will be melted and deep brown in color; watch carefully that it does not blacken). Let custards cool to room temperature, then chill for 45 minutes or up to 3 hours. Serve the same day once the topping is caramelized so that the topping is crisp. The topping will soften if chilled overnight.

PEACH COBBLER

12–15 Servings

6 tablespoons (¾ stick) butter
or margarine, softened
¾ cup sugar
1½ cups all-purpose flour
½ teaspoon salt
1 tablespoon baking powder
¾ cup milk

2 (29-ounce) cans sliced peaches
in syrup, drained, reserve syrup
¾ cup sugar
1½ cups reserved peach syrup

This recipe is from Ardis Legleiter, Cottey's talented baker. She has been working with us since 1995. This is a recipe that she has served to her family over the years, and it is very popular with our students and staff. You can use this recipe with blackberries or other fruit in place of the peaches. If using fresh or frozen blackberries, use 1½ cups of apple juice in place of the fruit syrup.

Beat together the butter and sugar until light and fluffy. Combine the flour, salt and baking powder in a small bowl. Add to mixture, alternating with the milk. Beat until smooth. Spread evenly in a greased 9-by-13-inch pan.

Preheat oven to 350°F. Spoon drained fruit over the batter; sprinkle with the sugar. Pour the reserved fruit juice over the top. Bake for 45–50 minutes, or until golden brown. During baking, the fruit and juice sink to the bottom and a cake-like layer forms on top. Serve with whipped topping or ice cream, as desired.

INDEX

INDEX

INDEX

INDEX

INDEX

INDEX

INDEX

INDEX

INDEX